GOD'S CATALYST

GOD'S CATALYST

Rosemary Green

Hodder & Stoughton
LONDON SYDNEY AUCKLAND TORONTO

Scripture quotations are take from the HOLY BIBLE, NEW
INTERNATIONAL VERSION, copyright © 1973, 1978, 1984
by the International Bible Society. Used by permission.

Every effort has been made to trace quotations included in this
book. If any further acknowledgment is needed, the publishers
and author will gladly include it in any new edition.

British Library Cataloguing in Publication Data
Green, Rosemary
  God's catalyst.
  I. Title
  253.5

ISBN 0-340-55659-5

Published by Hodder and Stoughton,
a division of Hodder and Stoughton Ltd,
Mill Road, Dunton Green, Sevenoaks, Kent TN13 2YA
Editorial Office: 47 Bedford Square, London WC1B 3DP

Typeset by Hewer Text Composition Services, Edinburgh
Printed in Great Britain by Clays Ltd, St Ives plc

To Mary and Elly
who both expressed to me
that they felt like guinea-pigs
in the early days of my counselling

Contents

FOREWORD

Some years ago in London I watched a young Californian woman pray and counsel a blind woman in a church. As I did so I was impressed by the sensitivity and what appeared to be the professional skill with which she slid smoothly past the psychological defences of the woman she was helping. The performance – if performance it was – was more than could be accounted for by her sensitivity alone. I asked the woman where she got her training. She had received no training whatever. Can the Holy Spirit teach counselling skills?

Of the many remarkable things that are happening in today's world, one stands out to me as a psychiatrist. God seems to be restoring to the Church a knowledge of the human psyche that still eludes professional groups. One example concerns the ministry to homosexuals. Through Christian groups such as Exodus, and teachers like Leanne Payne and Dr Elizabeth Moberly, homosexual men and women are finding release from sin *plus a change in their sexual orientation*. This is one example among many.

God is imparting knowledge as well as skill, knowledge that illustrates the truth of Scripture and goes beyond the discoveries of science. Freud knew about the unconscious mind, but psychoanalysts have been largely unsuccessful in making proper use of that knowledge. The unconscious mind (or that *heart* that is 'deceitful above all things, and desperately wicked') is a result of the Fall – how else could it have come into existence?

Along with many of us, Rosemary Green, aware of this fact, makes it clear we must deal with forgotten pain-producing memories *theologically*, and not merely psychologically. In doing so, we will not only be successful, but more importantly, be faithful to the God of the Scriptures. Many Christian psychologists and psychiatrists seem to lack an adequate grasp of the 'whole counsel of God'. Is it that they lack it? Or is it that it has never gripped their hearts?

Mrs Green deplores the Christian patina with which many therapists cover their basically secular approach to human problems. We live in an age when we pay lip service to Scripture's authority, while our real respect is reserved for human learning and so-called science.

Older Christian cultures enjoyed a deep awareness of the difference between head knowledge and heart knowledge, between head belief and conviction of heart. In dealing with love, with forgiveness, with faith, Mrs Green is aware of the difference. She is not afraid of using mental imagery to oil the hinges of the doorway separating head and heart.

Imagery has to do with the brain's right hemisphere. It is a half of the brain that God Himself created, as important to total thinking (and to our ability to communicate with God) as the left hemisphere. Old Testament prophets had right hemispheres that were fully operative and used them extensively. Christians who fear that side of their brains reduce the number of channels through which they can hear God's voice. They join the ranks of mental cripples created by western education's over-emphasis on logical thinking and its neglect of intuitive and creative thought. Good thinking embraces both hemispheres, both rational and so-called intuitive.

Mrs Green knows that evil powers will contest the use of any form of thought. They are as eager to oppose our logic as our imagery, replacing either with their own brand of thought. Darkness fights on both fronts – and so must we! The battle of the Gospel must be fought with every weapon God has given us. When I practised psychiatry I learned very quickly how hard it was to fight an enemy I could not see. It makes no sense to come against Satan with one arm tied behind your back (or half of your brain inoperative).

To counsel is more than to help solve emotional problems. All counselling represents war with evil. Anything less is sentimental foolishness. We do not wrestle with flesh and blood, but against wicked rulers. It is a battle involving the client's own will. Scott Peck was not the first psychiatrist to be aware of this, and Rosemary Green is under no illusions on the matter. She knows that the counsellor must be a step ahead, seeing what lies ahead, and challenging the client to follow.

But she knows, too, that all the knowledge in the world is not enough. We need the leadership of the Holy Spirit as we seek to untie evil bonds. We must therefore be sensitive to the voice of the Spirit, not experts in evil. It is to help us know that voice that Mrs Green has written her book. To read this book will be helpful to any Christian interested in helping others. But the real help will come for those of her readers who learn to listen to the voice of the Spirit of God.

John White

A HUSBAND'S COMMENDATION

They come to the house, weighed down by depression, shamefaced from guilt, harassed by loneliness – or apparently relaxed and without problems. They look at me curiously if I answer the door, and say, 'No, it's not you I've come to see. Is your wife in?' Sure enough she is in, and is prepared to spend a great deal of time listening to their stories, which she has a particular talent for eliciting. She has enormous patience, lots of wisdom, and the ability to help people to lay their burdens on Christ to such notable effect that time and again they go away with a lightness of step which I would have scarcely believed possible.

This has been going on for a number of years now. It was not ever thus. She has had a demanding life putting up with me and bringing up our four children. Her counselling gift is comparatively recent, and one which she was led to ask God to give her at a critical juncture in her life. He did, and you will sense the reality and scope of His answer if you open these pages. First, she began tentatively to use the gift she hardly knew, as yet, that she possessed. Then as confidence grew she used it more, and one celebrated professional psychiatrist was heard to say, 'You are a natural in counselling.' She certainly is, and the more she did it the more dissatisfied she became with the various current approaches in 'Christian' counselling which seemed to have so little distinctively Christian content and to depend so heavily on secular models and presuppositions. As she worked with more and more people she found that when they came into the re-creative presence of Christ in an attitude that was genuinely willing for change and healing He had his own inimitable and individual way of setting them free. She was not the agent of healing: merely God's catalyst.

Rosemary has been greatly sought after in recent years both to counsel others and to teach laymen in the subject how they too can become God's catalysts. She has lectured in many parts of the world, and has at last given in to the repeated requests of many grateful 'clients' and the encouragement of her publisher that she should write about it. It is not many authors of first books who are pressed to write and given a generous contract for a book when they have never written anything since college days. I believe it will prove immensely valuable.

I am profoundly grateful to Rosemary for all that she means in my life, for her partnership in our very varied ministry, and for the way she sets me a model of self-giving care for other people in need. And I am delighted to see her gifts and insights shared with a wider public through this book.

Michael Green

INTRODUCTION

About The Author

After many years of spiritual decline, with four small children, with unrecognised resentment against a husband whose success and activism in Christian work had often left me feeling of little value, and with great suspicion against the charismatic movement, God broke into my life in a new way. His tools were the people who loved me when my husband was in hospital in South Africa with meningitis. The love I experienced then melted my barriers of reserve and apparent competence. As that love flowed from other people to me, it melted too my reserves against God. Three weeks after the onset of Michael's illness I flew out to Durban; whilst there I remember saying to him, 'I have learnt the value of a hug,' and, 'I have begun to be able to say "I love Jesus" '. I had been a Christian for over twenty years, and I knew that I had never been able to say, 'I love Him' in the way that others around me could. When I allowed God's love to reach me through other people, it was planted in me; I then found that loving others, and giving to others, was a joy, rather than the burden that I had feared it would be.

A few months after the start of the ongoing process of transformation, I was telling a friend what the Lord had been doing in me. As we prayed together, the Holy Spirit gripped us. I knew that He was pushing me into asking for a spiritual gift. Despite the change in me, I was still highly suspicious of charismatic gifts. 'Not tongues or healing for me, thank you Lord!' So I had to ask Him what I needed. I can only believe that it was the Spirit who prompted me into asking for a gift of *wise counsel*, for I would not have thought of that phrase by myself. So my counselling ministry was born.

A month later I had an unexpected chance to attend a day's seminar entitled *The Effect of Birth and Early Childhood on Later Life*. The teaching and experience of that day made sense. Something clicked into place as I saw how patterns of attitudes, expectations and behaviour can be formed by an infant's first impressions of life. Shortly afterwards we moved to Oxford, into a busy church where I found myself thrust into pastoral situations where I was out of my depth. It was as if I had been given a sixth-form lesson (call that Grade 12 if you live in N. America) when I had not even been to Primary School.

Despite my inexperience and my ineptitude in those early days I had to trust that God knew what He was doing, not only for me but also for the people who were coming for help. I deplore my primitive efforts and my glaring mistakes. I learnt a little from short courses, and something more from the early books on inner healing. But mostly I was learning from listening to individuals, from the Bible, and from the Lord Himself. I have asked His forgiveness for my many mistakes, and where possible I have asked forgiveness from the people with whom I was clumsy. Mercifully we have a perfect, sovereign God, and I am grateful that over the years He has progressively shown me about Himself and His ways of working. The confidence I now have has grown through experience in ministry and also through the necessary and major spring-cleaning that He has done in me. I look back at one particularly difficult year, and I am thankful for the pain that produced fruit in my own life, and enables me to share honestly about the way God works.

About The Book

It is several years since friends first suggested to me that I might try to share with others what God has been teaching me in fifteen years of prayer counselling. This ministry involves a relationship between one needing help, and the one to whom the perplexed person comes; that is the *counselling* in the term. But even more important than the normal counselling skills is the dependence on God, the recognition that it is as we open ourselves to Him that He works for change. That is the *prayer*. My own prayerfulness matters, but less than my ability to enable the other individual to come to God, maybe with unsure faith, maybe even with antagonism. What He looks for is honesty and some willingness to change. I count it a great privilege when another person lets me see into his heart, and when God uses me in partnership with Him in His work. Exciting things happen when the Lord is allowed to be in control, and He often takes me by surprise by what He does.

Over the past decade there has been a multitude of books on Christian counselling and on inner healing. So why add to them? This book is aiming to help lay Christians who have a love for God and for people, who see the needs around them and to whom others often open up. 'Counselling' can happen as easily over an informal cup of tea or in a chat after a church service as in a minister's study (often more easily). In a world where godless standards are increasingly the norm there is a constant need for help in discovering God's perspective and His resources for change. We need to be as sure as Peter and John were that 'Salvation is found in no one else' (Acts 4:12). We need both to be confident that the Bible is relevant and to be at ease in using it as a tool. We need to be relaxed in praying extempore, in down-to-earth language, in all sorts of strange places. (Have you ever prayed aloud with another in the washroom at an airport? I have!) And in a world that is often starved of love we need to be those who are loving, approachable and unshockable, willing to come alongside and to listen, and to demonstrate the love of God to those who have never experienced it. So I hope it will be a book that you do not merely sit back and enjoy (or refute), but one that will stimulate you to grow in your assurance with God, in your own character, and in your ability to help others in need. It is not a heavy theological tome, but nevertheless it has plenty of biblical theology, and a working knowledge of Scripture for human needs. Nor is it a psychology textbook, but it gives some insight into how people function or malfunction. It does not pretend to understand all the problems we may meet, but it aims to put into the hands of laypeople some basic tools that can be used for a wide variety of situations, both inside and outside our churches.

I first taught the basic material of the book in 1982, in a three-week Summer School course at Regent College, Vancouver, under the title, 'A layman's approach to Christian counselling.' Since then it has been augmented and adapted for different situations in England, Canada, New Zealand and Australia. It has been used for extended courses in churches, for weekend conferences and one-day seminars, and its core for one-session workshops. There have been small groups where participants were already acquainted with one another, and large lecture rooms where total strangers have sat side by side.

Whatever the place, the personnel or the time frame, I do not confine myself to speaking to those present. There is always time for the content of a lecture to be absorbed by questions or group discussion, or – most important of all – for those present to divide into twos and threes to share personally and to pray together. The exercises at the end of each chapter have nearly all been used in such situations. So I hope that you will not pass these by as irrelevant or unnecessary – in the way that I know I should be tempted to do if I were reading the book! Some can be worked through individually; others require a partner. This may be a friend who, like you, wants to be better equipped to help others. You can agree to meet regularly as prayer-partners and potential counsellors, and spend time working through the suggested exercises.

I hope, too, that the book may prove useful as a handbook for churches that want to train a group of people for visiting or for prayer ministry after services, as well as for counselling. A church group committed to learning about personal ministry is the setting that I have in mind when I have suggested small group discussion. Sadly, it is rare for members of a typical 'home Bible-study group' to reach a level of mutual trust that makes it feel 'safe' for one to burst into tears over current stress or long-standing pain. But anyone involved in counselling needs a place, in a group or with an individual, where it is acceptable to be vulnerable, to release stress and to ask for help. A group is enriched when this is possible for any member. Paul reminded the elders of the church at Ephesus that, 'The Lord Jesus himself said "It is more blessed to give than to receive"' (Acts 20:35). Christian leaders and counsellors need to know that there are also times when it is more necessary to receive than to give.

In any counselling training group I frequently ask those present to pair up with a stranger rather than with a friend for the time of sharing, and also to change partners from one meeting to another. This both enhances a counsellor's freedom to be at ease with a new client (and so to put the client at ease), and also facilitates the coherence of the group and mutual love and trust within it.

In teaching and in writing I use many living illustrations, stories of God at work in lives. Most of the stories are isolated events, single incidents in a process of healing and change, chosen to illustrate a particular point. Some have led to an obviously fruitful outcome; others I have been unable to follow through. Some seem, to my grief, to have arrived in a backwater named, 'Unfinished', or even in a dead-end of apparent failure. Whatever the situation, I have changed names and have tried to preserve anonymity in other ways. As far as possible, I have asked permission to use these examples. I apologise to those whom I have been unable to reach, yet have included their stories, believing that they have a particular contribution to make in helping others. If you meet yourself unexpectedly in these pages, do write to me. I would love to hear from you.

There are many people I would like to thank for different ways they have contributed to this book. Most important are those who have entrusted their inner selves to me; I have learnt most of my counselling through them. Meeyan Judge was the first person to suggest that I might have something to add to the store of counselling books, and David Wavre waited patiently for a manuscript to emerge. Carolyn Armitage has been an encouraging and helpful editor, working under great pressure. Edna Johnson lent me her computer and taught me how to use it, and Dianne Gustafson worked late hours perfecting the diagrams when my instructions to her had been imprecise. Dr John White read the manuscript when he was meant to be enjoying a short holiday, looked for glaring errors and wrote a foreword. Last but far from least I thank a husband who has sometimes feared that his supper would not arrive in time because I was engrossed with a 'visitor', yet cooked many suppers for us both when I was engrossed in writing. He has offered encouragement all along the way.

There may be times when I offend some with apparently sexist language. If I use 'mankind' it will be as 'humankind', remembering that when 'God created man in his own image . . . male and female he created them' (Gen. 1:27). When I write about God I follow the Bible in using *He*, but I should like to emphasise that in the Godhead are all the characteristics, both male and female, of perfect humanity. When I write about a nameless client I usually use either 'him' or 'her' indiscriminately to avoid being clumsy; please do not count, and then complain of my bias!

Most of my counselling has been with Christians, and I am often asked about counselling those who do not share my faith. If someone who is not a Christian comes to me with a need, recognising my faith, why should I be ashamed of being open about my conviction that Jesus is indeed 'the way, the truth, and the life'? That does not mean that I shove my viewpoint down the other person's throat! But it does mean that I can gently show that Christ has something relevant to offer. It may be that I do that by praying (aloud, on the spot) for the situation, rather than by persuasive talk.

I think of a flight from England to Australia, when I started to chat with the couple sitting by me. James was next to me;

he soon told me that he had been a Christian for about three years, while his wife Susan was still quite antagonistic. The three of us talked about the reason for their journey and about their daughters left at home, and before long she shared her phobia of flying. Her shaking hand when she lifted her cup was evidence enough to back her words – and London to Sydney is a long journey to endure, even without fear. At one stage of the flight I was silently praying that I would have an easy opportunity at the next airport to speak to her alone about the Bible's promises for fear. Almost at once James asked if I would mind sitting next to Susan for a time; he did not know what to say to help her.

That answer to prayer almost caught me off guard! Without asking her to express her doubts about God I gently explained that I had a God who could understand and could help, and I asked her if I might pray for her where we were sitting. She agreed very readily. I cannot remember exactly how I prayed, but I know that when we next emerged from the plane she told my husband how much help it had been. I wish we could have followed up on this meeting that some might call chance, but I call divine coincidence. This book is not about evangelistic counselling, but every Christian counsellor should know how to help another person to commitment to Christ.

If we are to be alongside and helping others, we must be willing to be open to change in ourselves. It is amazing that a perfect God chooses to use us despite our failings. If He were to wait for perfection in us, He would never have any employees! It is God's prerogative to choose whom He uses, and how. Just because He uses me as I am, that does not mean that He wants me to stay as I am; I become less usable if I refuse to pay attention to any personal challenge He may make. As you read this book in search of help in counselling others, you may well find God speaking to you about things in your own life, maybe things you have never recognised, that He wants to change. Several years ago I learnt an important lesson, very painfully. When God is speaking, do not procrastinate. If He loves me, He wants the best for me; that is logical. If He is all wisdom, He knows the best for me; that is logical too. So put those statements together. If He wants the best for me, and knows the best for me, what point is there in arguing, or in delaying obedience? He does not force His power on me, because He respects the free will that He has given me. But He will not ask me to do anything that He knows is beyond my ability, with the power of the Holy Spirit freely available.

So I ask that whenever you read this book you have a Bible to hand. Pray that God will show you clearly what He wants to teach you, either directly equipping you for ministry, or for the changes that He wants to make in you.

1

THE UNIQUENESS OF
CHRISTIAN COUNSELLING

Margaret was an American lady from California who was attending our church while she was in Oxford temporarily. Let her tell her own story:

At age fifty-one, nothing in my life was working and I had come to the point where I no longer cared. I had tried everything I could think of to help myself – books, therapy, etc. I was a born-again Christian, and I was miserable.

My emotions and depressions were hard enough to deal with, but what pushed me over the edge was my health. In 1976 there was a Swine Flu scare in the United States and within forty-eight hours of the inoculation administered to me I fell gravely ill. The vaccine attacked my optic nerves. I was left with diminished eyesight and excruciating headaches. One of the big plusses in my life had always been excellent health, perfect eyesight and I could have counted the number of headaches on one hand. I was forty-six then and for the next five years I suffered daily with grinding headaches.

In 1981 I travelled to England to visit my daughter Helen who was living in Oxford next to St Aldate's Church. Helen saw the pain I was in and urged me to see the pastor's wife, Rosemary Green. I did not want to meet her or anybody else about my problems. I was sick and tired of being sick and tired, and believed nothing was going to change the way I was.

About this time, Helen and I were invited to an English

couple's home for a dinner party. I am a naturally curious person and was delighted at the prospect of seeing an English home, how it was run and furnished. Little did I know that the food and furniture would be the least of my experience. At the end of the evening, we were conversing in a cosy, warm room (September in England!) with a glass of port when our hostess, Mary, started talking about the baptism of the Holy Spirit and what it had done for her life. The baptism of what? My curiosity exploded again!

Even then, however, I was still balking at seeing Mrs Green, and when my daughter made an appointment, I wanted to back out. Helen gently continued to urge me to go and finally I went. Keeping that appointment was really my curiosity again and to show my daughter, 'Okay, I'll try.' Oh me of little faith! The date was September 25th, 1981.

The big, old, red rectory house was where warm and friendly Rosemary received me. I was ushered into an upstairs sitting-room where I was served hot tea and a sweet. That place will always be my 'Upper Room'. After we had finished our tea, Rosemary asked me to get comfortable and she then sat on the floor near me and said nothing. Finally I began to talk and cry for the next five hours. (Rosemary never looked at her watch once!) I was familiar with this process because I had been through this part with therapists before. Nothing new so far. Then Rosemary began showing me Scriptures in the Bible explaining to me about the Comforter Jesus had left for us and speaking in tongues. I thought, 'Give me a break!' Rosemary said she wanted to pray for me in tongues the next week and wanted Mary (the hostess at the dinner party) present. I was still very sceptical but my curiosity won out and I agreed to be back the next week.

The second meeting was on October 1st, 1981. Mary was with us and I told them about the circumstances of my birth and never knowing my parents. Even after half a century, that pain was very acute. I had told my story before and so what, nothing changed.

But gradually that afternoon my understanding and feelings did begin to change. The healing had begun as well as the realisation of what God, Jesus and the Holy Spirit really were in my life. The understanding of God who truly is my Father, of Jesus who died on that horrible Cross but encircles me in His arms, and of the Holy Spirit whom I can talk to in a language that expresses my heart of hearts took shape.

On October 8th, 1981 we met for the last time. The life lesson I learnt that was to become the most important to me was forgiveness. If Jesus could forgive His executioners from the cross and could spill His blood for me, could I then not forgive people in my life? Of course I could. A very freeing thing to do that leads straight to the peace that passes all understanding.

Through Jesus, my life did change, and what a gentleman He was. He led me right to the door and I still had no faith. Then He gently took my hand and led me through. On October 8th, 1981 my headaches ceased to exist. Thank you Jesus and the players, Rosemary, Mary and my daughter Helen.

That is the power of counselling that allows God full sway. I did not meet Margaret again for nearly eight years. It was a joy to find how much her faith had matured and that her healing had been maintained. She finished her testimony with this note of praise. 'I am the daughter of a King and I know it! "I will sing to the Lord all my life; I will sing praise to my God as long as I live" (Ps. 104:33).'

Why Is Counselling Needed?

We look around us, and we see broken homes, political corruption, illness, divorce, depression, anger, abortion, sexual abuse, addictions, and we hardly need to ask the question,

'Why counselling?' Here is my compact but comprehensive answer:

> We live in a fallen world
> in which sin and lack of love cause disjointedness of personality and relationships
> into which the Redeemer has come to rescue and change us.
> He has put us into a body, to help and encourage one another
> that we might grow into the people that He intended us to be,
> 'made in the image of God'.

Too often, we think of the word *sin* as meaning only the thoughts, words, deeds and attitudes for which each of us is personally responsible. But we are not as independent as we like to think. We have all been brought up by parents who, however good and well-intentioned, were far from perfect. We are surrounded by people who by and large ignore the Creator and His standards. The world in which we live was created by God; all that He had made was very good (Gen. 1:31). Yet that world was spoilt through the disobedience of those who had been put in charge of it (Gen. 3:17), and a chain reaction has carried on throughout history, affecting individuals and nations and even the environment itself. The word 'disjointed' sums it up well; we are out of sorts in a multitude of ways. We are not each personally responsible for many of the things that happen to us, but we do have to take responsibility for the ways in which we react to the pressures we face.

When God saw His good world marred by mankind's disobedience, He could so easily have discarded the world and its inhabitants and started again. Easily, except that it would have been out of character for a God who loved the people whom He had made. So even in the story of the Fall we see His tenderness in providing leather clothes for Adam and Eve (Gen. 3:21), and we see too His strength and His promise. In the Lord God's warning to the serpent that the woman's offspring would crush his head we find a hint of the saviour who would come (Gen. 3:15). Jesus came to our world; He lived and died and rose again; He sent the Holy Spirit to make real to us all that He offers. He has made provision so that we might be able to enjoy freedom from the chains of sinfulness. There is a thrilling phrase in Paul's prayer for the Ephesians in 1:18–20. We find that 'his incomparably great power for us who believe' is 'like the working of his mighty strength, which he exerted in Christ when he raised him from the dead and seated him at his right hand in the heavenly realms'. That is an astonishing statement. If we allowed that power full rein we would change dramatically, although none of us will reach perfection this side of the grave.

There is a simple diagram that expresses that, as Christians, we are citizens both of this fallen world and of God's Kingdom, and we are subject to the opposing forces of both.

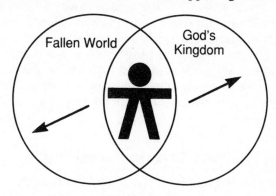

As Christians, we are citizens in God's kingdom, but are still subject to the environment of fallen-ness.

I remember hearing about a comment made when this illustration was used at a convention in Nairobi. It came from one of the Africans present. 'Of course,' he said, 'what really matters is which side of the face the nose is on.' That is a brilliant observation. If a person's life is basically directed towards God's Kingdom, then there will be victory and joy. If that life, although Christian, is being modelled by the ungodly climate around, there will be defeat and gloom.

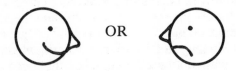

Our relationship with God is of prime importance. But if everything were to happen just between Him and me, then I could ignore everyone else around. Indeed, our whole understanding of God is largely moulded by our experiences with other people. If poor human models – especially early in life – have marred our concept of Him, then new relationships (with friends, spouse or counsellor) are needed to demonstrate the reality of God's character, and the possibility of a fresh and joyful relationship with Him. He has not created us to function in isolation; He has made us as social beings. As we love and encourage one another, as we teach and challenge and pray together, then we can grow, corporately and individually, into re-created people.

How Can We Define Christian Counselling?

In all counselling there is a relationship between two people that has a specific element of 'helper' to 'helped'. Christian counselling does not merely add biblical concepts and ethics to this two-way relationship, but it brings a new dimension. The relationship becomes a triangle, with God at its vertex. The one who comes for help may be feeling very unsure of his relationship with Him. The 'helper' seeks to communicate, by being, doing, and praying as well as by talking, who God is. He encourages the one in need to pray himself, and the whole triangle is strengthened. The helper and the helped may be mutual friends; they may be acquaintances; they may be strangers before the counselling process starts; the helper may be an ordained minister or an experienced lay counsellor. The same principles apply. Although *counsellor* and *client* may seem formal words to describe the people involved in this relationship, I have been unable to find better.

'Counselling between mutual friends?' I hear you ask in surprise. A friend once gave me a Peanuts card. On the front Lucy was bouncing along. 'Let us live! Let us love! Let us share the deepest secrets of our souls!' Inside she said, 'You go first!' We adopted that phrase, and we took turns in choosing the roles of counsellor and client. It worked. We let down our defences and allowed the Lord to work in our lives, and the friendship was undergirded through it. There is one word of warning, however. If the friendship is exclusive a point is reached where it becomes a hindrance rather than a help to growth.

What is the counsellor's aim? Paul writes in Colossians 1:28–29, 'We proclaim him [Christ], admonishing and teaching everyone with all wisdom, so that we may present everyone perfect in Christ. To this end I labour, struggling with all his energy, which so powerfully works in me.' We want to see the client and the immediate problem changed by the encounter in such a way that there is growth towards maturity in Christ. Teaching and admonition are part of the process, not in hardness, but with Christ's love and gentleness that enable us to come alongside with understanding love. Because of the 'energy' of the Holy Spirit at work, and the love for the client that He gives, it rarely feels like hard labour. Rather, it is a privilege to be allowed to be a junior partner with God in His work. So we can define Christian counselling as an intentional relationship between one person who is looking for help, and another who is instrumental in enabling God's means of help – indeed, God Himself – to reach the one in need.

The Individuality Of Every Counselling Relationship

Every person is unique. Even 'identical' twins are distinguishable, despite their similar appearance and their amazing sensitivity to each other's feelings. It may seem obvious to say that no two clients are identical, nor are any two counsellors. This means that there is rarely one 'right' way to help a client. Yes, there may be certain inescapable steps to be taken, determined by God's standards and His ways of dealing with wrong, but the route to those steps is not uniquely defined. The ways in which you and I relate to the same person will differ, without either of us being right or wrong. The means that we use in counselling do not have to be the same in order to bring the desired change. The exclamation, 'I wouldn't have done it that way!' does not need to imply 'She's wrong. I would have done it better!'

A counsellor is an artist. The art teacher can show his pupils how to use the tools of brush and pencil, of watercolours and oils. Some of them will draw and paint in a style that is almost indistinguishable from his. Others will produce pictures that are utterly different. In the same way you can take the counselling tools that you are offered (in this book and elsewhere) and make them your own, submitting to God your gifts and temperament. Even while you follow God-given principles remember that, whatever the apparent similarities, no two clients, or their situations, are identical. Our knowledge and skill grow with experience, but we cannot escape the need for humble dependence on the Lord that we need for each individual.

Counsellor As Catalyst

There is a variety of ways in which the relationship between counsellor and client can be expressed. The most important is to see the counsellor as a catalyst. In chemistry, a catalyst is the substance that enables a reaction to take place between two other substances; its presence is vital to the reaction, while it is not itself altered. In counselling, my prayerful, encouraging, challenging presence, is often used as the factor that enables the client to meet with God in a new way. Unlike the chemical catalyst which is unchanged, I thank God that I am not left exactly the same as I was before, but rather I am enriched as I relate to the client and as I share in the Spirit's work.

Counsellor As Parent

The counsellor and client can be seen as parent and child. A good parent will want to help a child grow up into maturity and independence, by teaching and modelling, by helping the child to think for himself, not afraid to confront and discipline, but allowing for mistakes to be made that are part of the learning process. We want to convey, by our words and by who we are, who God is and what He wants to do in our lives. But just as He has given us free will, and respects that freedom, so must we respect the will of those who look for our help, even if we disagree with the choice they are making. As a child grows up, the relationship between parent and child changes; through the rebellious teens (which may have its parallel in counselling, as the client moves from dependence towards maturity), and into a new adult to adult relationship.

That transition may be as hard for counsellor and client as it often is for parent and child. I remember the time when our older son returned from his first term at university, saying, 'I'm not a youth now, I'm a man.' I could feel myself almost physically hit below the belt. It was not that we had kept him tied to our apron strings. Indeed, he had been away at boarding school for eight years, and during the year between school and university he worked in Pakistan as a lay minister in a church. But it still took me two years to dispel that feeling. I could allow him to approach me as an adult; then after a time I would begin to feel threatened, and inwardly I would say, 'No, down you go, back to where you belong.' He once expressed, 'Mum, I can go so far with you, and then I have to back off.' It may be much the same

for counsellor and client. If we are truly wanting our clients
to grow into maturity we must be willing for a change in
our level of relationship, so that instead of acknowledging
'upper–lower' levels we can move into a measure of equality
in friendship.

The Issue Of Dependency

The model of parent–child raises a common question. How
are we to avoid the client becoming too dependent on the
counsellor? There is a fine line here. A certain measure of
dependency may not be wrong, as it is often because of the
client's immaturity or sense of helplessness in the current
difficult situation that she is looking for help. A child *needs*
to be dependent on parents, and for many people the effects
of bad experience in childhood need to be rebuilt through
the counselling. The human relationship between counsellor
and client is used to model a new pattern that she may
never have experienced in life; then the Holy Spirit works
change in both the effects of past deficiencies and the present
experience of God as Father.

An alert counsellor can guard against wrong dependency.
First I should examine myself to ensure that my needs are
not being fed by feeling indispensable. At the same time
I must watch what is happening in the client. If I detect
that she is leaning on me too hard I can be firm and gentle
in rebuke, and maybe make myself a little less available.
If she is trying to set me up as the 'perfect parent' she
never had, I must remind her of my fallibility and of her
impossible expectations – for me, or for her real parents.
However clearly this is said, she may be unable to grasp it.
If that is the case the relationship between counsellor and
client can expect some rough times.

I look on myself as a funnel, through which God's resources
are to be poured. The ideal is that the client extends both
hands under the neck of the funnel, in order to receive what
is being poured through. She may need to hold on to me with
one hand, in order to keep steady enough to keep the other

hand stretched out. But woe betide her and me if she tries to keep both hands hanging on to the neck of the funnel! That will both stop her from receiving anything from God, and will pull me down, so that I will be in danger of being angry at the strain she is putting on me.

Anger Against The Counsellor

I referred earlier to the parallel of the 'rebellious teens'. I have sometimes been shocked in counselling by the anger being vented against me. Perhaps I have made a small mistake. Suddenly there seems to be a barrage of stones hurled at me! I have learnt to apologise for my insensitive comment, and then, mentally, to duck from the onslaught, as I sense that I have probably tapped a hidden store of anger that has neither been recognised nor freely expressed. Once I have understood that I am not the real cause of the anger, I can actually be glad about the outburst, because something important is being uncovered in the 'safety' of the counselling room. Then we can move to talk and pray about the underlying reason for the anger.

Counsellor Alongside And In Front

We cannot normally be in two places at the same time! But another way of expressing how the counsellor relates to the client is just that. First the counsellor must come alongside. That means listening in a way that tries to understand, as closely as possible, the client's perspective and feelings about the situation. The measure of understanding can be communicated by words, looks or actions. We have already considered that no two counsellors are going to behave in exactly the same way, nor do we find two clients identical. Counselling involves people, not robots, and we are not carbon-copies of others. So the responses that indicate the understanding of 'alongsideness' will differ. Some will reflect back what is being said; others will merely say 'yes', or grunt, or nod silently. Some will move closer and put an arm round a shoulder or a hand on a knee, to express understanding; others will be cautious about any physical touch. Communication has many languages. What matters is that we communicate the desire to understand, and that this is a safe place for the client to be, and to unload both the facts and the emotions of the problem. Never pretend to understand 100 per cent how another person is feeling. Only the Lord can do that. A friend once said to me, 'It's marvellous to have somebody who understands exactly how I feel.' It was a mistake to accept that comment, for it cannot be true.

There is no point, however, in merely being alongside, to be bogged down in the client's confusion and uncertainty. We assume that he is in search of change, albeit that the change he wants may not be exactly the Lord's plan for him. So we also need to stand out in front; not inaccessibly far, but far enough to offer new perspective on the scene. Paul urged the Thessalonians, 'Warn those who are idle, encourage the timid, help the weak, be patient with everyone' (1 Thess. 5:14). At different times there will be encouragement, challenge, rebuke, or teaching. Usually some relevant piece of Scripture can be explained and applied. We do not need to be afraid to hold clearly to the norm of God's truth. In these days of relativism it is fashionable for people to choose their own beliefs and codes of behaviour, regardless of God. The common approach today is, 'Well, it is all right for you to believe what you want, but my way is . . . ' In this climate we need to stand up for a God who is truth, a God whose ways must be respected if wrongs are to be righted. Our place is to show principles, not to give commands to direct another's actions. As we highlight relevant Scripture, those principles may show very clearly what the Lord's commands are.

Suppose someone is looking for help in deciding which of two job offers to accept. You could show him Psalm 25 verses 9 and 10, verses which underline the importance of humility and obedience in following the way of a God who is faithful:

He guides the humble in what is right
 and teaches them his way.
All the ways of the Lord are loving and faithful
 for those who keep the demands of his covenant.

Ask him what these verses show about God's character.
What do they show us about our attitude? So what should
we look for in the ethics of the two firms? Think about these
questions; then pray with him for his ability to know if God
is giving him decisive direction between the two jobs, or
allowing him to make a free choice if there is no clear 'right
and wrong'.

The Counsellor Like The Holy Spirit

The counsellor's role is a reflection of that of the Holy Spirit.
Jesus said to His disciples, 'The Counsellor, the Holy Spirit,
whom the Father will send in my name, will teach you all
things and will remind you of everything I have said to you'
(John 14:26). 'The Counsellor . . . the Spirit of truth . . .
will testify about me' (John 15:26). We are to point to Jesus
and to help anyone in need to meet with Him in a new way.
Counselling that is merely talk is unlikely to reach the heart.
Counselling that helps the client to meet with Jesus can be
used to bring change and to deepen the relationship with
God. Jesus also spoke of the Holy Spirit as one who comes to
'convict the world of guilt in regard to sin and righteousness
and judgment' (John 16:8). Looking at this verse simply,
we can see that we can be partners with the Holy Spirit in
making clear that sin is sin, and cannot be ignored. We are
also partners with Him in affirming that guilt is not meant
to rest on us as a burden, but rather to be a motivating
force towards the two-part righteousness of forgiveness and
holiness. To use theological words, there is justification and
there is sanctification. The Holy Spirit assures us of the
first, and enables the second; the counsellor's role is
similar.

Counselling In Pairs

It is easy to assume that counselling is a one-to-one relationship, but many find it valuable to work in partnership.
It may seem threatening enough to a person who has never
dared bare his soul to another to face one person, let alone
two others at once, and I rarely insist. However, once this
initial hurdle is passed, there can be a real strength in such
a situation. While one of the pair takes the lead in the
counselling the other is mainly praying and observing in
the background. Then roles can be reversed, as the quieter
one has insight to be shared, a question to be asked, or a
corrective to the direction of the counselling.

Jane was a Christian of many years' standing but a novice
in this ministry; she once joined me with a young man
called Richard. We found that he wanted help over his
sexual orientation, and I began to search out the pattern of
relationships in his family background. He did not appear to
be blocking the exploration, but every avenue of questioning
seemed only to lead to a dead end. Jane was quietly listening
and praying, but she eventually took the opportunity of
Richard's temporary absence to tell me that I was on the
wrong track. Beware the assumptions of a standard format!
His return from the washroom gave us a fresh start on a new
and fruitful path that led to some decisive prayer.

Such teamwork needs love, trust and humility, and most
counsellors like to develop partnership with the same co-
counsellor. I tend to approach it differently. I sometimes
ask the client, either when the appointment is first made
or after the first meeting, whether he has a friend he would
like to bring with him. This has several advantages. He has
the 'safety' of a friend who is already trusted; then instead
of having to go home and report what has occurred in the
counselling room he has a companion who is part of the
experience, and is well placed to help with the ongoing
process. I value not only the other's prayer support, but
also the knowledge he has of the client in normal life, not
only in the comparative artificiality of the counselling room.

A friend, or a spouse, often refers to an event which the client might forget. 'Do you remember when . . . ?' This can bring some helpful insight. It may be useful to turn to the companion, particularly if he has been largely silent, to ask for a comment, emphasising that he has a valuable part to play.

Take a medical analogy. A consultant sees a patient with junior doctors in attendance. They probably have the day-to-day care of the patient, and they offer information at the same time as being trained by the consultant. Apprenticeship is a useful method of training. The friend who has already proved trustworthy probably has counselling gifts waiting to be developed. He is as grateful for the lessons he learns in this shared experience as I am for his participation and support.

Framework For Counselling

I see four main stages of a counselling encounter. Probably all four will be part of any meeting, in varying emphases, and they will be explained further later in the book. Earlier in this chapter we thought of the triangular relationship between God, client and counsellor. Each side of the triangle is important. It is not just the words but tones of voice, gestures, responses, a sense of caring – all these contribute towards the quality of relationship that is forged between counsellor and client. The counsellor's awareness of God and obedience to Him make another side of the triangle strong. Those two sides together make it easier for the third element, the client's relationship with God, to be either forged or strengthened. In that three-fold relationship, deep changes can be made and mountainous problems overcome. The different stages of the counselling process can be expressed in a diagram, with the arrows showing the main direction of communication at each stage. Throughout their time together the counsellor keeps one ear cocked towards God, wanting Him to be in control of all that happens.

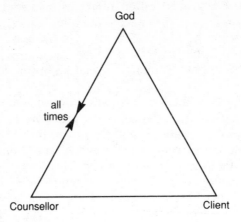

At first the counsellor is primarily listening, asking a few questions, seeking to understand the problem, avoiding snap judgments.

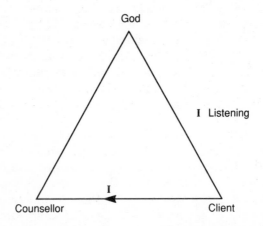

Next she is teaching and explaining, helping to re-structure thinking, by acting as a sounding-board, by unravelling a tangle, or by turning to the Bible and showing God's viewpoint. The point comes when the client needs to be challenged about her willingness to change and to be re-directed by

God. That challenge is the link between the second and third stages.

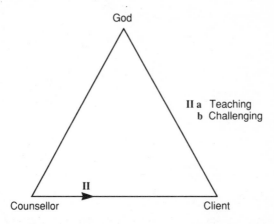

As they then move into prayer, the catalyst-counsellor enables her to turn to the Lord, and to pray for herself, even if faith is small and feelings are negative.

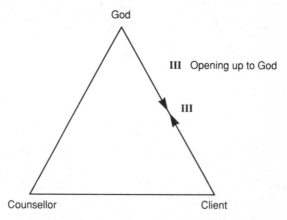

Finally she is sent out into the real world, with some goals to work out in her life (see over).

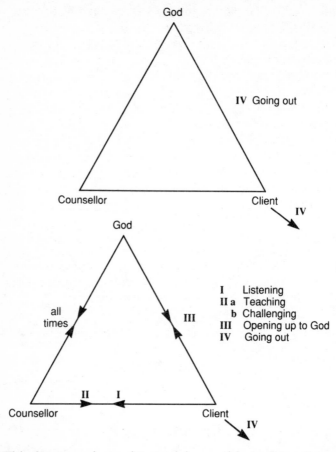

This framework can be used for a wide variety of needs.
We do not have to be experts in every problem; more
important is our growing expertise in using God's tools to
meet varying needs. Crises in life and long-term personality
problems; a need for guidance and chronic depression; emotional or sexual abuse; the recognition that over-reactions are
a symptom of underlying needs; uncertainties in friendships
and doubts about God; stress in marriage and guilt over past
failures; anger against parents and anxieties over children;
difficulties in relationships at work; sexual sin or involvement

in the occult. The needs tumble over one another, and the list is almost endless. We will constantly be meeting new situations, and variations on old themes. We do not need to be afraid of the problems that may surface, so long as we are humble, and confident that the infinite God offers help to all. We need to be flexible in His hands, open to anything He may want to do. That humble flexibility may include referral to another source of help, for confidence in God does not mean pride in ourselves. The biggest key is prayer that expects God to communicate, prayer that learns to listen to a God who can do the apparently impossible and who leads us into our obedience. I like to put together Jesus' saying 'apart from me you can do nothing' (John 15:5) with Paul's 'I can do everything through him who gives me strength' (Phil. 4:13). We can approach any client with love and with quiet excitement, knowing that we are junior partners with One who is infinitely greater than we are.

The Richness Of God's Resources

I fear that much 'Christian counselling' is represented by this small diagram:

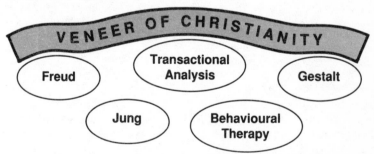

So often Christians, who ought to be in the forefront of research that is exploring any aspect of God's truth, are slow on the uptake. Then we see that others have entered a new field of understanding, and we run to catch up. I suspect that this has happened in the realm of psychology, therapy and counselling. Others have become 'the experts'.

We absorb their teaching, add a veneer of Christianity, and call it Christian counselling! I venture on dangerous territory here, knowing that I am not 'professionally' qualified in this area. But I humbly believe that God has given me qualifications, and I have a passion for God's truth to be obeyed and for Him to be acknowledged and known. I have a passion that He should in no way be put into a corner, when He is the ultimate psychologist and therapist. This means that we do not assume that 'the experts' have it all together, and that all we need to do is to add a little private prayer and repudiate some glaring ethical errors. Rather we start with a core of biblical truth: God's teaching on His character, on the nature of man, on His means of rescue, and the richness of the spiritual resources He gives us. Round that central core we put a filter. We are then able to test the teaching and therapeutic methods of the secular professionals to determine which parts can go through the filter and which have to be left outside. We certainly do not discard all that modern psychology has taught, but the new diagram looks like this.

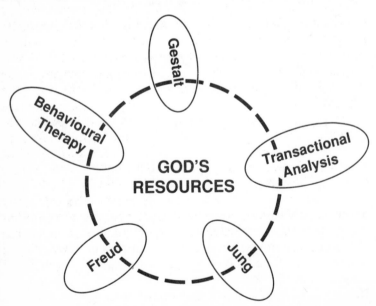

I once attended a weekend to learn about Gestalt therapy. There were only about a dozen of us there, all Christians except the leader of the weekend; she was the Gestalt expert, a sensitive, caring person. We were told the guidelines for our time together by the Christian psychiatrist who was the hostess. 'This is a Gestalt weekend. We will do everything the Gestalt way.' I felt slightly uncomfortable about this, but I was the shy newcomer to the group, and I was there to learn so I tried to conform. I did indeed leave that weekend with some new tools that I was glad to adapt and use in my own counselling. At the same time I was sharpened in my alertness to the need to subordinate all that we do to biblical standards. Two examples stand out in my memory. The first is a statement I heard. 'You have got all the resources for change in yourself.' When that sentence is put through the filter of biblical truth, we realise that it is true only when the Holy Spirit is resident in a life.

The second example was in my own experience. Intense, unidentified frustration was rising in me. I expressed it physically as I lay on the ground, feeling imprisoned. I pounded the floor; I fought and kicked. Then I deliberately chose to release my feelings on to the Cross, and I quietly prayed and relaxed. I was told by one person that I was 'copping out,' and that I should have fought through to the end with my own energy. He acted as spokesman for the whole group. I experienced a painful rejection at a moment when in my soreness and my vulnerability I looked for accepting love, even for commendation. Yet I am glad now, as I was even then, that my choice was to allow Christ's submission on the Cross to be my example, rather than the Gestalt methods we had been told to follow.

God's truth and His resources are huge. Who can really show us how to meet rejection, apart from Jesus? Who has an answer for guilt without knowing the forgiveness that Christ brings through the Cross? Paul has much to say in 1 Corinthians 1:18–2:16 that is relevant here. 'My message and my preaching were not with wise and persuasive words, but with a demonstration of the Spirit's power, so that your faith might not rest on men's wisdom, but on God's power' (1 Cor. 2:4). It is worth taking time to consider the whole of that passage, and let it shed light on these pages.

I started this chapter with Margaret, the American lady whose headaches were healed and whose life was transformed when she let God's Spirit work in her in a new way. Counselling under the direction of an infinite loving God is an exciting privilege.

Before You Read On

These exercises are designed to help you to be equipped as a counsellor who draws on all the resources God has given us. You can work through them on your own or with others.

1) Draw a big circle. In it list the resources that are uniquely available for the Christian counsellor. You will find some answers in Appendix I.

2) Here are some statements that might be made by either a counsellor (*a* to *e*) or a client (*f* to *h*). How much of each comment is fully in accord with God's truth? What amendments should be made?

a) You have got all the resources for change in yourself.

b) I haven't seen people affected by evil spirits, so it doesn't happen.

c) You need to experience love, so try sex outside marriage.

d) Recognise the extremes in your character, and incorporate them all.

e) Jesus loves us so much that He accepts us as we are and says that we are all right.

f) Surely it doesn't matter that I used to play with a ouija board.

g) My father never bothered about me, so why should I bother about him?

h) I had an abortion when I was a student. I'm so guilty that God cannot forgive me.

3) List six verses or passages in the Bible that excite you about God's character of love and reliability. Then prayerfully assess how deeply you believe those qualities in Him.

4) Think of some of the experiences you have had of being the 'helper' to another person. Would you describe yourself as catalyst; as parent; as 'alongside and in front'; or in other terms? Note the ways in which such helping/counselling situations have arisen.

2

CHARACTERISTICS OF A CHRISTIAN COUNSELLOR

If I were to ask you to describe the sort of person you would choose to approach with a personal problem it would probably not take you long to list at least ten qualities you might hope to find. Some are natural attributes of personality; others grow through study or through trial and error in counselling, or develop as the fruit of the Spirit matures in lives. Many are common to any counselling, while others are special for the Christian; being approachable and trustworthy would be high on any list. So what do I look for in a Christian wanting to share in this ministry?

An Assured Christian

Paul has high standards for Christian leadership. Here are some selections from 1 Timothy 3. The Christian minister should be self-controlled; hospitable; able to teach; not an alcoholic; gentle, not violent or liable to pick a quarrel; not set on making money; in good standing in family relationships; not a new Christian; worthy of respect; not a malicious talker; trustworthy; sincere in relationships and with a deep grasp of the faith. It sounds a formidable standard, but I am encouraged when I remember that God always uses us *in spite* of what we are more than *because* of what we are. He does not wait for perfection before giving us opportunity for ministry. If He did, He would have no ministers!

I wrote in the first chapter about Margaret. She came to see me at a time when I was turning emotional somersaults in my own life. I would rather have crawled into a corner to hide than keep the first appointment. However I was committed to the meeting, and the Lord honoured it in a way that I could not have dared to imagine. At one point I turned her to some part of the Bible, and admitted that I needed to grasp it as much as she did. That honest vulnerability was just one part of me that He was able to use that day.

God is a sculptor, and each one of us is like a hard lump of granite; it takes a lifetime for each piece of stone to be carved into the Christ-like figure He wants. Our desire to grow in obedience and in character will make us as willing to receive counselling as to offer it. Our openness to God and our readiness to change are more important for our usefulness than the standard we have already reached.

I like Paul's phrase in verse 9: 'They must keep hold of the deep truths of the faith with a clear conscience.' A deep confidence in God and in His power over the apparently impossible enables us to stand firm, unshaken by the mountain of problems that may assail the client. Moses sang at the end of his long life:

> He is the Rock, his works are perfect,
>   and all his ways are just.
> A faithful God who does no wrong,
>   upright and just is he. (Deut. 32:4)

If we share that solidity of conviction we shall be able to be rocks to others who are shaky. That does not mean that we will never be assailed by doubt in our own lives, but it does mean that there will be ballast to give us resilience when knocked, like the Wobbly Man toy our children had when they were small. When hit it would lean over, wobble around, and return upright.

Not long ago my handbag was stolen from a table during the after-service coffee-time at church, the day before I was due to leave for two months away from home. It was an uncomfortable experience to lose house keys, driving licence (with home address), cheque books, and a VISA card, and it was ironical that in my Bible were the notes of next evening's sermon – on God's sovereignty! I searched; I prayed with others (and confessed the folly of my carelessness); I telephoned the police and the bank. Then there was an internal battle between my natural fear and my faith in an omniscient, omnipotent God. I had to make a decision. Could I really trust that He was in control, whether or not that bag and its contents were to be found by next morning? I have been sure for years that He is a God who makes no mistakes, but my conviction was tested afresh. As I chose to trust Him, and prayed, the Wobbly Woman came upright with God's peace, and the rejoicing was all the greater when the bag was found that afternoon.

Able To Love

Top of the list of qualities needed for a counsellor is a real love for people of all sorts. Jesus commanded us to love one another (John 15:17); that love can grow through the Holy Spirit at work in us. When I was in the trough of my spiritual barrenness I realised that I knew little about loving other people. I read Paul's well-known passage about love in 1 Corinthians chapter 13, and prayed with one hand stretched out, 'Lord, please give me that love.' But as long as my other hand was tightly clenched, with my fear that it would be too difficult to love and to give, I was stuck. Change came only when circumstances pushed me into a corner; I began to let down my barriers and to receive love. As God's love reached me through other people it was planted in me. I then discovered that it was not the hard and costly thing I had feared. That new love was the soil in which the counselling gift could germinate and grow.

Loving, however, does not always include liking. I do not have a natural inclination to like everyone, and if I find myself being asked to counsel someone whom I do not like, love may actually mean that I back off before my dislike is sensed. I am not called to meet every need, and if my natural inclination is to dislike a person, I either pray that

God will give me a special gift of love in a way that I have sometimes experienced, or I look for another counsellor.

Jesus told us to love one another. Look at 1 Corinthians 13, and try to read aloud verses 4–8 in this way: 'I am patient, I am kind. I do not envy, I am not proud. I am not rude, I am not self-seeking, I am not easily angered. I keep no record of wrongs. I do not delight in evil, but rejoice with the truth. I always protect, always trust, always hope, always persevere. My love never gives up.' It is almost impossible to reach the end of the passage before we have to stop to confess the poverty of our love. Then we remember that the Spirit of Jesus is resident in us, and there is hope. 'Jesus in me is patient, Jesus is kind. He does not envy, He is not proud. He is not self-seeking, He is not easily angered. He keeps no record of wrongs. He does not delight in evil.' So the impossible goal of His quality of love becomes instead an aim for which we dare to hope.

His love enables us to be approachable. That is important, for people do not find it easy to display to others the weaknesses they would prefer to ignore. It is a great privilege when another person risks exposing inner confusion and pain. Never take it for granted, even if it happens frequently. It is never my right to pry into the inner sanctum of a soul, and I cause surprise when I thank a client for trusting me. She for her part, is amazed that anyone else should count it a privilege to see through the opened windows of her inner being into the rubbish lying inside.

His love will help us to be sensitive and unshockable, so that we do not trample with hob-nailed boots on the sores that have been exposed. We may hear some vile and appalling tales: a seven-year-old raped by her great-uncle on the floor of a church; a boy forced by his mother to eat dirty nappies; a boy whose older brother had oral sex with him; a mother who confessed that, ten years earlier, she had deliberately smothered her three-year-old daughter and had succeeded in passing it off as an accident. These are among the appalling events I have heard.

I was once told, 'Always appear interested' and, 'Never

show you are shocked.' Both those statements are weak.
If we are to be worthy of another's trust our love will *be*
interested, and we will never *be* shocked. What causes us
to react in shock when we hear these wretched stories?
Surely it is not our purity. Even a holy God does not
recoil from the pain and the grime; that is the garbage that
took Jesus to the Cross. No, we shrink back when our own
incompleteness is touched. The shock waves we emit are
barriers to protect our own vulnerability, steel barriers that
hurt those who have risked sharing painful things with us.
We do not have to pretend that these things do not matter.
They do. They are sin. They are vile. But the more God's
holy love reaches to our core and makes us whole, the more
resilient we become. Instead of the hard unyielding surface
covering our own weakness there is india rubber that does
not hurt those who knock on it, and whose dent quickly
returns to normal.

Think of it another way. You can imagine yourself speedily
hiding behind the Cross, so that the filth lands there. You can
then reach out with tenderness towards the hurting person,
and point to that Cross as the place for sin, for grief, for
anger, for all the feelings of hurt and dirt and betrayal.

Unshockability does not exclude the compassion that is
literally 'being moved in the bowels'. That is the compassion
that moved Jesus when He saw the crowds 'harassed and
helpless, like sheep without a shepherd' (Matt. 9:36). We
may feel it physically, but we do not need to be overwhelmed, because we can offload it on to Christ, who has
'carried our sorrows' (Isa. 53:4).

His love includes, too, a genuine interest in others as
people, not just as 'souls'. That means that we will want
God's best for them, a high goal that is often reached by
hard paths. 'Tough love' is the phrase to use here, for rebuke
and discipline can be partners with gentle encouragement.
I try to look at the other person through God's eyes, not
just my own. A good question to ask is, 'What does she
really need?' rather than, 'What does she *think* she needs?'
Strangely, the answer to that sometimes comes when I ask

myself 'What is right for me in this?' It can be a question that brings great freedom, so long as it springs from a genuine desire to help the other person rather than from selfishness.

I think of a day when I was called out of a midweek chapel service to meet a Christian student who was looking for counselling. Much as I would dearly love to be able to help everyone, I know that if I tried I would then be of no use to anyone. I explained the limits of my spheres of work without the false guilt that often makes us defensive; I showed her that I was not ignoring her needs by suggesting she might talk with another mature Christian who lived in her residence; and I prayed with her. Those ten minutes gave her a constructive suggestion and left her feeling that I had cared; at the same time I had not over-stretched my own resources.

I learnt the hard way this lesson about not over-extending myself. Penny had become too attached to me, and I had reached the point where I was drained. I felt I had nothing left to give her, yet I was afraid that if I took one step back from her that her enormous sense of rejection would swamp her. So I hung in, trying to give to her out of my vacuum. The inevitable result was my own exhaustion, anger against her for (supposedly) causing it, and worse rejection that could have been avoided if I had been wise.

Able To Listen

Listening is a big word, and is a major part of any good counselling. On the wall of my study is a poster that shows a worried-looking chimpanzee with one finger to his mouth. He says:

> I know you believe you understand
>   what you think I said.
> But I am not sure you realise
>   that what you heard
>   is not what I meant.

I am afraid there are too many times when our clients feel like that! But they may be too polite or too frightened to express it.

How do you react when your friend finishes your sentence for you as soon as you pause for a word? How do you feel when your husband assumes he knows what you are going to say, and comes in with 'I've heard that before'? What if your wife asks you the same thing six times in ten minutes? Here from the Samaritans in South Africa are some extracts about listening:

> You are *not listening* to me when . . .
>> You do not care about me;
>> You say you understand before you know me well enough;
>> You have an answer for my problem before I've finished telling you what my problem is;
>> You cut me off before I've finished speaking;
>> You finish my sentence for me;
>> You find me boring and don't tell me;
>> You feel critical of my vocabulary, grammar or accent;
>> You are dying to tell me something;
>> You tell me about your experience, making mine feel unimportant;
>> You are communicating to someone else in the room;
>> You refuse my thanks by telling me you haven't really done anything.

> You *are listening* to me when . . .
>> You come quietly into my private world and let me be me;
>> You really try to understand me even if I'm not making much sense;
>> You grasp my point even when it's against your own convictions;
>> You realise that the hour I took from you has left you a bit tired and drained;
>> You allow me the dignity of making my own decisions even though you think they might be wrong;

You do not take my problem from me, but allow
    me to deal with it in my own way;

You do not offer religious solace before I am ready
    for it;

You give me enough room to discover for myself
    what is really going on;

You accept my gift of gratitude by telling me how
    good it makes you feel to know that you have
    been helpful.

We can sum that up by saying that a person's sense of
being valued and loved will be enhanced or diminished by
the quality of listening. A real love for people will lead to
good listening. We can train ourselves to listen with our
eyes as well as with our ears, as we observe posture and
mannerisms, as we notice when tears are near or certain
topics are avoided. *Safety* and *space* are two important
words, so as I listen and watch I ask the minimum number
of questions. The danger is that the moment the client pauses
for breath I start to reply; often the most revealing comments
emerge in the second and third 'paragraphs', when I have
shown that I am accepting whatever is being said without
being shaken. The first 'paragraph' is testing me out, before
the really tender spots are revealed. While I listen I keep
one ear tuned into God, at the same time drawing on my
experience to begin to decide what the real needs are and
what should have priority. I pencil in a mental assessment,
ready to erase it when I see I am wrong or to ink it in if I
seem to be right.

Janet was in her mid-twenties when she came to see me.
As she talked about her happy home I began to wonder
whether her ties to the family were unnaturally close. She
had already mentioned that her parents would soon be flying
across the Atlantic on holiday, so I asked how she would
feel if the plane crashed. Obviously no one with healthy
family ties would rejoice at such a supposition, but the
speed with which tears came to her eyes confirmed my
suspicions. That showed where we needed to focus our

thinking. Old ties needed to be cut so that more mature ties could grow.

Some Signs To Watch

The apparently irrational

'It's stupid, but . . . ' is a phrase that immediately sets my counselling antennae quivering. Here is a sample conversation:

> *Client:* 'It's silly . . . I know this is ridiculous, but . . . '
> *Me:* 'Can I break in for a moment? I often hear people say that, and I want to say that it is all right. You see, your adult mind is saying that it is stupid, but what you are saying is pretty strong, isn't it?'
> Client breathes a sigh of relief.
> *Me:* 'Let me try to explain. There is something you have always felt, probably tied up with an event when you were a child. That colours how you see things now. The grown-up in you can't understand why you are making such a fuss, but the child in you is screaming out for you to pay attention. Does that make sense?'

Of course it is not totally *all right* to be in this state, but I convey, in simple words, that such confusion is normal and need not be feared. Then we can go on to explore the underlying reasons. I do not believe there is any such thing as an irrational feeling or an irrational fear. *Ratio* is the Latin for reason. The feelings have their reasons, with invisible roots that live underground. Roots can be dug up, even if the ground is hard and the roots are as obstinate as ground elder.

My example here is Diana. She was a lively Oxford student, who had decided to teach five- to eleven-year-old children. She came one day sheepishly admitting an apparently irrational fear of spiders. It would not be too good for the teacher to jump on a chair in the classroom at the appearance of the first small spider! She did not want to make a fool of herself in front of the children, nor to pass on her fear to them, so she was determined to eradicate the long-standing phobia. We explored first the general background of fear in her life, in a home that was less secure than her vitality indicated; in prayer she forgave her mother for the erratic outbursts whenever her daughter made a mistake.

We then turned our attention to the spiders. She told me that when she was about nine she regularly watched the science fiction series *Dr Who* on television. One episode showed huge spiders which leapt on to people's backs, slowly killing them, and she screamed in terror as she remembered them. Again she prayed. She confessed her addiction to the programme and asked God's forgiveness. She was the one who recognised that there had been sin in something that I would have passed over as normal childish activity. We asked the Holy Spirit to clear the fear in the memory, and told Satan that if he had any part in it he had to disappear. The next time I saw Diana she was keeping a small spider as a pet in a jam jar, and after the teacher-training course she went to work in Kenya, no longer daunted by the insects (worse than English spiders!) she might meet.

Exaggerated shame

Another signal to notice is shame. If I detect abnormal hesitation as a client's story unfolds, more often than not there is guilt that is false or exaggerated; this is frequently over a sexual problem. This may be a time to break the normal rules of listening, and to interrupt. By asking a gentle question I open a door marked SEX and I express that it is safe to talk about it.

I met June at a church weekend away. Late one night she confessed that she and her boyfriend had slept together. Sadly, this is so common that I have come to expect it; indeed, I may even ask. When there are sexual difficulties in a marriage it has often had a poor start because there has been intercourse before marriage, with each other or with a variety of other partners. We have no right to ask God to clear things up if there is sin ignored and unconfessed; the ground needs to be cleared first before the current problems can be tackled. As June prayed, she seemed unable to be sure that God would really forgive her.

Then her confession moved to 'something worse'. I asked her to be more specific, not because I wanted to be inquisitive but because I believed she needed to uncover the matter. Suddenly I had a hunch. Was this 'something worse' an abortion? Guilt over this is real. Murder has been committed. The Holy Spirit wanted to bring home to her that even though her sins seemed as impossible to bleach as the scarlet dye used in Isaiah's day, they would be made 'as white as snow' (Isa. 1:18). Satan the accuser wanted her to be kept under the ton weight of her guilt. It was important for her that I asked her outright whether my suspicion was right, because I do not believe she would have dared to tell me. If I had been wrong, she might have been slightly offended, but it would not really have mattered. In fact it would probably be such a relief to deny it that it would then not be too hard to tell me the truth. As it was, June's tears of confession led to her relief in receiving forgiveness.

Able To Relax

That was at a conference, but I like working at home. There are comfortable chairs, and I take off my shoes and curl up after offering a cup of coffee; I have a box of tissues and a Bible (often needed in that order!) available but not obtrusive. My own ability to relax can defuse some of the tension that is almost inevitable on a client's first visit. 'What is going to happen? How am I going to start? Is she going to like me? Is this going to be worth the effort? Is she really trustworthy? I have heard she helps other people, but can she really help me? I'm ashamed that after being a Christian for so long I cannot get it all together. Will she despise me? Will it all seem silly, because I know the answers in my head but I can't get it all together? Will she show up my ignorance of the Bible?'

My initial answer to these unspoken questions will be communicated by the way I act as well as by the words I express, and may make or mar the whole counselling process. A short time of general conversation leads into a short prayer. I usually pray simply for the Lord's guidance, sometimes with picture language, such as asking for a wall of protection round us and space inside to move. I pause long enough to give the client a chance to pray aloud if he wants to, but not so long that he is embarrassed by the silence. Then I ask a simple question, perhaps, 'Where do you want to begin? I don't mind if you feel as if you are talking in a tangle. Part of my job is to help you sort out the muddle.' My own way of putting a person at ease may make you shudder. This is all part of our individuality, and you will find your own ways of imparting relaxation.

Our own ability to be at ease is enhanced if we are not scared of a number of things. We should be unafraid:

   of silence, often a sign of honest thought
   of a torrent of words, indicating tension
   of tears, God's gift to release pain
   of touch, which often releases the tears
   of anger, a reaction to pain or injustice
   to be honest about our own failures, if this seems appropriate
   to apologise for mistakes in the counselling
   to confront or to challenge, as Jesus did
   to be realistic about the situation, not offering lightweight solutions
   to receive as well as to give
   of not having an immediate answer
   or of seeing no immediate success.

All these develop as we grow in the right sort of self-confidence. This is the confidence that God gives us, as we come to Him with our strengths and weaknesses, with our gifts and limitations, with the moulding from our past and the circumstances of the present. There is no need to fear recognising our own limitations. Rather we should be afraid of wearing blinkers that would cause us to stumble over obstacles which we ought to avoid, hurting others as we crash. The joy of ministry can so easily mask self-gratification, and the cries for help can make us feel indispensable.

It is not only God to whom we turn in our weaknesses. As counsellors we also need to have people around, people we can trust for their support and for their readiness to confront us when they spot stresses and failures. A good counsellor can be very choosy about accepting critique from others. (When he read this chapter my husband's amendment to *choosy* was *extraordinarily allergic*!) Unfortunately the supposed expert is frequently the most reluctant to receive in his own field, even when he gives the appearance of being open. When we are tired and under stress we are prone to lose perspective; those are the times when we most need help.

Able To Receive

A friend of mine teaching counselling used to write on the blackboard:

'Input = output = input = output = input'

Output without input will lead to starvation, aridity, ineffectiveness. A pond dries up without a stream to feed it, even if no cows are coming to drink. Even a machine needs sustenance! A car cannot keep going without petrol, oil, water, air, regular servicing and an occasional overhaul. We too need nourishment for body, mind, emotions and spirit. That means taking time for the physical input of food, rest and exercise. It means time for stimulating the mind with reading or with thought-provoking discussion, and also for recreation that gives the mind a complete rest. It means time for friendships, for relationships other than in counselling. The very fact that a bond grows between the two of us during the counselling process is a tonic to me, but

I must not be dependent on this for my emotional input. Last but not least we must keep fresh with God, with resources that I hope are obvious: private devotions of Bible reading and prayer, corporate worship as part of the whole body of Christ, and more intimate fellowship in a small group. All these are streams to prevent us from becoming parched.

Much of this chapter is relevant to any good people-helper. What is special for the Christian? Two basics need to be underlined. The first is Scripture; the second is prayer. Paul has a striking phrase in 1 Corinthians 2:16, 'We have the mind of Christ.' It is astonishing when we put it alongside Isaiah 55:8–9:

> 'For my thoughts are not your thoughts,
> neither are your ways my ways,'
>   declares the Lord.
> 'As the heavens are higher than the earth,
> so are my ways higher than your ways
> and my thoughts than your thoughts.'

If our minds are to be re-moulded we must absorb biblical teaching, open to the Spirit of truth who wants us to understand who God really is and how He looks at us. Our thinking has been largely formed by the attitudes of a world that omits God, and it is sad that often even Christian teaching has been distorted by attempts to create God in our own image. Among the hardest people to counsel are those who have grown up in a home that was bound by evangelical rules without the living truth of God or His accepting love. Jesus once said, 'You diligently study the Scriptures because you think that by them you possess eternal life. These are the Scriptures that testify about me, yet you refuse to come to me to have life' (John 5:39–40). I have this afternoon spent time with a young pastor's wife who is grateful that her years of chronic fatigue syndrome have wiped from her memory many of the distortions of truth imparted by the teaching she received from her church during her early years.

Minds that understand should be partnered by wills that

obey. In fact, minds without obedience will be very limited in their understanding. James puts it clearly enough, 'Faith by itself, if it is not accompanied by action, is dead' (2:17). We are cheats if we try to use the Bible as a tool to help others without living by it ourselves. At the same time as we read it for our own lives we can try to memorise parts. Many of us find it hard to remember verses and their references; there will be more about this in chapter 13. We should pray that ability to learn and memorise will be sharpened, so that the Bible will become a resource we can use in our counselling.

What about prayer? We know little about Epaphras, a Christian who came originally from Colosse. We find him alongside the imprisoned Paul. 'Epaphras, who is one of you and a servant of Christ Jesus, sends greetings,' writes Paul in Colossians 4:12. 'He is always wrestling in prayer for you, that you may stand firm in all the will of God, mature and fully assured.' That is a model of prayer for a Christian counsellor. I confess that I rarely wrestle as deeply as that for my clients, but I am glad when I know that others are praying in this way. Yesterday evening a man committed himself to two hours of prayer while I was with his wife, and I believe the time with her was far more effective than it had been on our previous meetings.

Even if we do not wrestle in prayer as Epaphras did, our counselling can be immersed in prayer, prayer that can listen to God as well as talk to Him. We pray aloud at the start of a session. We pray silently as we listen to the client, praying for insight and for direction, keeping one ear cocked to the Lord. We pray out loud with him, and seek to free him to pray for himself. We will take a closer look at that in chapter 15.

Some Ways To Absorb This Chapter

1) *Practise meeting strangers* Instead of sitting in the familiar 'safe' seat in church every Sunday, sit in a completely different place each of the next four weeks. Do not leave

without talking to someone who has previously been no more than a face to you.

2) Read Paul's prayer for the *Colossians* in *1:9–14*. Read it again, in the first person, and make it a prayer for yourself. 'I ask God to fill me with the knowledge of His will . . .' Take time to allow the Spirit to show you some of the changes He wants to make in you.

3) Over the next week, *jot down the ways you receive nourishing input* for your own life and take note of the approximate time you spend.

4) *With a partner* Find someone who is also interested in developing skills in prayer counselling, preferably one whom you do not know well. Spend a few minutes thinking of some incident in your life in the past two days that has touched you emotionally. It does not matter whether it has been major or minor, happy or difficult. Spend time sharing about these events and the feelings they evoked. Then pray together for each other; for the emotions, for other people involved, and for the implications. After this spend a few more minutes in silence, and assess the interaction between you. Ask yourself questions like these. Did I have difficulty in exploring my feelings? Did she seem really interested in me and in what I was saying? Did the way she listened make it easy for me to talk? Did I enjoy coming alongside her? Did her sharing make me feel vulnerable? How easy was it for us to pray together? Did our praying touch on anything we had not already talked about? Would I like to spend time with her again?

Now spend a few minutes sharing the answers to those questions. 'I found that I . . .'; 'I felt that you . . .' Point out what was good, and what could have been better. If necessary, tell her what was awful! Do it gently and honestly. Remember that you can help each other to grow as caring listeners by your loving rebuke as well as by your affirmation. Finish by praying together again about the ways in which you need to learn and about the opportunities you will have to help others.

3

THE POWER OF THE CROSS

It was a time of stress. Anger in my own life, affecting my friendships, my marriage and my children had been confronted. I had been receiving counselling, some helpful, some misguided. I had for a time been laid aside from ministry, and my self-confidence had been severely undermined. Thanks to the God who rescues us, this time of devastation had also been a time for re-building. Then one afternoon, as I was about to visit a young woman who had come to Christ out of drugs and occult involvement, I was walking round a field in Oxford, praying in tongues as my mind roamed round many events and people. Suddenly I saw a huge cross in front of me. It was plain and empty, gilded but not shining. It stretched towards the clouds, a few hundred feet tall. As I looked at it, God underlined for me four strands of truth about the Cross of Christ that were relevant for the young woman, for me, for everyone.

Four Strands Of Truth About The Cross

Two strands were about forgiveness – God's forgiveness for me and my need to forgive others. First, that Cross was so tall and its arms were stretched out so wide that there was nothing, absolutely nothing, too bad to be covered by them. ALL the sin of my life was forgiven. The second fact He brought home to me was that in the Cross are contained all the resources we shall ever need if we are truly to forgive others. I reckon that nearly all counselling situations need at least one, often both, directions of forgiveness.

Third, it is in the Cross that we find the possibility of

healing and restoration for anything that has been spoilt through the Fall. People come knowing that things are amiss and looking for help to get them straight, even if they have not seen that it is through the fulness of Christ's salvation that help is to be found. We need to see the doctrine of the Cross on a broad canvas. Jesus' death was not merely for individual sin, which is the first thing I understood when I became a Christian, but for the sinfulness of the whole world. His redemption is intended to be worked out in the whole of creation, and in counselling we are allowing that redeeming power of God to be focused on individual need. The suffering of the Cross and the triumph of the Resurrection are both part of our ministry of reconciliation. That is thrilling!

Finally, the Cross is the place of victory over Satan. The *4* more we are aware of the devil and his activity, the more sure we need to be that he is a defeated foe. In the next few chapters we shall look at these four strands more closely.

Forgiveness For My Sin

There are many Christians who know the theory that God forgives but who lack conviction about it. When they are honest they say, 'I know that God forgives everybody else, but I'm not really sure that He forgives *me*.' God wants us to be sure. The Holy Spirit brings home the reality of sin and guilt, not in order to crush us with its burden, but to motivate us towards the Cross. The Bible is full of it, in Old and New Testaments alike. 'He himself bore our sins in his own body on the tree, so that we might die to sins and live for righteousness' (1 Pet. 2:24). Peter has in mind Isaiah chapter 53:

> We all, like sheep, have gone astray,
> each of us has turned to his own way;
> and the Lord has laid on him the iniquity of us all (v.6).

Try this simple illustration with someone who needs to grasp this truth. Stretch out both your hands, and cover the left hand with a dark book, while the right hand stays empty. The left hand represents an individual, estranged from a holy God by his sin; the right hand represents Jesus, with nothing between Him and His Father. 'And the Lord has laid on him . . . ' Move the book from left hand to right. Now the left hand – the guilty person – is free; the right hand – Jesus – is carrying the weight. Think of Jesus on the Cross, calling out, 'My God, why have you forsaken me?' The answer is clearly portrayed by your hands. 'He bore my sins in his body on the tree.'

True Guilt And False Guilt

We do no one a service by ignoring that wrong is wrong, that sin is sin. I was deeply struck recently as I read in Leviticus 4:27: 'If a member of the community sins unintentionally and does what is forbidden in any of the Lord's commands, he is guilty.' In the following chapter we find this: 'If a person sins and does what is forbidden in any of the Lord's commands, even though he does not know it, he is guilty and will be held responsible' (5:17). At first sight this seems hard. Why should I be called responsible for sinning when I did not even know it was wrong? Simply because it is sin against God's rules. We have a holy God, whose 'eyes are too pure to look on evil' (Hab. 1:13). This means that His character is such that He cannot just ignore wrong, however it is committed. In the Levitical law the person responsible had to bring an offering for sacrifice. For us that offering has already been made, by Christ on the Cross. We do not need to bring another sacrifice; we do need to come and claim the forgiveness that is freely available.

How is this going to affect our counselling? An illustration helps. If milk is spilt at the table, it needs to be cleared up; the mess is there, however it was caused. The measure of reproof and punishment to the child who was responsible for spilling it will vary according to the measure of carelessness or deliberate act of disobedience – and, sadly, according to the temper of the parent. The *child was responsible for spilling it*, however the mug was overturned. A good parent will convey the right measure of reproof, the child apologises and promises an effort to change and the incident can then be forgotten. A parent who is carrying other stress is likely to take it out on the child. 'You stupid child! You're always like this!' The child is likely to leave the table carrying anger at the unfairness mixed with a message, 'It's always me that is wrong. I must be stupid.'

The 'good' parent is modelling God's attitude. The milk has been spilt; the mess is there; but there is not a heavy hand of judgment. That means that we do not land heavily on the client with, 'What you did was BAD, BAD, BAD,' when we point out that the sin committed unintentionally or in ignorance was still sin that needs to be brought to the Cross to be confessed and forgiven. Unfortunately there are too many parents whose behaviour is not godly; the child grows into an adult who has a very confused concept of true and false guilt, as well as a distorted concept of what God is like. Feelings of guilt have strong elements of false guilt, and fear of God the Judge is stronger than safety with God the Lover. Such a client needs careful re-educating, by our biblical teaching and by our firm but gentle attitude towards sin.

Satan's Distortions

The Holy Spirit's deep desire for us is to be sure that we are forgiven. But there is an unholy spirit, Satan, who wants to misrepresent God to us in any way he can. He has two main ploys with Christians on this matter of sin. He is both liar and accuser.

On one hand he is the serpent in the Garden of Eden, the liar. I should say at this point that it does not matter to me whether or not Adam and Eve are historical figures, and Eden a geographical place on the map. What is important is all that the story teaches, about God and His ways, about people and what we are like. This is authority and truth as much as Jesus' parables are. So look at Genesis chapter 3. The serpent sneaks up to the woman whining, 'Did God *really* say you must not . . . ? He wants to spoil things for you . . . He won't do what he says . . .' That is typical of the father of lies, the deceiver. He whispers in the ears of Christians, 'Surely that is outdated . . . No one will find out . . . Your friends would be much happier if you joined them . . .' He is constantly undermining God's rules, which are designed by the Creator for our good.

At the other end of the scale Satan comes as the accuser. He bangs his fist on the table, shouting, 'You're guilty, you're guilty, and don't you forget it! What you have done is much too bad for you to be forgiven. Remember the unforgivable sin . . .' So he goes on, often feeding on childhood experiences, when forgiveness has not been deeply demonstrated even if the theory has been taught.

Zechariah chapter 3 has an interesting picture which I often use in counselling. Joshua the high priest is dressed in filthy rags; he stands in front of the angel who is the Lord Himself. Imagine how Joshua is feeling!

'I wish I wasn't here. I'm ashamed, and there is nowhere for me to hide. What is the angel going to say?'

To make matters worse for him, Satan is standing at his right side. 'Joshua, just look at you! What on earth are you doing here?' A dark finger points accusingly.

Now read verses 1–5. First, the Lord directs His attention to Satan. The 'burning stick' (Joshua) has been rescued from the fire's destruction, and the accuser is rebuked in no uncertain terms. In fact, he disappears from the scene, and I have pencilled 'Exit Satan' in the margin of my Bible. Then the Lord turns gently to Joshua.

'I have taken away your sin,' is first stated, then demonstrated as Joshua is re-clothed from head to toe. Imagine now how he feels! The activity of Satan and the reality of forgiveness can both be demonstrated through this passage.

Using Scripture To Teach Forgiveness

Helping the client to identify with a Bible character is a useful tool for helping him to bridge the gulf between head and heart. Do not waste energy arguing the existence of Satan. Let the Scripture speak as it stands.

Misunderstanding about forgiveness is so prevalent that it is good to keep a mental storehouse of references, but I may well start by asking the client what comes to his own mind before I produce any verses. 1 John 1:8–9 is often familiar. Ask him to read it aloud, and follow with some simple questions; here is a sample conversation:

Q. 'What does it say about God?'
A. 'He is faithful and just.'
Q. 'What does that imply to you?'

His next answer may be somewhat grudging, because his feelings are reluctant to admit God's faithfulness. So suggest he reads it again, in the first person. 'If I claim to be without sin, I deceive myself and the truth is not in me. If I confess my sin, he is faithful and just and will forgive my sin and cleanse me from all unrighteousness.' That is powerful. He finds it hard to argue when he has read it in that way, and you may find that he is ready to confess his sin with a new measure of faith that God will actually forgive him.

The Old Testament is full of pictorial verses about God's forgiveness. Psalm 103:12 is another that is often quoted when I ask what verse comes to mind. 'As far as the east is from the west, so far has he removed our transgressions from us.' There are a number of ways in which this can be brought alive. I used to think of standing on a cliff, looking out to the sea with a wide horizon in front of me; God has banished my sins as far as my eye can see. This image was superseded by a pilot who told me that he thought of the far more extensive view from the cockpit of his plane.

I was once flying over the Canadian prairies which seem to spread endlessly, and I imagined dumping the load of sin

in Toronto, and then flying 2,000 miles west to Vancouver.
A mental image like this can make a familiar verse more
vivid. Cultivate a habit of visualising what you are reading
in the Bible.

Isaiah 43:25 is a verse that the Lord highlighted to bring
home to me the completeness of His forgiveness. Scriptures
that have spoken to me are often ones that I can use
effectively to help others:

Q. 'What are the phrases here that show how completely
God forgives?'
A. 'Blots out . . . Does not remember.'

Again, you can illustrate from everyday life, as Jesus so often
did. A word processor on which you press the wrong button,
and the essay is lost; or an acetate for an overhead projector,
on which the client has written all his sins with a soluble pen.
Put it under the tap, and watch the colour being washed
away, leaving the plastic utterly clean, and ready to be used
afresh. That is how God treats our sins.

There is a phrase in the middle of this verse which it is
easy to overlook. 'For my own sake.' God does not blot
out our sins just because He loves us, although that is true.
He does it to satisfy His own character of love and holiness.
That takes the weight off the person who is not sure whether
God loves *him* and on to God Himself.

There is one more verse I want to look at before we move
on. Micah mixes his metaphors in a way that would make
my English teacher turn in her grave! Chapter 7 verse 19 is
highly picturesque: 'You will tread our sins underfoot.' That
conjures up for me a foot stamping on the ground, squashing
the sins into tiny fragments. 'And hurl all our iniquities into
the depths of the sea.' Those pieces are scattered over the
water. Or we can think of a liner sailing into the deepest part
of the ocean. Lead weights are tied on to those sins before
they are dropped overboard, so that they sink straight to the
bottom. No diver is to be sent down to rescue the bundle,
and the liner must sail on.

Other Ways To Emphasise God's Forgiveness

There are other means we can use to help the client understand God's forgiveness. Illustrations from everyday life, hymns and the use of imagery in prayer are all in my toolbox. For example, I refer to a scene at an airport, where passengers are standing by the carousel delivering luggage, each person hoping to recognise his own suitcase. He needs to claim his own; he should not walk away with anyone else's. Foolish is the passenger who tries to collect every suitcase, and even greater his folly when he staggers along, carrying them all, ignoring the trolley provided! Think of each of those cases as filled with individual guilt. I must claim my own guilty baggage. But I must not clutter myself by trying to be responsible for another's wrong; that is false guilt. So I pick up my own suitcase from the carousel, and load it immediately on to the cart that has a huge red cross painted on its side, and Jesus waiting to push it away.

It is useful, too, to have a hymnbook handy. Many of the hymns that are traditionally used for an evangelistic altar call are relevant for a Christian struggling with guilt. The one I use most frequently is 'Just as I am':

> Just as I am, without one plea,
> But that Thy blood was shed for me,
> And that Thou bidd'st me come to Thee,
> O Lamb of God, I come.

'Waiting not, to rid my soul of one dark blot . . . Thee, whose blood can cleanse each spot . . . I am poor, wretched, blind . . . Thou wilt receive, wilt welcome, pardon, cleanse . . .' The language is old-fashioned, but the truths are still up-to-date, and can be used as a prayer, even by young people.

I will say more about the use of imagination later in the book, but I would like to tell one short story about Dorothy, whom I met at a conference. She carried a bundle of assorted guilt and resentment. I had suggested that she should think of the Cross with an enormous pit next to it, ready for her to throw in all that she might unload. In prayer she brought her load and toppled it in, and asked that God would help her to leave it there. He showed her the Cross falling on top of the tip, sealing it over, a sign to her of the completeness of His work.

'How Can I Forgive Myself?'

God's forgiveness is indeed huge; 'ginormous' is the word I would use if it were in the dictionary! He stretches His hand right out to us with His offer of forgiveness for our guilt, but He does not force us to grasp it. We need to confess our need of it, and to reach out our hand to accept – accept, and not drop. I am sad when I hear a client say, 'Oh yes, I know God forgives me, but I can't forgive myself.' It is as if she claims she has accepted a rich present, and then promptly discards it.

Many counsellors emphasise the need to forgive ourselves. It is certainly important that our lives are not weighed down by our guilt and our regrets. But 'I must forgive myself' has a basic flaw when it stems from counselling theory that has no room for God and no understanding of the Cross. So guilt becomes merely subjective. 'I am holding against myself the mistakes I have made.' Without the Cross there is simply no place to leave the guilt; with the Cross it is blasphemy to hang on to it.

Our God is both holiness and love. One way to tackle 'I can't forgive myself' is something like this:

Counsellor: 'You say that you know that God forgives you. That means that He is dropping any charges He might hold against you. Right?'

Client: 'Yes.'

Counsellor: 'Can you tell me anything in the Bible that tells us what He is like?'

Suppose the client remembers Jesus saying to the disciples, 'If you have seen me you have seen the Father.' (Quick think on my part. Where does that come? John 14. Would it help to turn to it? No, not at the moment.)

Counsellor: 'So is it fair to think that the way He treated people is the way that God treats us?'

Client: 'Seems so.'

We might then look at the story of the woman taken in adultery, in John chapter 8. Jesus made it clear to her that He both forgave her and expected her to change. Or we could turn to Luke chapter 23, and the penitent thief who was assured of a place in heaven.

Counsellor: 'Well, if a holy God forgives you, and says that He is going to forget, what right have you to hold on to your guilt and refuse to let it go?'

Client: 'I suppose not . . . but it's so hard.'

Counsellor: 'I'm not pretending it's easy, and things will happen that will remind you of your mistakes. You have actually got a choice here. You can choose to believe that God really wants to let go, or you can say that you want to carry on listening to the Enemy's whispers about the mess you have made.' I pause, and give her a chance to talk. She seems to be thinking, and wanting to hear more, so I carry on.

'May I tell you about something that happened to me a few years ago? I had had a tough year, and I had been struggling to deal with the violent anger that had become a habit. I thought I was winning, when one morning I blew up on someone. She touched a very sore spot, and I exploded in anger. I knew it was wrong, but she was too hurt to accept my apology.

'So I went off on my own, and I prayed in a way that I have never prayed before or since. I asked God to pour a river of His blood over me for my forgiveness, and then to pour it into the roots of the jealousy or anything else that had caused my explosion. He met me; I was sure of it. But the aftermath of my explosion was like a mushroom cloud that billowed out and affected me and others in the church. I kept thinking, "If only I hadn't . . ." That was true. If I hadn't flared up in that way, the consequences would not have happened.

'Then I realised that, while I was wholly responsible

for what I had done, I was *not* responsible for the way that other people reacted, and I did not need to carry the whole load of the situation. Even so, Satan the accuser made his inroads for months, and once, when I was feeling particularly guilty, Michael (my husband) and I prayed together about it. We needed to confront the accuser, and I was at last free to put it behind me.'

That is a long testimony to use. I do not do it to draw attention to myself, but it shows that I understand something of the struggle she is having, and it contains several teaching points. I do not underline all the details of the story, but I pray that she will ask about anything that the Holy Spirit knows is relevant for her, and that she will ignore the rest. I could pick up on the process of change that may be an unsteady, 'two steps forward and one backward', or on the 'blood' that we tend to think is old-fashioned phraseology about the Cross. I might enlarge on the question of differentiating between my responsibility and that of another.

God used that incident in my life to show me clearly that my bad behaviour gives other people excuses, but not reasons, for their poor reactions. We only have to look at the Sermon on the Mount to find Jesus asking for perfection in our attitudes towards our enemies (Matt. 5:43–48). Or we could talk about Satan and the way to resist him. I will let her take the lead in asking the questions and in applying whatever is relevant to her. I do not want to divert her from her path of discovering how to be really sure of the Lord's forgiveness for her.

Forgiveness Leads To Change

There is one more thing to be said in this vital question of grasping God's grace in forgiveness. In the early chapters of Romans, Paul emphasises God's free gift of justification for sinners. (I heard a crude but useful definition of that long theological word in my early days as a Christian.

God looks at me 'just as if I'd' never sinned.) Then He poses a question. 'Shall we go on sinning, so that grace may increase?' (Rom. 6:1). His answer is emphatic. 'By no means!' Forgiveness should be followed by change in our thinking and in our behaviour. This may, for instance, mean restitution, as it did for Zacchaeus (Luke 19:8), or an attempt to restore strained relationships. We may need to think through with the client the implications of grace received, but common experience is that if the Holy Spirit has really been at work in making forgiveness real He makes the next steps abundantly clear.

Second Corinthians chapter 7:8–13 gives us some insight here. Paul had written a tough letter to the Christians at Corinth, a letter that had caused sorrow. He was encouraged that their sorrow had not left them stuck in the bog of self-pity; instead it had led them to repentance and to a positive change in their attitude. The unholy spirit loves to see us drowning in self-pity and in false guilt. The Holy Spirit rejoices when we are freed from the burden of guilt and when that leads us into a new quality of life.

Homework

1) Re-read p.50. Try the movements that use your hands to illustrate Isaiah 53:6.

2) Learn, with their references, three verses you might use to teach about God's forgiveness. Think out an illustration to use in explaining each one.

3) *With a partner* Decide which one of you will 'be' the client, and which the counsellor. Let the 'client' tell her story, true or fictitious, of guilt. The 'counsellor' will then use her Bible to try to help the 'client' to understand the reality of God's forgiveness.

After the role-play discuss the strengths and weaknesses of the counselling, and pray together about what you have learnt from it. Then reverse the roles, either with the same partner on a later occasion, or immediately by a change of partners if you are in a group.

4

THE CROSS – RESOURCE TO
FORGIVE OTHERS

So far I have implied, but not clearly stated, my definition of forgiveness. 'Dropping the charge' is one way we can put it. Literally, it means 'cutting loose'. A lady once told me that she used to think that forgiving meant pretending that she had not been wronged. No, it means that, whether others have actually done wrong, or I feel that they have, *I choose not to hold it against them*. I choose. That is a commitment of my will. My feelings may be tugging hard in the opposite direction, or they may seem to be dead. I choose to drop whatever charges, real or imagined, I may be holding against another person, or even against God.

Jesus' Teaching About Forgiving

Jesus made it abundantly clear that this is a matter of prime importance. How often do we pray the prayer He taught His disciples? 'Forgive us our trespasses, as we forgive those who trespass against us.' I used to mumble that bit! After Matthew's record of the Lord's Prayer this is the one part he underlines. 'For if you forgive men when they sin against you, your heavenly Father will also forgive you. But if you do not forgive men their sins, your Father will not forgive your sins' (Matt. 6:14–15). It looks straightforward, but it is all too easy to modify it mentally. 'Well, it means that if I do not forgive others it shows that I am not fully grasping His forgiveness to me.' That is true, but incomplete. Certainly it is logical. If I am clutching on to resentment with one hand I cannot be coming to God with my hands open, ready for

Him to take and drop everything for which I need Him to forgive me.

The parable of the unforgiving servant in Matthew chapter 18 makes it impossible to slither over the truth that God will not forgive us if we are unforgiving. Indeed He can't. In verse 21 we find Peter coming to Jesus with a question, and some pride. 'Lord, how many times shall I forgive my brother when he sins against me? Up to seven times?' I wonder which of his brother disciples was niggling Peter at the time! He thought he was setting himself a high standard. The Pharisees taught that letting a matter go three times was ample. Peter, with a smirk on his face, was in for a shock as he listened to Jesus' story. The master remitted a debt of a million pounds in response to his servant's plea. The man went to a fellow servant, demanded repayment of the few pounds he was owed, and refused to be lenient in any way. In due course the master heard of the affair, and he was livid. ' "You wicked servant. Shouldn't you have had mercy on your fellow-servant just as I had on you?" In anger his master turned him over to the jailers to be tortured, until he should pay back all he owed.' Then comes Jesus' punch line. 'This is how my heavenly Father will treat each of you unless you forgive your brother from your heart.' Evasion is impossible. God will be as angry as the master in the story if we refuse to forgive others with the same quality of forgiveness He offers us.

That is a solemn thought, but it is good that there can be no argument. I do not really help the client if I sympathise with 'There, there, you were badly treated, weren't you,' and fail to show Jesus' crystal-clear teaching. His example matches His instruction. When He was on the Cross, for no misdemeanour of His own, He prayed, 'Father, forgive them, for they do not know what they are doing.' That is an astonishing prayer from one who was in such pain. In one way they did know what they were doing, the soldiers who banged in the nails, Pilate with his conviction that Jesus had done nothing wrong, the members of the Sanhedrin with their falsified charges. But they had no conception whatever of the whole weight of the world's sin that was loaded on Jesus. He asked His Father to let it all go. That is the example He set us. If you are inclined to argue, 'That was Jesus. He was unique,' then look at Stephen, who died in similar circumstances with a prayer of forgiveness on his lips (Acts 7:60).

Illustrations About Forgiving

When I saw how fully God forgives – that He blots out, and forgets (Isa. 43:25) – I soon recognised that the quality of my forgiveness must copy His. That was not easy for one whose habit was to blame others fifty times before blaming myself, for one who found it easy to cry over spilt milk. There are many different images I can use to illustrate the fact that God wants to help me to forgive others as surely as He has forgiven me. For example I can imagine myself hiding in a dry, warm cave, the cave of forgiveness. Then I turn round, and from the entrance to the cave I reach out a hand to forgive others. Or I can picture myself going up towards the Cross. I can stretch out against it, feel its solidity and claim the forgiveness He gives; then I turn round with my arms still stretched wide, to face those who need my forgiveness.

Another image is of walking up to Jesus to thank Him for His death. I take His hand and I ask Him to lead me towards those who have hurt me. I find it hard to go by myself, but I know He wants to take me there. 'Forgive *whatever* grievances you may have against one another,' says Paul (Col. 3:13). This is a vital truth, frequently needed in counselling. We do well to be unequivocal in our own understanding, honest in personal experience and well equipped with tools to help others to grasp it.

'Forgive your brother from your heart,' says Jesus (Matt. 18:35). Does that mean that as soon as I have decided to obey Him all my resentment and anger will immediately melt? No; that is a common misunderstanding. See if this simple equation makes sense to you:

CHOICE + PRAYER + PROCESS = CHANGED ATTITUDE + NEW FEELINGS

The starting point is the choice to go the Jesus way instead of the Self way. The Jesus way forgives. The Self way claims a right to feel aggrieved. By myself, my choice to forgive may last as long as the typical New Year's resolution! I need to pray that I may let go of grievances, so that I consciously ally myself with the Holy Spirit and His power. Then the process starts.

Think of an ant deciding to walk from one end of the carpet to the other. There is a point at which it steps on to the edge of the carpet and the journey begins. There are then many steps before it reaches the other end, and there may be a number of obstacles along the way to discourage it from persevering. Sometimes a client feels able to go no further than, 'I am willing to become willing to forgive.' That is like the ant turning round to face the rug, before it takes the first step on to it. But that decision, if brought to God in prayer, is usually quickly followed by, 'All right. I will forgive.' There is then a process. Often repeated prayers of forgiveness are needed to clear both the deep-rooted feelings from the past and the ongoing niggles of the present.

A Personal Example

I was in my forties when I suddenly remembered a shopping excursion that took place when I was about six years old. My mother and I went to buy a new coat and a new dress. There were two possibilities for each, and she offered me a choice; the more expensive of one, and the cheaper of the other. That seemed fair, and I had no problem with my decision; the yellow coat, which was cheaper (I liked its matching hat!), and the flowery dress. No problem – until she over-ruled. We came away with the blue coat and the flowery dress, both of them the expensive ones. I forgot this incident for nearly forty years. When it surfaced I was furious. 'How stupid,' you might say. 'You must have grown out of those clothes after two years. Why should it bother you still?'

Think what happened for the child. Choice was first offered, then taken away. I felt ignored, squashed. The clothes had indeed been long discarded, but the feelings had remained, buried. There had probably been a number of times when my mother had appeared not to listen to me, or had over-ruled. That one memory surfaced, encrusted with the anger of countless other incidents. By then I had learnt the principle of forgiving, so I prayed:

'Lord, please help me to forgive.'

A few days later I would remember it again, and the rage still flared. So, 'Lord, please help me to forgive her.' Gradually the fury diminished, but it took me about six months of working, repeatedly praying, before I could think of the blue coat without a growl.

The Damage Of Resentment

Choice, prayer, process. Choice, prayer, process. The proverb says that 'time heals'. Time usually helps us to push memories into the background, but it will only really bring healing when the resentment at the source of the infection has been cleaned. A wound may heal on the surface, but it will go septic if the dirt remains inside. Scripture has a clear warning about the bitter root that, 'grows up to cause trouble and defile many' (Heb. 12:15). The person who is the most damaged by an unforgiving attitude is the one who harbours the cancerous unforgiveness. However badly we have been hurt, however unjustly we have been treated, whatever the cause of our resentment, the Bible's message is the same. Forgive. Let go. Cut loose.

Whatever The Feelings

It is worth noting that resentment may be sitting dormant, unnoticed. David, talking about his childhood, had referred to one incident when his father had clearly wronged him. I suggested that, in prayer, he should affirm to God that he forgave his father.

'But I don't feel resentful,' said David.

'Well, you were obviously treated unfairly, so it would do no harm to pray like that anyway.'

David appeared to have no difficulty in praying, quite simply assuring God that he forgave his father for that incident. Then he commented, 'Hm, I *was* resentful. I hadn't realised it.'

The very act of speaking aloud the prayer of forgiveness uncovered the resentment that he had not felt, and had genuinely believed to be absent. Whether feelings are rampant or quiescent, the same choice needs to be made. Follow Jesus' example, and tell Him that you want to obey Him by dropping the resentment you hold against another.

Whatever The Situation

The forgiveness process does not only apply to past events. People and situations in the present disturb our peace and make life difficult. There will constantly be jarring, at work, at home, in church, in recreation. A simple basic rule is this. Come to God with, 'Lord, please change me,' before you come to Him with, 'Please change my circumstances.' That prayer is likely to be uncomfortable but fruitful! We must never let go of the need to forgive again and again and again. The alternatives are that we are forever complaining, or that we grit our teeth and bear it, storing up a pile of resentments until a last straw causes an explosion over some trivial matter.

When someone comes with complaints about the current situation he may first need to be faced with the inescapable truth of the Bible's teaching. The combination of the Lord's Prayer and the parable of the unforgiving servant is potent! He may then need encouragement to persevere in his forgiveness, however much he feels affronted. You may have to help him see that these feelings do not just belong to the current situation, but are part of a pattern in his life. Or you may need to help him discover how to confront his opponents with graciousness but firmness. He needs to hear whether God is asking him to persevere in the difficult situation, or using it to nudge him into a new direction.

Whatever The Difficulties

I do not pretend that it is easy to keep a hand stretched out, offering reconciliation, particularly if the offer is rejected and the hand knocked away. It is not easy to forgive from the heart, and then to tell another gently when he has been in the wrong (Matt. 18:15). It is not easy to keep forgiving from an underdog position, when right confrontation may seem to be impossible. It is discouraging to believe that I have forgiven someone else, and then realise that the process is unfinished. Perhaps I hear him being praised, and realise that I would prefer to hear him slandered; that signals that my forgiveness is not yet complete. No, this is not a smooth path. But it is Jesus' path, and so we can count on His Spirit of power and love to help us all along the way.

I recall a woman I met in 1985. She was deeply shaken at first to recognise that she still harboured feelings of dismay against the man who raped her when she was in her early teens. She had thought the matter was buried. As she struggled to pray her forgiveness towards him, and towards his father and brother and their caresses, she wondered why she was finding it quite so hard to find release. Suddenly, late one night, it became clear to her. There was an element in the experience that the pubescent teenager had enjoyed; there was a small part for which *she* had to ask for God's forgiveness. I remember her passing my window next morning, giving me 'thumbs up' as a signal that she reckoned that the matter was now CLOSED.

Nora was another person who found that forgiving, and being forgiven, often go hand in hand. During a counselling course, she told us what God had done since she had told Him that she wanted to change. 'You may remember that at the end of last Monday evening we were asked to pray together in twos and threes, and to apply something from the evening. In my prayer then I told the Lord that I suspected there were people that I needed to forgive that I wasn't aware of at the time, and I asked Him to bring that about in my life some time during the week. The next evening I had a bit of time, so I just asked the Lord if there was some work He wanted to do in showing me anyone I needed to forgive.

'Rather than the name of a person, two words came to mind. "Church camp." As a child I had spent a number of summers at our church camp. I thought I enjoyed those times, and every year I wanted to go back. But as I began to review teachings that I had received from people there, I realised that some had instilled fear into my life – *real fear* of God. My very tender and sensitive heart had been really crippled in a number of ways, and I had been unable to open my heart to the Lord because these nagging fears were around.

'So I started with a couple of fellows, and forgave them for their teaching, and another who had pamphlets, "From the Dance Floor to Hell." Then there were a number of events that were painful as I remembered them. They brought anger in my heart as I thought about them that evening. So God was gracious in helping me to forgive quite a number of people and events over a period of time, just encapsulated in those two words, "church camp". Then I asked Jesus where He was in all of this. I thought He should probably be there somewhere at church camp! I was thankful that I was able to see Him in a number of places.

'This paved the way for what happened later in the week. I thought "It wasn't so bad on Tuesday night, so I'll try it again on Thursday." This time He brought a specific person to mind, someone who is close to me in my life. I wrote almost a page of resentments against this one person, and I was able to forgive each one. A lot of them were quite petty, but under the Lord's light it was easier to release my judgment, and my demands, on this person. I went back over the list, and the tables just turned. After each one I could name a sin in my own life, for which I needed to ask forgiveness. So that was a two-pronged evening of forgiveness that the Lord worked for me.'

I like the combination of ways in which God worked in Nora's life. He led her on one step at a time. The first prod came through the human agency of the counselling seminar; the next ones came directly from the Holy Spirit as she prayed.

Steps To Reconciliation

After the commitment in prayer to forgive comes another question. How do I put things straight with the one who has wronged me? Do I go and visit? Do I write a letter? Do I keep quiet? The answer is rarely clearcut. It is too easy for such a visit to be (or to appear) an excuse for a backhanded way of telling the other person how badly hurt and angry we have been. In Matthew 18:15 Jesus says, 'If your brother sins against you, go and show him his fault, just between the two of you.' The teaching on confrontation is followed by the teaching on forgiving. So much sensitivity to God's leading is needed in reaching out. The motive must be reconciliation, not rebuke; the time may not be immediate. I will hope that the other person will receive me with my apology and my forgiveness, but I need to be secure enough to cope with whatever reaction meets me.

A letter arrived recently from a woman I had met just once, in a prayer group in her church. 'I had been holding a lot of anger, hurt and resentment against the church I once went to. You told me to forgive, forgive, forgive. Well the Lord never let me forget that. I put off going to the pastor, but to grow as I knew I wanted to, I had to forgive and forget. It was very difficult; I put it off for a good year. But I finally did it. And boy does it feel wonderful! It was hard even going into the church, because instantly it brought back all the hurts. We talked, prayed, cried and forgave. And now we're friends.'

For her, forgiving meant going – fearfully, but in obedience to the Lord – to the person and the place where there had been pain. For another person, Harriet, it meant writing a letter. Her own struggles, as she worked through a storehouse of

fifty years of resentment and insecurity, showed her some
of the wrong things she had passed on to her son. This is
how she wrote to him. John is her husband; Susan is her
daughter-in-law; Jane is a friend; and Granny is her own
mother:

During the past year I have been going through a period
of 'healing of the memories'. This has been very painful
at the time of each bout of revelation and eventual giving
over to God, but has left me with a greater certainty
of His existence and personal involvement in my life. I
believe I'm much more mature in my faith and able to
put it to the test and accept the consequences, and to
see God's hand at work in my life. It's a very prolonged
up-and-down existence, but God's love and power are
really real to me now.

I would have retracted long ago, if Jane had not been so
constant and supportive. Her and John's love and vision
to see me whole have given me the impetus to want to go
on. Time after time either a Bible reading or sermon or
chance remark on the radio has just led on to the next step.
And more than anything I have been conscious of people's
prayers, especially Jane's, and I have faced with her many
individual fears, failures and memories of childhood, and
have prayed them through.

Poor old Granny has been the butt of most of my
reactions. Lately I have been able *at last* to forgive her
for things which, unknowingly, she allowed to happen or
which she did to me, which I have resented ever since.
Some things have come up in my consciousness only as
the result of prayer and talk. But, praise the Lord, a lot
of these have been blotted out since I was able to forgive
her for them individually. (This forgiveness has been a
recent gift from God.) There's one major fear which I
still can't let go of, or have the confidence to face and
give over – so pray that this may soon be revealed, faced
and abolished.

The crucial phrase 'failed me' which I used just now has

made me think to my dismay of what, unknowingly, I have done to disturb *your* subconscious, even to inhibiting your life, and your reaction to others, Susan included. And it has made me think of things you may resent about me, or of deep-seated fears caused by my or John's handling of the situation.

If Granny knew of all this about my attitude towards her I'm sure she would want to say from her side, 'I'm sorry.' But she's too old and too vulnerable to talk to about such things. But we are not. So I just wanted to ask your forgiveness for anything in the past twenty-five years that I have done to hamper a free and joyful life for you. For Susan's benefit, too, I have endeavoured to cut the ties of mother-son relationship. I hope I've let you go.

The day after Harriet wrote this letter she sent a copy to Jane, with a note. 'I wrote this letter yesterday – freely and without hesitation; it all came out of the blue. John was astounded and moved. I posted it immediately even before he saw it. Since writing the letter I've had a great and special joy.' Her letter to her son is wise and sensitive, as she draws him alongside, explaining what has been happening in her own life before turning to involve him. She has done her best to put matters right with him. Years later there is much pain in the way her son and daughter-in-law behave towards her and John, as parents and as grandparents. She is *not* responsible for their reaction; that is their choice, their responsibility before God. She and John *are* responsible to behave as wisely and lovingly as they can now, constantly forgiving the anger and rejection that meet them.

'Granny is too old and vulnerable to talk to about such things.' That is exactly what I thought about my own relationship with my mother. As I have said, I struggled for months to forgive her for buying the wrong coat; I forgave her 'from my heart' (Matt. 18:35), and I remember saying to myself with surprise as I drove home from one visit to her, 'I was able to stand up to her!' I had released the chains of unforgiveness that had bound me, but I had no intention of talking to her about it, and visits remained dutiful and stilted.

Another surprise awaited me. She was ninety-two when our move to Canada was planned. One day she told me how glad she was that we had given our teenage children so much freedom to travel alone; then she talked about her own resentment. When she was twelve her mother had vetoed a possible visit to Italy, and had discouraged a possible job in Russia some eight years later. An eighty-year-old resentment – partnered by seventy-year-old anger with herself for not asserting herself against her mother!

I started to talk about the principle of forgiving; then I had a dilemma. Should I tell her that I knew from personal experience what I was saying? I decided to take the risk. As soon as I began to talk to her about the shopping excursion nearly fifty years earlier she replied, 'I've always regretted that. You would have looked sweet in the yellow coat!' Not only was I then down on my knees in front of her, imploring her to accept the forgiveness I was holding out to her. It drew out of me the ability to thank her for all that she had done well, in the battle she had as a young widow on a limited income to raise three children alone. That freed her to express the disappointment she had felt at my failure to show my appreciation over the years, and now it was my turn to ask her to forgive me.

This utterly unexpected conversation was a gift from God that seemed to seal over the work He had begun in me years earlier. We did not talk again in this way before she died, only a few months later, and I do not know what else God did for her; but I do know that she was as glad as I was for that breakthrough in our barrier of artificiality.

Three situations, all different in the way they were handled – a visit, a letter, a long wait. I believe that each way was right for its situation. In our counselling we show the relevant part of the Bible; we make clear the unalterable principles; we offer suggestions of possible courses of action. Then we help the client to take it to the Lord in prayer, and we leave him with the freedom to work it out with God.

The Confidence Of Experience

You may think it strange that, as well as stories about God at work in the lives of other people, I have written much of this chapter in the first person. I have learnt deeply from God through my own experience. That means that when I am with a client I can speak with the assurance that comes from my heart. I am not teaching mere theories, but sharing what I know about a God who has proved Himself real. I do not expect Him to work in exactly the same way in two different lives, and I must be a flexible pipe in His hands, to show His character (as much as I am able) and to teach His truth. Over the years I have become more sure about God. So I have dared to become more assertive in applying His principles to particular cases, at the same time as growing more sensitive in the way I approach people.

My conviction about God's utter goodness means that I can echo Abraham when he says, 'Will not the Judge of all the earth do right?' (Gen. 18:25). That has tremendous implications for our ability to forgive. We do not have to be worried about whether justice will be done, because God is a judge who makes no mistakes. The Bible has a theme about vengeance. 'Do not take revenge, my friends, but leave room for God's wrath, for it is written, "It is mine to avenge; I will repay," says the Lord' (Rom. 12:19, quoting Deut. 32:35). I do not need to take revenge, because I can trust a God whose vengeance is His righteous judgment on all evil. That will come to pass in *His* time, which may well be outside my own lifetime. So instead of taking personal revenge we are called to forgive, and do positive good towards those who have hurt us. Jesus told us to pray for those who persecute us (Matt. 5:44). Paul who, after telling us not to take revenge, suggests instead, 'On the contrary: "If your enemy is hungry, feed him"' (Rom. 12:20).

I was talking today with a father who had just learnt that his teenage daughter had been raped. He hoped that he, personally, would not find the man who assaulted her, for fear that he might want to kill. It was his eighteen-year-old son who suggested that they should pray for the rapist. That is our Lord's way.

Some Work To Do

1) Re-read in your Bible all the references mentioned in this chapter. Then follow Nora's example. Spend some time on your own in prayer, and ask the Lord to show you if there is anyone, past or present, against whom you are harbouring resentment.

2) *With a partner* Do some role-play. One of you will be the client, talking about a grievance (real or imaginary). The other is the counsellor, who will *use her Bible* to help the other to the place of choosing to let go of her grievances.

If you cannot find a partner, write, in full, how you might explain the need to forgive. Then put yourself in the place of a client. Read what you have written, and check out your use of vocabulary and illustration.

3) *On your own, with a partner or with a group* A person says he is willing to forgive but the hurt is an obstacle. What would you do?

5

WHAT ABOUT ANGER?

Righteous Anger And Selfish Anger

Our thinking about forgiveness and about God's vengeance leads us on to considering two sorts of anger. There is anger against injustice and unholiness; that is the righteous anger of God. There is anger against personal hurt; that is the unrighteous anger of a sinner. Confusion is caused when the second is super-imposed on the first; and it is compounded by the teaching of humanists who have a measure of God's truth, particularly in their concern for injustice, but ignore God Himself. It is too easy for an angry Christian to refer to Jesus' anger against the money-changers in the Temple, and to say that He sets us an example of, 'It's all right to be angry.' He follows that by, 'Anyway, Paul tells us to "Be angry but sin not" so he expects us to be angry.' He quotes part of Ephesians chapter 4 verse 26 – in the Authorised Version, which he probably rarely uses! – and ignores verse 31, 'Get rid of all bitterness, rage and anger.'

Think first about Jesus and His life. We do indeed find Him furious in the Temple (John 2:13–16). We find Him angry with the Pharisees for their hypocrisy about sabbath observance and their hard-heartedness about deformity (Mark 3:5). He shared His Father's anger about the violation of the holy place and about injustice against the poor. But when He was on the Cross, we find Him wholly forgiving towards those with whom He had every right to be angry – or so we might think! John Stott explains the difference superbly in his commentary on Ephesians,

God's New Society, and he then comments (p.185), 'There is such a thing as Christian anger, and too few Christians either feel it or express it. When we fail to do so, we deny God, damage ourselves and encourage the spread of evil.'

But most of the anger we meet in counselling is the unrighteous anger of the personally hurt. So take another look at Ephesians 4:26. ' "In your anger do not sin." Do not let the sun go down while you are still angry, and do not give the devil a foothold.' Paul quotes from Psalm 4:4, 'In your anger do not sin; when you are on your beds, search your hearts and be silent.'

Are the psalmist and Paul not telling us to examine the quality of our anger? It is far easier to look at the one who is wronging us, to shout at him or to complain to our friends and to God, than it is to look at ourselves and our own reactions. 'In your anger do not sin.' Ensure that your anger is not the sin of assuming that you have a right to be angry because you have been hurt. As you lie awake at night, fuming about the day's events, 'search your hearts.' Ask God to show you His perspective on what has been happening. You are likely to see how you have been wrong; then choose to forgive, and so become at peace, and silent.

I have referred earlier to my own violent anger that had grown into a habitual pattern. It was a shock to recognise how distorted my attitude was. In effect I was saying that because I had been hurt, I had a right to be angry. Yes, I was indeed angry because of past wounds, and I often used that, unconsciously, as an excuse to be angry. But as a follower of Jesus I had no right to hold on to that anger. Once I saw that, and was willing to renounce my angry attitude, the spring-cleaning started. The anger did not disappear overnight, but I reckon that the process was one of the three most important periods of growth in my spiritual life.

Anger – The Devil's Weapon

Paul continues with a warning about the devil. 'Don't give him a chance to get in!' Clutching on to anger is one of the ways in which we give easy access to the Enemy's infiltration into our lives. John Stott comments (*God's New Society*, p.187), 'He loves to lurk around angry people, hoping to be able to exploit the situation to his own advantage by provoking them into hatred or violence or a breach of fellowship.' Sadly, I can endorse that from personal experience, knowing how my anger was a major cause of fellowship broken longterm.

I can add to it, too, another aspect of Satan's destructive work. There was a period of a year when, time and again, the devil found a crack of resentment that he could exploit. Physical symptoms of an ashen face or heavy limbs would show either my husband or me that something was wrong, although sometimes we were slow to recognise it. (It may seem preposterous, but once I even spent five days in bed, thinking I had 'flu, before perceiving the Enemy's influence!)

When we had finally been alerted to the trouble, we would pray together. My turn first, dolefully. 'Lord, what have I got to confess *this* time?' The answer usually came quickly. Nearly every time the Lord showed me someone I needed to forgive, and He used that year to teach me just how much He minds about bitterness and resentment. Once I complained, 'Lord, it's not fair! That was only a tiny crack.' It was as if the evil one had taken a knife, squeezed it into a hairline fracture, and wriggled it round to enlarge the crack into a chasm. I am sure that God allowed it so that I would learn a lesson I could not forget. Ashamed confession on my part would be followed by confident resistance against the foe, and physical symptoms disappeared very soon.

Do you want to argue that it all sounds very far-fetched? A few years ago I would have agreed with you. The New Testament repeatedly invites us to, 'resist the devil and he will flee from you' (Jas. 4:7). That is not the same thing as asking God for His help. It requires that we come, positively, against the Enemy, strong in the power of Jesus. And then he really does turn tail and flee.

Dealing With Personal Anger

Simple drawings of three boxes are helpful in showing a client about different ways of dealing with personal anger.

I *The stiff upper lip*

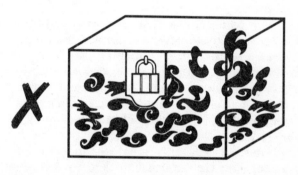

This is the traditional Christian approach, or 'the stiff upper lip.' The negative emotions seethe around inside the box. When they ooze out in criticism their source is unrecognised, and when a wall of silence is built, it is seen as self-control.

Depression frequently springs from this source. Emotional energy is consumed by subterranean anger and guilt; then more energy has to be used in the effort to repress them. Little energy is left for living; result – depression. That is an incomplete view of depression; some will say it is simplistic. But there is truth in its simplicity. Denial of anger is dishonest, and it brings no peace either to the owner of the box or to family and friends. A depressed person often appears weak. There is, actually, much strength around, but it is being dissipated instead of being harnessed for good. Nuclear energy can be used for electrical power, or for an atomic bomb!

When anger appears to be locked away, deep inside a person's being, I explain about the inner walls that a child often has to erect as a defence against emotional pain. Those walls become a habit, and the person does not know how to change. In this situation I suggest that the adult Christian prays that he is able to give God permission to remove those walls in whatever way He knows is best. The client's head understands and makes that choice, although he may recognise that his gut-level feelings find it hard to trust people or God, and are terrified of the consequences of such a prayer.

Anne had emerged from a long period of emotional instability after a hysterectomy, and was holding a responsible job as a warden in a residential hostel. Many of her friends commented to her that she seemed unable to show any anger, even when it might be appropriate to do so, and she reached the point of wanting God to change this.

It transpired that her anger had been locked away all her life. She was born within a year of her parents' marriage, when her mother was only nineteen and her father was unemployed. The Holy Spirit unlocked for her some deep memories, and she verbalised feelings that she carried from a time when she knew no words. As she replayed some of the experience of her own birth she shouted angrily, 'I know you didn't choose for me to be born, but I didn't choose it either!'

The anger she felt against her unwelcome arrival in the world was submerged in the need to win acceptance, and had remained hidden all her life. When its source was uncovered she was able, as an adult Christian, to forgive her parents, and she was then able to move into handling anger in a realistic way. This was one part of an extended time of counselling that was simultaneous with her growth in relationships and in her work. It is an example that is extreme but not unique.

II *The secular way*

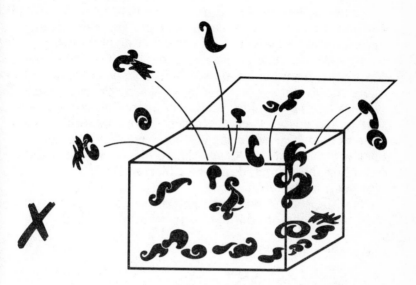

The second box is the approach that was in fashion with the humanists a decade ago. 'Admit your anger. Release it, and that will get rid of it.' A small event is allowed to trigger an explosion. As bricks are hurled through the air (metaphorically or actually!) relationships are damaged, sometimes permanently, and the aftermath is likely to be an increased sense of guilt. The explosion does not even clear the box of its mess. Although it may, initially, release tension, the seeds of anger remain in the box, where they again start to multiply.

It is all too easy to let anger out inappropriately. Have you ever stubbed your toe? There is pain, and so there is anger. You cannot usefully be angry with the leg of the chair that hurt you, and you do not particularly want to admit your own carelessness. Your friend hears your squawk of pain and comes alongside to sympathise – and cannot understand why you bite her nose off! Or your husband comes home tired at the end of *your* frustrating day, expecting an instant meal instead of greeting you with the understanding you want. You shout at him, and at the moment of explosion you feel as if he has deserved it all, not seeing that you have hurled at him the day's accumulated feelings. The habit of anger grows stronger daily, and its owner is caught in a trap.

Beware! Cold anger can also be a habit. Cold anger, expressed from behind pursed lips, is as destructive in the long run as hot anger. It is just more subtle in its tactics. I think of one couple I knew. The more volcanic she was, the more like an iceberg he became. When he turned round and walked away when she was in the middle of her diatribe her wrath increased. As she chased him down the corridor shouting, he retreated into his office and shut the door of his heart as well as his room.

No, the second box is no improvement on the first as a long-term solution, but here is the third picture.

III *The Jesus way*

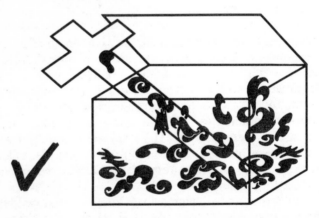

This is the box that Jesus offers us. The lid is partly open; the anger is recognised, and a Cross has been slid through the opening. Remember that it is through the Cross that we find forgiveness for all our sin – including our sinful anger. It is through the Cross that we find the resources to forgive others – for anything that has caused our angry reaction. So all the debris is sucked up, and the box is cleaned out.

Can forgiveness start too soon?

There is one school of counselling that fears a 'quick fix' if we encourage a client to start the process of forgiving others before he has unearthed all his anger. I am sure this is a fallacy. If a basement is full of rubbish you do not need to identify it all before you begin to use the dustbin! When we discover that there really is a 'safe' place to bring our anger we do not need to deny the feelings that we feared would overwhelm us if we let them loose. If you use these drawings with a client you can suggest that Jesus is asked to keep His hand on the lid, to hold it open as long as necessary. That will ensure that the box is not shut on top of anger that is being ignored.

Mary was using a different image to pray forgiveness towards her ex-fiancé. In prayer she had imagined that she had a large sheet of paper on which she had drawn a cross. Under one of its arms were her resentments, under the other were her sins. I suggested that when she had finished praying about everything she had 'written' she should roll up the paper and carry it to Jesus.

She paused. She had concentrated on the things she felt she needed to forgive in her fiancé, but then the Holy Spirit showed her one part of her own sin that she had ignored. Afterwards she confessed that Jesus unexpectedly moved towards her in her 'prayer picture'. He helped her to roll up the paper and He took it away Himself. If a client is really open to letting God do what He chooses He will not allow superficiality in prayer – and I reckon that I can usually detect if a client is being deliberately dishonest before God.

Remember that forgiveness is a process. We never have to pretend that one prayer of forgiveness will clear away all the feelings. But it is a help, not a hindrance, to start that process. It becomes easier to empty the box when peace starts to replace the turmoil. We can dig out *all* the anger and resentment, for we know that we can bring it to the Cross. There it will be destroyed instead of being destructive.

One day I visited Wai-Ling, and found her in the depths of depression. She told me of some of the crises of her life. The youngest of a family of eight children, she was born at the time of her father's bankruptcy. Her father died when she was studying overseas, and she was unable to cross the Pacific for her father's funeral; her mother's death had also been an exceptionally difficult time. Her favourite sister had committed suicide, and finally her first child died in a cot death. There was certainly plenty to cause anger and depression. I suggested that her anger was like a black lake, into which she needed to plant the Cross. Even as I spoke she found herself visualising the scene, and she could see the black anger being sucked up into the Cross. This spoke to her about the power of the Cross to neutralise the grief and anger. There was still plenty that she needed to work through in more detail, but she now knew the direction she had to go. The lake and the box differ in their imagery, but they express the same truth about the way to deal with the anger against being hurt.

Anger Against God

What if there is suffering for which we cannot blame any particular person? 'That must be God's fault. Why has He allowed it? He should have stopped it!' This is not the place for an exhaustive treatise on the problem of pain, but let me attempt a summary.

God created a good world, and He put mankind in charge. Human disobedience led not only to the inherited taint in human nature, but also to disruption in the world for which we are responsible. We find the first hint of this in Genesis 3:18, in the 'thorns and thistles' that God said would grow. Earthquakes, famine, war, illness, deformity, abuse, divorce; all alike are part of the way the world has been spoilt. The totality of sin leads to the totality of suffering. At times we can see a direct link between one and the other;

for example when a drunken driver kills a child, or the chain of suffering set up when a victim of abuse becomes in turn the abuser. At other times the pain appears to be nobody's fault – except God's.

He made us for a love-relationship with Him. In that relationship He showers gifts upon us, and in return He looks for our trust and our obedience. Love does not force its own way. It is generous; it leaves us free to choose. God is deeply grieved by sin. It evokes both His righteous anger and His profound compassion. So why doesn't He do something to intervene?

He has. He sent His Son, to live and to die for us. 'This is how God showed his love among us: He sent his one and only Son into the world that we might live through him. This is love: not that we loved God, but that he loved us and sent his Son as an atoning sacrifice for our sins' (1 John 4:9–10). The Cross of Jesus, who died and rose again, has the fulness of God's provision for our redemption. We can only appropriate that for ourselves by allowing His Spirit to work in us, in His way, according to His rules.

Think of a child coming to parents with a complaint. 'Hey Dad. Hey Mum. This watch you gave me doesn't work.'

'Chris, did you set it the way I showed you?'

'No, I did it my way.'

There's plenty of Chris in every one of us! We disobey the Maker's instructions – and then complain to the Manufacturer!

The Cross is the supreme act of love in history, but not the only one. God is constantly demonstrating His love to us, but our worm's-eye view is limited. We do not share His bird's-eye view which stretches to infinity. We see merely what is happening in one corner of the universe in one moment of eternity, and the pain we feel blinds us to the reality of His love.

So what are we to do with our anger against Him? He does not actually deserve it. He has not done anything wrong; that is an intrinsic part of His nature, that He makes *no* mistakes. So come to Him with it. He knows about it anyway. He understands. He is not angry, and He wants to help. So why not let Him – however you feel? I often say to a client, 'It does not matter how much you shout at Jesus, but give Him a chance to reply. That is only fair.'

One afternoon I was leading a workshop on prayer counselling at a conference in Alberta. In the course of this I asked the group to spend some minutes in silence, praying for God to be in control of this time. Then I asked each person to imagine herself walking along a path in a wood, and to look for someone to come towards her. We waited for the Holy Spirit to meet each individual.

That evening a couple approached me. The husband started by asking for me to pray for a young man with cystic fibrosis whom they knew. Then it came closer to home; their own five-year-old son had the same terminal disease. Next his wife spoke up and told us what had happened for her in the afternoon workshop. As she prayed, she found Jesus coming along the path. To her surprise she found herself striking Him repeatedly. She had never before recognised how angry she was with God over her son's illness. His reply was beautiful. He just put His arms round her, and held her. That spoke of His love and acceptance of her, even with her anger. He showed her that He cared, that He was holding her and her family when it might seem that He was ignoring them. He met her that day in a memorable and totally unexpected way.

A few months later I was telling this story to a young woman in Oxford. Her beloved only brother had died earlier that year after a specially nasty train accident and I asked her whether she had allowed her genuine feelings towards God to emerge; in particular, had she been angry? Her experience had been amazingly similar to that of the lady in Alberta. One day when she was praying with two friends she had a sense of Jesus standing next to her, wearing a cloak. She, too, was hitting out at Him in anger. His reply was to wrap His cloak round her, a token of His love and care.

Yes. God understands. We need not be afraid of showing Him our anger, even shouting at Him. But we should stop to give Him a chance to reach us in the middle of it. He may not change the circumstances. He *will* help us, so long as we do not demand that His help comes on our terms.

As we look at Jesus' struggle in the Garden of Gethsemane we find that even He would have liked the situation to be different. It encourages me to find that even He needed to pray in the same way three times before He was ready to say to His Father, 'Not what I will, but what you will' (Mark 14:36). But He did not turn aside. With His jungle knife He has cleared a path for us to follow, though that path may be narrow and overgrown with poisonous thorns. 'God is faithful; he will not let you be tempted beyond what you can bear. But when you are tempted, he will also provide a way out so that you can stand up under it' (1 Cor. 10:13). He knows our capacity for pain better than we know it ourselves. There have been times when I have cried out to Him, 'Why are you stretching me to breaking point?' But He knows what I can endure with His help. The stretching is painful, but it brings growth and lasting benefit if I allow it.

Homework

1) Think about the things that make you angry. Prayerfully try to sort out which are matters of righteous anger against injustice and against God's holiness, and which are matters of anger against personal pain.

2) If possible, take the matters of righteous anger against injustice to a small group (perhaps a house fellowship group or a group of your friends). Talk and pray together about whether you – individually or corporately – should use the energy of your anger to take any action towards righting a wrong.

3) *On your own, or with a partner* Take time to think, talk and pray about your personal reactions of anger. There are two main questions: a) Are you choosing to forgive the people concerned? b) Is your current anger linked up with past unresolved events in your life?

6

THE CROSS FOR HEALING
AND FOR VICTORY

The Cross clearly spells out the two directions of forgiveness, vertical and horizontal. There are two other huge truths about the Cross that are particularly relevant for counselling. We consider both in this chapter.

The Cross For Healing

I have written earlier that we should not restrict our use of the word sin to personal misdeeds. It is a broad word that reminds us that the whole world is distorted. So the concept of salvation through the Cross does not merely focus on each individual, nor on one period of history. I was greatly helped by C.S. Lewis' thought of the infinite God, outside time, viewing a page in a book as a whole, seeing everything as NOW, while we finite beings run along the lines, bound by the past, present and future of history. To Him salvation is NOW, while for us we look at three tenses. We have been saved, by Christ's death at a moment in history. We are being saved, as we appropriate the effects of that death and resurrection through the Spirit at work in us. We shall be saved, when the Second Coming brings triumphant fulfilment.

God's huge resources

That thought is an important one as we consider the resources for healing that are to be found in the Cross: healing for body, emotions, relationships. It means that we can come to God in prayer, confident that nothing is outside the bounds of His ability to heal and restore. We must also come humbly, not demanding, but trusting Him for whatever measure of healing is best for us at the time.

That humble confidence will affect the way in which we pray with a client who may have a variety of needs. I often suggest that we bring in prayer all the individual needs of which we are aware, and give God permission to start wherever He wants. We can be sure that He is not a capricious God, waiting to satisfy His own whims, but one who knows and desires our highest good. The more confident I am about Him, the more I can communicate, with a sure and gentle touch, that He really is trustworthy.

While I talk I draw a simple pin-man picture:

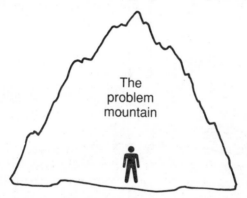

The
problem
mountain

That is how the client often feels, a tiny person in front of a huge mountain of problems and needs. The mountain may be made up of present circumstances and relationships, with feelings about those situations that ring bells with past experiences. Guilt, despair, anger, practical needs, temptation, failures, lack of direction; each need is piled on the other, and the whole mountain is overwhelming. Then I do another simple drawing, and explain to her what some of these resources are (see over).

Then we put the two together. The figure is no bigger, but because it stands under the Cross and the rainbow there is a different perspective on the mountain.

Healing for the body

How do we find the Cross relevant for particular needs? Isaiah chapter 53 is a rich source of teaching.

Through the Cross there is *healing for the body*. 'Surely he took up our infirmities' (v.4). Matthew quotes this verse after writing of an intensive time of Jesus' healing ministry, showing Jesus fulfilling this Scripture. All healing, whether it is administered through normal channels of medicine, or by His direct intervention, comes from God.

An atheistic doctor might not be too pleased to be told that! It is grievous that the advance of medical science often leads to medical practices that are utterly against God's ethics; indeed, the danger is that a doctor can be allowed to assume the place of God over matters of life and death. But however healing comes it still fits into the picture of disease as one aspect of sin, and healing as one dimension of salvation through the Cross.

I do not want to be drawn into a discussion of 'holistic health'. The concept of the relationship between different aspects of wholeness – physical, emotional and mental – is right. Unfortunately those who are in the forefront of promoting the concepts are often in the New Age movement, with its subtle but definite undermining of Christian truth, ethics and spirituality. I was once asked to speak on 'A Christian approach to inner healing' to a group of nurses interested in holistic health. The led meditation that opened the meeting asked us to 'open ourselves up to the light that is within us'. The intention had been a Christian meditation, for my benefit. Instead I sensed a subtle false doctrine, and I found myself quietly praying in tongues as a protective barrier against any false spirits to which we might be exposing ourselves. When I spoke about the uniqueness of Jesus and the Cross for emotional healing I could feel a silent wall of hostility, and I was dismayed and sad that the Christian who had invited me to speak had not seen how she was being deceived.

Healing for emotions

Healing is indeed not only for the body but also for the emotions. '*He carried our sorrows*' (Isa. 53:4). All *grief* can be taken to Jesus. On the Cross His suffering was deeper than any we shall ever know. Even when He was praying in Gethsemane, in the anguish of knowing what He was facing next day, 'his sweat was like drops of blood falling to the ground' (Luke 22:44). When He was dying the suffering was limited in time but infinite in its intensity.

'He was *despised and rejected* by men' (Isa. 53:3). Jesus identifies with all our *rejection*. How necessary it is to know that when we are counselling, for we meet rejection in many guises, with a variety of roots. On the human level 'even his own brothers did not believe in him' (John 7:5); that thought gives encouragement to many Christians who feel unwanted and misunderstood in their own families. On another level we remember His desolate cry, 'My God, my God, why have you forsaken me?' (Matt. 27:46). Was He actually being rejected by His Father at that point? Not rejected, but cut off. The alienation from the Father as Jesus carried the load of our sins means that He can identify with any sense of rejection experienced by a client, even if the counsellor cannot.

Jesus is there, too, whenever we are being *humiliated*. 'Like one from whom men hide their faces he was despised, and we esteemed him not' (Isa. 53:3). We can return to the story of the Crucifixion, and we find Jesus being mocked and taunted by Jewish leaders and ordinary passers-by alike (Matt. 27:39–44). Not only did He endure it, He showed us how to face it. 'He was oppressed and afflicted, yet he did not open his mouth' (Isa. 53:7). This is a thought that Peter picks up. 'When they hurled their insults at him, he did not retaliate; when he suffered, he made no threats. Instead, he entrusted himself to him who judges justly' (1 Pet. 2:23).

The same chapter looks forward, too, to the *Resurrection*. 'After the suffering of his soul, he will see the light of life, and be satisfied' (Isa. 53:11). We thank God that the Cross is now empty. There is help for the *bereaved* person in two ways. Jesus is risen, to be a living friend. And because, 'Christ has indeed been raised from the dead, the firstfruits of those who have fallen asleep' (1 Cor. 15:20) there is assurance for us of life after death.

It is good, too, when we are alongside someone who is mourning to remember that Jesus' human experience included the grief of losing a close friend and a relative. He was only a young man when Joseph died, and later we find Him weeping outside the tomb of Lazarus.

Great sensitivity is needed to have the gentle patience to stay alongside, and weep and wait, as well as to point to the hope of the Resurrection. Two people come to my mind. One was Donald, the day after his parents and his only brother had been killed in a car crash. All he could say in his brokenness was, 'Thank you so much for coming. Thank you so much for coming.' There was little for me to say; I just needed to be there, in silence, loving, quietly praying.

The other was an Anglican bishop, a few months after the death of his wife. He told us how he used to glance quickly through the day's pile of mail, and sort the letters into two piles before reading them more carefully. The helpful ones spoke of her as a person the writers had loved and known, while the ones that were filled with confident verses of Scripture were left on one side until later. His head knew they were true, but his grieved feelings were not ready to absorb them.

Healing for divisions

Another vital aspect of the Cross for counselling is that it is the place of *reconciliation*; reconciliation between God and man, and between man and man. Paul spells out clearly in 2 Corinthians chapter 5 that he is 'Christ's ambassador', that he brings 'the message of reconciliation'. 'We implore you on Christ's behalf: Be reconciled to God' (vv.18–20). We, too, are ambassadors in the same ministry. In Ephesians chapter 2 he writes of the barrier between Jew and Gentile being broken down. 'His purpose was to create in himself one new man out of the two, thus making peace, and in this one body to reconcile both of them to God through the cross, by which he put to death their hostility' (vv.15–16).

Paul had the big picture: Jew reconciled with Gentile. In counselling we normally work with individuals. We may be counselling one person, to help him to see how he can work towards reconciliation with another whom we may never meet. Or we may be in the middle of a marriage or some other family relationship, or with friends or partners in business at a time of disagreement. Counselling both parties is more difficult than just meeting with one individual, because we have a natural inclination to identify more readily with one side than with the other. We must try to convey that God is impartial in His love. I often say, perhaps to a married couple, 'It is not that I stand in the middle, on nobody's side. I'm on the side of both of you, because I want to see the best thing happening for both.' But of course, as soon as I confront the husband on some issue, he will feel that I am siding with his wife. Then the moment I turn round to challenge her, she feels aggrieved that I have changed sides! I need to develop the hide of a rhino with the heart of a gazelle, while all the time I seek wisdom from the Lord.

A glance at marriage counselling

Marriage counselling, or indeed counselling of any broken relationship, is not easy. Genuine willingness for reconciliation is only the start, but it can give the foundation of commitment to working through a mound of problems. One big difficulty arises out of the fact that we start by counselling three things at the same time: two individuals, and the relationship itself, with the tangles of many years. Many of their tussles arise because each one has failed to understand the assumptions that both have carried into the marriage from a quarter of a century of upbringing, or to recognise the painful feelings from past experiences that cause eruption in anger or withdrawal.

Last evening I was with a couple who postponed their wedding two months ago, when she felt that she could not cope with the stress of their frequent arguments. We examined the factors that trigger their explosions and then cause them to escalate. We finished our time together after she saw her need to break the unhealthy ties with her family, and he recognised that there is unresolved pain from his teenage years that smarts whenever she snubs him without listening to him fully. Each of them needs to work on these individual concerns, whether or not they are going to commit their lives to each other.

An image for prayer

It is sometimes helpful to suggest to the client that she imagines herself in front of the Cross, bringing all her needs. First she pictures herself clutching the Cross with both hands, to claim the forgiveness that is assured. Then she holds tight with one hand, while stretching out the other hand towards those who have wronged her.

Next she holds out cupped hands towards God, with the humility that does not demand any particular aspect of healing and with the faith that believes that He wants to give good gifts to His children. That attitude saves us from the brash arrogance of those who assume that God will always do what they want, in the way and at the speed they demand. At the same time we maintain, even develop, our confidence in Jesus who said, 'With men this is impossible, but with God all things are possible' (Matt. 19:26).

Why does God not always heal?

We cannot expect perfection in this life, and it is the prerogative of the God who is all wisdom and all love to decide the priorities of the agenda for healing and for change. So when we come to Him with confident humility, open to receive whatever He wants to give we can be certain that He always answers prayer, even if it is not in the way we had hoped or expected. We used to work with a minister who was particularly interested in healing, and I know of a number of people with cancer for whom he prayed.

I visited one lady with him many times. We saw her grow

in faith and in character. When she developed a large malignant growth on her liver we prayed for healing, alongside her medical treatment; successive X-rays showed the tumour shrink and disappear. As far as I know she is alive ten years later. Others with cancer for whom he prayed died, but there was always some visible intervention from God. One received Christ into her life; another had far less pain than was expected; yet another died more quickly than she 'should'. Yes, prayer was answered, although there was no miraculous extension of life. Instead these people found the ultimate healing, the freedom from sorrow and pain that death brings.

The Cross For Victory Over Satan

Do you remember the enormous cross that I saw one day as I was praying my way round a field? The fourth strand, the victory of the Cross, is also relevant to counselling. 'Having disarmed the powers and authorities, he made a public spectacle of them, triumphing over them by the cross' (Col. 2:15). The evil powers and authorities cannot be ignored. But they are defeated. As Jesus was dying He cried out in a loud voice, 'It is finished' (John 19:30; Matt. 27:50). We hear a shout of triumph. Jesus knew that the devil, whom He encountered face to face at the outset of His ministry, was indeed vanquished. But he refuses to acknowledge his defeat, and Peter warns us, 'Your enemy the devil prowls around like a roaring lion looking for someone to devour' (1 Pet. 5:8).

I look back to World War II. There could be no real doubt about the final outcome after the Allies had invaded France on D-Day in June 1944. But Hitler did not stop fighting. The Allies advanced steadily towards Berlin, but their progress was resisted all the way. There were many casualties, and Hitler's forces won some notable battles. Finally VE Day came in May 1945. Hitler was dead, and peace was declared. In our war with Satan, the Cross shows that Christ's victory is assured. But we are living in history between the D-Day of Jesus' death and the VE Day of the Second Coming, and Satan refuses to surrender.

Think again of that image of clasping the Cross to claim forgiveness, reaching out from it to forgive others, and then standing with upturned hands to receive healing. It is as we stand close to the Cross that we have the confidence to resist Satan. The Cross is the supreme evidence of God's love to me, and Satan cannot abide love, not real self-giving love. The Cross is a place of light, and Satan and his forces are of the darkness. It is often useful to take a client through those four steps. I explain that if we are standing apart from the Cross, with unconfessed sin or resentment in our lives, we are vulnerable to the enemy's attacks. But if we have brought in prayer all the wrong things we have recognised, then we can hold up Paul's shield of faith against the 'flaming arrows of the evil one' (Eph. 6:16).

I finish this chapter with a story. Ruth was a university student, a deeply committed Christian. When she first came to see me she had been ill for eight months with little intermission; the doctors had done all manner of tests, and could not see any medical reason for illness continuing.

A discerning friend saw that the root of her trouble was probably emotional rather than medical. She came from a Christian home where she was sure that love was real, and her mother had cared well for the family as well as sharing in her husband's work. There was no doubt that there was much that was genuinely good. Yet I detected symptoms that showed that things were probably less solid than Ruth thought.

On our second meeting she began to talk about some of the negative experiences in her childhood. There was a tight budget, and resentment that her father was never able to sit in church with the family; even when they were on holiday he was 'paying' for their accommodation by leading services. There were good reasons for her parents' sacrifice in sending her to school out of the neighbourhood where they lived; she was grateful for their generosity, but it entailed a tiring daily journey, and school friends lived a distance away. Their home was tied to her father's job; it was large, and her mother was often out at meetings in the evenings.

Ruth remembered that she was only about seven when she made a decision that she would never cry. After all, if she cried in bed, probably no one would hear; if anyone did come, it would only be the babysitter. Gradually she saw the connection between the feelings she had denied for so long and the illness caused by the suppressed tension, and she began to allow God to bring different aspects of the Cross to bear on these hidden needs.

One afternoon she told me about a visit to the hospital when she was a teenager, and she was able to see some of the feelings left behind from that day that were still clogging her. When she was ready to pray, I suggested that she use the imagery I have already mentioned. God gave her a very clear picture. First there were attitudes and resentments she needed to confess. Then she imagined herself reaching out towards the two or three people that she had seen, during our afternoon's discussion, needed her forgiveness. To my surprise she named others, because God reminded her clearly about other people against whom she was harbouring resentment. Next she held out her hands, to ask God for whatever part of her healing He knew she was ready to receive.

Then her image of the Cross changed. Instead of being solid and firm in the ground, it became like a processional cross used in some churches. She picked it up and marched forward, confident that the devil must retreat in front of it. She saw a fence almost surrounding her, but marched forward, and out through an opening at the far end. Then she turned and looked back, and she saw that the gap through which she had come was closed behind her. She could not return. She knew that God was at work, leading her forward, bringing healing, gradually overcoming the devil's destructive work in her life.

When Ruth read the first draft of this she asked for some details to be changed. Then she commented, 'I must admit that I found it very interesting to read your account of that time together. It's strange how I remember such different things about it; different details that were important to me have stuck in my mind.' This underlines the fact that the counsellor will *never* understand 100 per cent what it is like for the client, in the problem, in the teaching, in the prayer, in the changes to be made. God alone has the perfect understanding, and I am thankful that He is at work, picking up on my mistakes.

For Your Own Work

1) *Alone, with a partner, or in a counselling support group* Think back to times in your own life when you have been in physical or emotional need, or when your relationships have been awry. a) In what ways have the intervention or the prayers of other people been a known help? b) In what ways do you feel that other people let you down?

Make brief notes to answer those questions. Then use your notes and your discussion a) to learn how you can better help others in need, b) to pray with thanksgiving for the helpers and in forgiveness towards those who have failed you.

2) Think of one person you know who is in need of healing in any area of life. Is there anything in this chapter that sheds light on how you should be seeking to help that person, by prayer or in any other way?

7

THE FAMILY INHERITANCE –
FOR GOOD OR ILL

The topic for an essay at school was, 'What do you want to be?' One child wrote, 'I would like to be myself. I tried to be other things but I always failed.' That quotation from a *Reader's Digest* could be echoed by many of the people who have opened their hearts to me.

Patricia was a primary school teacher, good at her job. She was a single woman in her early thirties, reserved, not too sure of herself. She told me that her father had great expectations that his family would be 'a model family', to compensate for his own inadequate childhood. It was not surprising that she, the oldest of four children, had a highly developed sense of responsibility. She had begun to recognise her anger with him, initially about the way that her mother was expected to be the 'perfect farmer's wife', without the chance to develop her personal gifts. On Patricia's first visit we talked about forgiveness, and she prayed that she would not be stuck with this anger. Afterwards she commented that she felt as if she had been turned inside out and shaken!

Her next visit was prompted by her younger sister's imminent wedding. After talking about her feelings over this, we prayed. She was surprised that God gave her a simple picture. There was a baby, dressed in white, sitting up in her cot; not doing anything, just sitting. We saw in this a symbol of the way she had been expected to be a perfect child in this supposedly model family, and she prayed that she would be able to forgive her father for this burden that even the baby could sense. We did not think that God had finished with her for the evening, so we turned to Him again.

Her next picture showed a toddler on a tricycle, riding

around in front of the house. The focus here was not on the child but on the front door, where 'a parental figure' (to use her phrase) was standing, propped up by the door jambs, unable to leave their support. It seemed that God was showing her that, whatever the child's needs, neither of her parents had the inner strength to meet them. So she now needed to say to God that she recognised that they did not have the resources to give her all she had needed emotionally, and to ask that her anger might be replaced by compassion for their weakness. At the same time the 'child' in her still needed to forgive them for not giving her the support she needed.

It may seem strange to ask her to forgive them for something they were unable to do. The adult in Patricia was able to see their weaknesses, but the child in her was still carrying the feelings of being deprived. Those were the feelings that she chose to drop by praying forgiveness.

We felt that the Lord had still not finished the evening's work, and He gave her yet another picture. 'I'm standing next to a bonfire!' she told me. I envisaged a huge Guy Fawkes bonfire, flames leaping, but she described the ashes of a burnt-out fire, and herself as 'THE NEW ME' standing there.

In the following weeks I asked her from time to time how the 'New Me' was progressing. It was not that she had an immediate, total transformation. God gave her a promise that what He had started He would continue; Philippians 1:6 comes to mind. 'He who began a good work in you will carry it on to completion until the day of Jesus Christ.' That 'New Me' was a decisive sign for her of God's renewing work. Over the years I am watching the continuation. The completion will not happen until Christ's return.

To return to my story about Patricia. One Sunday evening the following year she and her sister returned from a weekend at home, distressed at their father's condition. He was both deeply depressed, and full of wild, aggressive thoughts, saying, 'The devil is in me.' They told me some family history. I have forgotten details, but have an impression of some eccentric characters in previous generations, a sign that the pattern of disturbance might be inherited.

A few days later I spent several hours with their father. He explained his sense of utter defeat, the tax demands weighing heavily on him, his extreme sense of guilt and his desire to lash out when cornered. I shared with him the experience God had given me earlier that week, when He had shown me that the arms of the Cross were wide enough to cover anything at all about which I might be feeling guilty.

Was *his* guilt too huge? His immediate reply was, 'Yes'. Then he paused, and with a wry smile he admitted that perhaps the Cross was big enough to cover even his wrong. That became the turning point that enabled him to ask the Spirit of Christ into his life, and he left, having fixed a return visit a few days later.

When I had listened to the family history from his daughters and had learnt that the family had lived in the same farmhouse for five generations, I began to suspect a demonic presence lurking. On Graham's second visit my clergyman husband joined us, and we talked in matter-of-fact terms about the reality of demonic spirits and that, there might be an essence of truth in his own statement, 'The devil is in me.' We did not need to know how some evil strand might have entered the family, maybe many generations back. We needed to attack it, with Graham's consent. As we claimed the power of Christ to release Graham from whatever dark force had affected him from past generations, Michael sensed an evil presence depart, and Graham left our house that day a more free man.

I could not continue to give him the ongoing help he needed, and I am sad to say that I do not know how his faith has progressed. But Patricia was still in our church, and a year later she was in my sitting-room again.

'It's a funny thing,' she commented. 'I seem to come to see you once a year, but last summer I sent my father instead.'

A bell tinkled inside me. 'It hadn't occurred to me before. You are your father's daughter, and it may be that the spirit that was affecting him has touched you.' She saw the logic, but we put the thought on one side while she talked about her current need.

When she came to pray, she could feel a physical block in

her throat, impeding her ability to talk to God. It seemed to be divine coincidence that Michael returned to the house at that moment. He joined us when I had briefly explained the situation to him. She assured us that she had not dabbled at all in the occult herself, and then in Christ's name he commanded any evil force affecting her to leave. He was again aware of a dark force present, and departing. She sensed something lifted from her, and she looks back on those few minutes of prayer as the most decisive time she has ever known of God's work in her life.

What Is Our Rightful Heritage?

It is an old, old question. How much are we determined by our heredity, and how much by our environment? Add to that another question. What is basic and unchangeable in our characters, and what is open to the Lord's re-moulding? We will look in the next few chapters at some of the factors in heredity and in environment that mould us, that determine our attitudes and our expectations of ourselves, of other people and of God.

The very first chapters of the Bible show much of what we are meant to be. Our relationship with Him should be open, and He gives us one another for companionship and partnership. There are rules to obey; there is work to do; there is responsibility for the rest of creation; there are supplies for our physical needs.

How quickly the mess started! Disobedience, greed, lust, jealousy, murder, revenge; we find them all in the first few pages of Genesis. Later in Scripture we read that we are to love God whole-heartedly, and we are to love one another. 'We love,' John tells us, 'because he first loved us' (1 John 4:19). God undoubtedly has good purposes for us, but sometimes you might think that we do our utmost to see that His good intentions are not fulfilled!

Good Foundations And Solid Building

Think of the beginning of a child's life. Ponder the ideal situation of a married couple, secure in their love for each other, with their basic material needs met, looking forward to a child. The baby is conceived and born in an environment of love and stability, wanted just for itself, irrespective of whether that 'it' is 'him' or 'her'. He or she is the fruit of love between the parents, overflowing into a newly created person, wanted and *loved unconditionally*.

As he (or she) grows he needs nurture for the different aspects of human personality. He needs food for his *body* and stimulus for his *mind*. He needs to be fed *emotionally* by love that is expressed in word and touch and action and discipline. He needs to be taught about *right and wrong*, with the ethical standards of the Ten Commandments as a framework. He needs security and *stability* in his home, from which he can reach out and learn how to *relate to other people*. He needs to be *shown who God is*, both by words and by a demonstration from his parents of the Father's love.

Basic human needs and fulfilment

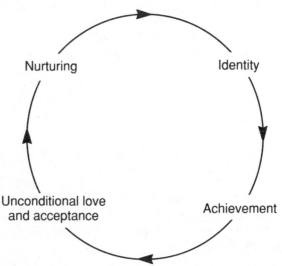

Those foundations of unconditional love, followed by good nurturing, lead to an adult who has a sense of identity. He is a person who can say, 'I know who I am; I'm all right.' His achievements in life spring from a stable, confident core, and he is free to do, to love and to give without needing to prove anything to himself or to others. He will then be a person whose marriage; work and relationships are stable, laying a solid foundation for the next generation.

It is interesting to see the parallel between human development viewed in this way and our spiritual birth and growth. God's grace, with its free gift of love, acceptance, and justification, is showered on us. He nurtures us through the Bible, through prayer, through church teaching and discipline, through fellowship with other Christians, through the family meal of Holy Communion, through the Holy Spirit. So we grow in the assurance that, 'I know that God loves me.' Paul wrote, 'For you did not receive a spirit that makes you a slave again to fear, but you received the spirit of sonship. And by him we cry, "Abba, Father." The Spirit himself testifies with our spirit that we are God's children' (Rom. 8:15–16). Any ministry we offer should spring from that security of relationship with God, unencumbered by any ungodly fear.

The spiritual parallel

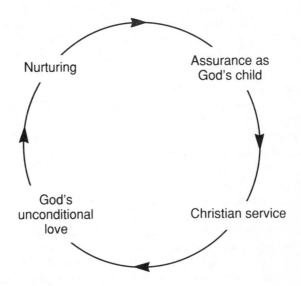

Where Are The Flaws?

Sadly, the person who has not grown in the ideal situation of acceptance and nurturing, who is unsure of his real identity, finds it hard to know God with joy and freedom. We will meet in counselling very many Christians who know in their heads that God loves them but who lack any heart-experience. They know in theory that God forgives but they have little assurance about it.

There are too many Christian workaholics, over-busy in their need to prove themselves. There are too many Christian counsellors who are being fed by the need to be needed. There are too many Christian parents who teach right theory about the Father but who demonstrate the opposite. It is not surprising that the adult finds it hard to know the invisible God of love, if the infant and the growing child have received a message from visible, tangible parents (whether Christian or not) that love is conditional or non-existent.

Many of the problems we meet in counselling are insoluble until they are viewed in the context of the past as well as the present. Many of the changes people would like to make in their lives are impossible unless there is a readiness to see how the events of the past are still affecting the way life is viewed and lived. We often need to work on two levels simultaneously. We have no right to ask God to heal the effects of our past unless we are willing to put matters as straight as we can in the present; but often we are unable to rectify the present, however hard we try, until God has changed the strong feelings and attitudes left inside by the past. If a dandelion is about to seed the gardener does well to cut it off immediately; but it will grow again unless it is dug up by the root.

Mercifully, God is in the reconstruction business. The beginning of Isaiah chapter 61 has a marvellous message of hope for the brokenhearted, for the captives, for the mourning and the despairing. Verse 4 speaks of ancient ruins being re-built and of 'places long devastated' being restored. Even 'ruined cities that have been devastated for generations' will be renewed. When we see a chain of insecurity and lovelessness from one generation to the next we do not need to be overwhelmed, because God can break the chain and can re-make broken people.

The great joy in counselling is to be a partner with God in His re-building. He actually needs us. He needs us most of all because we can demonstrate Him in visible, tangible relationship. We cannot by ourselves make up for all the deficiencies of the client's past, but we can be agents for the Holy Spirit to work. It amazes me to be a living tool in God's hands, ready to be used or to be put on one side. It is exciting to watch Him at work, like an apprentice who watches a skilled craftsman with awe, giving help here and there. It is a mighty privilege, and a big responsibility. He allows us to help Him with wounded, fragile people. So we want to learn to diagnose the causes of the wounds. That is what we shall do in the next three chapters.

Some Things To Do

1) Re-read the story of Patricia and her father on pages 98–101. Note the clues that indicate deficiencies in any of the four elements of the first circular diagram (p.102).

2) See over the page.

2) Draw a circle like this.

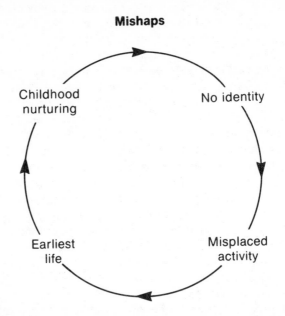

Mishaps

Under each of the headings of *Earliest life* and *Childhood nurturing* list some of the mishaps there may be in a child's life.

Under the other two headings list the signals people give that all is not well in these areas.

3) Draw a similar circle and use it to think about the positives and negatives in your own life. Ask God to remind you about good things and bad, in your past and in your present, in your 'natural' life and in your Christian walk. Let these thoughts lead you into prayers of thanksgiving and of forgiveness. You might well share your thinking and your praying with a friend.

8

DURING THE BUILDING PERIOD

In the last chapter we thought about the ideal foundations for a life, and the way in which the building ought to continue. But when we read the newspapers, listen to clients, or even think about ourselves, we cannot ignore the fact that the perfect does not happen. So what goes wrong?

In The Foundations

Charles was a young man whom I met in the very early days of my counselling. He was small in stature, and carried himself stiffly. He was quite withdrawn, but he gradually told me about himself. He was an only child, born when his parents had been married for several years. One day he cautiously stated, 'I'm afraid of my mother. I'm afraid of her body. I'm afraid of this part of her body' – pointing to his lower abdomen. 'I'm afraid of being conceived.' I can only conjecture why that fear had started. Perhaps his mother was scared of sex; perhaps she was afraid of giving birth or of being a parent. Whatever the cause, it appeared that her fear had touched him at the very start of his life. My very first lessons in counselling had taught me that the trauma of birth can leave deep impressions that last to adulthood. I then understood from Charles that the uncertainties can start as soon as the baby is conceived.

Conception should happen in the context of a man and his wife, thrilled with each other and enjoying the union of their bodies. But if there is fear or anger the foetus may sense it, and the child grows up tempestuous, insecure, afraid. If conception is outside the bounds of marriage there is real guilt even if it is not admitted, often there are fears and uncertainties that lead to an unstable pregnancy. Or the child may be conceived as a deliberate attempt to rescue a rocky marriage. What expectations that puts on the child, right from the start of life!

During pregnancy the foetus is kept safe in an enclosed environment. But even there, arguments can be heard and fears transmitted, and the infant's impressions about the meaning of life start to be formed. In the course of counselling, Marlene told me that her twin brother was miscarried at six months, and in her mid-thirties she still felt responsible. After our time together she wrote to me about the vivid experience she had when she was praying. 'I actually went back in time and was in the womb, foetus size, seeing Mark's eyes registering fear. Knowing it's too soon and we are not ready to come out. Reaching to him, holding on, feeling my own connection tearing away under the added strain. I let go to save myself.' In her life, different friends have committed suicide, always leaving her feeling that she is responsible, that she is the bad one to be around. I believe the roots of those feelings lie in the accident of her brother's miscarriage.

The time of birth, too, is an especially vulnerable time for a child. Think what it is like for the baby. After nine months of comparative safety, comfort and stability he is propelled erratically into an alien environment. There are bright lights and lots of people. Instead of being dependent for life on the umbilical cord he starts to breathe – maybe by being hung upside-down and slapped! – and becomes dependent on his lungs. That is a traumatic experience. Leboyer is a French obstetrician who introduced some novel ideas: birth in a semi-darkened room, and the child lain immediately on his mother's naked body, and soon into a bath. One picture in a book about Leboyer's work stands out in my memory. A newly born baby is being held by its feet, dangled upside-down. Delighted adults are watching. The next photo shows a close-up of the baby. The face spells anguish. I cannot help wondering if a fear of heights in an adult often stems from such an experience. The baby fights its way into the big outside world, and then finds that *this* is what life is like!

I admire parents who adopt a baby, because inevitably they have a child who has, deep down, a sense of being rejected by the natural mother, whatever the circumstances of pregnancy or birth have been, whatever happened in the early weeks of her life, however loving and secure the adopting home. Lesley grew up as the youngest child in a home where her mother was a secret alcoholic. So there were different layers of fear and false guilt, but underneath was 'That R word'. Rejection was a word that she could not even bring herself to say.

There are other ways in which a newborn infant may receive a message that seems to say, 'We don't really like you this way.' What if the parents have longed for a boy, and find they have a girl? Or vice versa. The initial reaction of disappointment, even if it is only momentary, can be sensed by the baby as rejection. Only too easily is that reinforced by parents as the child grows. The message is subtly conveyed, 'You should have been a boy!' The girl strives to please, and a tomboy has been born, who inevitably fails in her efforts to be what her parents wanted.

I think of a man I knew in Oxford; tense, often angry in his home, subject to periodic spells of hyper-tension, loving to help people, always feeling a failure, but rarely at peace. His brother, ten years his senior, was slightly physically handicapped, and was a bookworm. Peter was born to forty-year-old parents four years after his infant sister had died. He is an enthusiastic ball games player, and I imagine that as a child he was a typical, active boy. His sister's death made them over-anxious and over-protective in his early years; the question he heard regularly was, 'Peter, why can't you be good and quiet like Bob?' I suspect that question also disguised the thought, 'We really wish you had been a girl, a replacement for Sheila. She loved playing quietly with her dolls.' I am sure he could have echoed the child quoted at the beginning of the last chapter. He tried to be other things than himself, to conform to his parents' disappointed hopes, and he always failed.

The Building Grows

Think of the different strands of nurturing that we need in order to develop as balanced people: physical, mental, emotional, ethical, social, spiritual, in a secure environment. There are many ways in which a mixture of parental failings and unavoidable circumstances cause cracks in the building of personality. It is worth saying at this point that, by definition, parents want to do the best they can for their children. But that desire can be submerged under their selfishness and blindness. And 'the best they can' includes the flaws that are due to their own backgrounds, as well as their failures, through choice or weakness, to overcome their own sin.

Respect For The Body

I have this morning been reading a letter from Julia. I first met her when she was in her teens, and had glimpses of her life ruled by a father who was immature, autocratic, and manipulative to the Nth degree, despite his professional success. It is only now, more than a decade later, that she has lifted the veil of secrecy that is typical of the unrecognised, involuntary collusion in a family whose dominant members want to appear respectable and successful.

When I saw her six months ago she told me a little about the beatings on bare buttocks that, as a teenager, she received from her father. With her letter today she enclosed a copy of a newspaper article about male violence against women, and she wrote this.

'This article was saying that men who are violent *are* in control and they choose to do it – otherwise they wouldn't stop, nor choose the time and place. Therefore there is *no* excuse. I think that is one of the things that has really hurt me, to realise that my father chose to behave like that, to confine it to the house or to times and places where no one else would see or hear, to say, "Wait till you get home, I'll teach you . . ." Or to wait in the car till he stopped, to beat up my mother and leave her standing there while he drove off a few yards.

'And he *chose* not to hit us so we were spectacularly physically injured or bruised, just so we were crushed or destroyed and afraid, too afraid to speak. He never even told us not to tell – didn't need to. I was livid when I realised (ages ago) that one of the reasons I had to tell my mother when I had my period must have been so that she could tell him, and he could remember not to make me take my pants down to hit me, as he might have been embarrassed. What is that if not self-control?'

Julia was violated. Instead of nurturing there was abuse, physical, emotional, ethical, social. It is not surprising that Julia struggles now in her relationships, and finds it difficult to hold a job or to expect anything good for herself. As I read that letter I share her anger, God's anger, against her father for his utterly unrighteous behaviour towards his family, and for his own self-righteousness and self-pity. Then I recall my first visit to her home, and the pathetic signs of her father's immaturity. That enables me to share a little of God's compassion for a man so wounded.

I do not expect the same of her; perhaps it will grow later. But I am delighted that she has broken the silence and that she is receiving professional help. I have hope for her in her honesty, and I pray that she will experience God doing the apparently impossible in her. I count it a privilege to be trusted by her.

That abuse is blatant, as it is in many of the stories that we hear, and its effects on self-image are similar to those of outright sexual abuse. Sexual abuse itself is probably on the increase; certainly it is more recognised than it was.

There is inevitable damage to a person who is abused, whether male or female, inside or outside the home, as child or as adult. The damage is increased when the event is hushed up, when the victim keeps quiet – frightened, feeling dirty, ashamed to talk. Sometimes the child tries to tell a grown-up, and no one wants to believe; the ensuing inner confusion is deeply damaging. When a child's body is attacked, it is not only the body that is damaged. All areas are affected: mind, emotions, social relationships, comprehension of right and wrong, and even the concept of God.

Marlene's tale is also horrific, quite apart from the way her twin's death (before birth) affected her. When she was seven the teenage cousin who lived with her family began to molest her. One afternoon she was in an empty church, praying aloud, 'Jesus, please tell me whether I should tell Daddy about Johnny.' Her beloved great-uncle entered the church, heard her, told her to tell him more. Then he said, 'If Jesus is really going to know what happened, we must show Him.' There, on the floor of the church, he raped her. Her older brother did the same, and years later, as a young teenager, she was sucked into vile satanic ritual.

Marlene received years of psychiatric treatment before I met her as a woman of thirty-five, in training for full-time Christian ministry. The first time she told me her story she did not talk about her great-uncle; that memory was unblocked only after she had prayed in detail about the other incidents. As the memory about her great-uncle unfolded she rolled round on the floor, all 280 lbs of her, praying out loud, while two of us supported her in silent prayer.

Her prayer was utterly genuine. 'Oh, Father, you don't really want me to do that, do you? . . . All right, if you tell me to . . . Father, please help me to forgive him.' There was no denial of the pain and horror, but her prayer of forgiveness echoed Jesus at Gethsemane. 'Not what I will, but what you will' (Mark 14:36).

That prayer brought release for the next stage: confession

that she, the abused, had in turn become the abuser. 'There were eight children I abused.' In prayer, she named six of them, and asked God's forgiveness. Later she admitted that the other two were her own younger brothers. It is common for the abused to become an abuser of others, as well as an abuser of self by physical neglect and abysmal self-esteem. In this lengthy tale there is a mixture of talking, remembering, confessing and forgiving that are all part of the long process of healing.

Not all the tales we hear seem as appalling as those of Julia and Marlene. The abuse does not have to be as vile as it was for either of them to lead to distorted feelings about life, about oneself, about sex, about other people, about God. Basic physical needs may be in short supply, from poverty or from neglect. For example Barbara grew up fifty years ago in a home where there was too little money to buy new shoes. Her toes today are bent under, and her back bent from insufficient food.

Feeding Of The Mind

The child needs stimulus for the mind, and encouragement in learning, in ways that are in keeping with that child's ability and temperament. It is abundantly easy to neglect on the one hand, or to force on the other. I think of James, aged fifty, with tears in his eyes because his ambition to be a student at either Oxford or Cambridge was thwarted by growing up in a home where books were absent and 'university' was scarcely a word in the vocabulary.

I met Sisilia, an Anglican nun, who was asked to undertake new responsibilities in her community on a Polynesian island. She came to share with me her trepidation about this, particularly as she felt that her English, which was the language in use in the community, was weak. She told me of the impoverished family in which she had grown up, and her limited school education; she had only a few years of learning English at school, and felt ill-equipped to fulfil what was being asked of her now. Our conversation then went like this:

> *Rosemary:* 'When you were a child, did God know what was going to happen to you as an adult?'
> *Sisilia:* 'Yes.'
> *R:* 'If He reckoned you were going to need more English later, could He have done something about it?'
> *S:* 'Yes.'
> *R:* 'Then why do you think He didn't?'

She quickly saw that she had been trying to tell God that He had made a mistake, that He should have organised things differently. It was a sad shock for her to realise that she had not really been trusting Him over this part of her life. Her nun's habit was a good substitute for Kleenex to wipe the tears, and her prayer of repentance and renewed trust was simple and genuine.

Neglect of academic stimulus is less common in my counselling experience than exaggerated pressure from parents, which can start when the two year old is taught how to count to ten in order to show off to relations how clever he is, or the eight year old is expected to enjoy history because dad did.

I remember Sarah, who was in Oxford studying for a Ph.D., with high expectations for herself and fear of disappointing her parents. As we talked one key memory stood out. Her first school had been a very small one, with classes covering a two-year span, so that she and her brother, a year apart, were in the same class. One day there was a mathematics test – a weak subject for her. At the end of the school day their father was finding out how they had done. John was younger, and his turn came first. Father was not too pleased.

'What, you only got eighteen out of twenty-five? Why on earth was that?'

Sarah waited with trepidation to report her mere seven marks. How her father received that, I cannot remember.

Certainly the fear of not living up to his expectations in spite of doing her best left a deep impression on her. That by itself is a small incident, but one memory like this is often representative of the atmosphere in which a child has grown.

The mistakes parents make may be less easy to define but nevertheless real. Our ambitions for our children should be born out of a genuine desire for our offspring to reach their full potential *with respect to each child's individual gifts and abilities*. It is only too easy for a father to want his son to follow his own successful footsteps, or else to fulfil his own thwarted ambitions, in work or at play. Mothers are not exempt from the same wish!

I caught myself out on both these counts with my own daughters. I had as a girl been a reasonably competent pianist; I was also an enthusiastic Girl Guide in a poor company. In the first I was successful; in the second I was disappointed. So when my daughters were flagging on the piano I urged them on, in my desire for them to achieve in the way that I had done. Then when they were Brownies and Guides, my pressure on them was for rows of badges, for stickability and for leadership status. Such parental pressure happens only too easily, and I am thankful that I saw what I was doing before I hurt them any more.

Real Love Matters

Emotional nourishment is all-important. Love is, of course, the key word. Love wants the best for the child, but unfortunately love may be mis-guided and unable to see what is best. Parents may be convinced that they have their child's best interests at heart in steering him away from the insecurity of an artistic career and towards a steady, 'safe', job, but the result may be an emotional cripple.

It is vital that 'I love you' is communicated to a child in as many ways as possible. It is said in words. It is said in companionship, in doing things together or just sitting on dad's knee. It may be said in gifts – but only if the gifts are actually right for the child, not what the parent thinks the child ought to want.

There are many ways to distort love. *Things*, even expensive things, that come accompanied by a label that reads, 'I do all this for you, so you must . . .' are emotional blackmail. They leave a child yearning for love, striving for attention, believing that love can only be earned by seeking to please. Gifts cannot be a substitute for time, for time spent in the child's way, not the adult's way. 'Read me a story, Daddy,' does not mean a book of Greek poetry! It may mean that he reads the child's favourite story even if they both know it by heart. The interest for the child is that he enjoys knowing exactly what comes next. The interest for daddy is in his child's joy and trust. Mum may hate going for walks in the rain, but her toddler loves splashing through the puddles while nobody minds about the mess.

One of the sad facts is that the negative nearly always shouts ten times more loudly than the positive. So any part of the relationship that spells out, 'I don't really love you,' is likely to make a deeper imprint on the memory than, 'I really care about *you*.' Memory is a strange thing. We think we remember facts, but actually we remember far more clearly the emotional impressions made on us by the facts. If dad is bored Tom will know it, and his pleasure will be spoilt. If mum is impatient when little Katie wants to help in the kitchen, big Katherine may hate cooking in later years. Both parents have conveyed the message, 'Don't bother me!' How does a child translate that inwardly? 'I'm not worth bothering about,' and that leads to, 'I'm a failure; I'm no good.'

Even over-protectiveness and smothering-love may spell out as strong a message of 'We don't *really* love you,' as outright rejection does. That seems surprising at first sight. But real love looks outward, while smother-love looks inward, unconsciously looking for the child to fill an emotional hole in the adult.

I am reminded of a simple physics experiment I watched when I was at school. A vacuum was created in a tin can which then collapsed under the external pressure of the weight of the invisible atmosphere. The tin was as dented as an aluminium Pepsi can after a heavy foot has stamped on it! There is often a vacuum in a child, in the space that ought to be filled by the knowledge of being unconditionally loved.

In order to resist the inner fear of collapse the child can build interior self-protective walls. The pain of feeling unloved becomes almost overwhelming, so it is subconsciously replaced by an attitude that says, 'All right then, I'll pretend to myself and to you that I don't mind.' In later years the adult may recognise that there are internal barriers that block the ability to feel. Eileen remembers the day she made a conscious decision to stop crying. Or a boy is told when his father dies, 'It's not manly to cry. Remember, you're the man of the family now. You must look after your mother.' He is not allowed to express his grief, and he locks it away behind steel shutters.

A vivid picture comes from Pavlov's experiments with his dogs. He rang a bell, and brought their food. At first these were simultaneous, but then he started to ring the bell before the food could be seen or smelt. The dogs were still excited by the sound, associating the noise with the meal. He gradually increased the timelag, until there was a cut-off point. Instead of greeting the food with joy, they turned against it, and against the man who brought it. Why? They had passed the threshold of their ability to wait. So it is with a child. He passes the point of desire, moves to anxiety, and reaches the stage of, 'I won't care.'

This section on emotional starvation is far from exhaustive. I have not, for example, touched on the specifics of the sadly common problem of what it is like for a child to grow up in a home where one parent is an alcoholic. But if we stay too long on analysing the problems we shall never explore the tools for healing, and there are other areas of poor nurturing to be examined.

Stop To Do Your Homework!

1) Return to p.106, question 2, and add to the list you have already begun. If you omitted it before, start now!

   2) *Only for those who like diagrams* Consider this:

Think of one or two troubled people you know. Does the diagram apply? Can you amend it for each one? Which part might be rectified first?

   3) Discuss with a partner how you might help a client who has built internal self-protective walls.

9

POOR BRICKLAYING

We have thought about some of the areas of life, physical, mental and emotional, in which a child may be malnourished in the formative years, and we have glanced at some of the results later on in life. There are other aspects of our personalities that also need to be taught and fed, and I shall deal with four further important formative needs in this chapter.

Discipline And Ethics

Discipline is an important aspect of real love, because it is concerned for the well-being of the child, who needs to be moulded by God's rules, not allowed to run wild under the influence of original sin. 'Train a child in the way he should go, and when he is old he will not turn from it' (Prov. 22:6). Consistent, loving discipline gives a framework that leaves a child clear about the boundaries and so brings security. I have heard complaints from young adults who recognised how insecure they felt when there was no discipline, and from others who did not really enjoy it when they were allowed to be in control, twisting the adults round their tiny fingers. It all starts young. My husband can remember sitting up in his perambulator (yes, we belong to the generation of the pram – baby-carriage in N. American!), deliberately, persistently, throwing his toys over the edge in order to have the pleasure of seeing his mother pick them up!

More common than sparse discipline is a hand that falls too heavily. It is easy for a parent to allow a child's small misdemeanour to become an excuse for unnecessarily strict punishment. What is the child's reaction going to be? Despite the bent of original sin, children retain an innate sense of justice. So start with the natural dislike of any rebuke, add in, 'This isn't fair!' and there will be anger. But it is unlikely that the child will vent that anger on the adult. After all, it is wrong to get angry, and the adult is top dog. More likely there will be squabbles between the siblings, one of whom will appeal to the authority, 'He kicked me!' Further rebuke follows, and further mutterings about unfairness.

At the same time as this is going on, the child, simply by being a child, needs a secure base. One aspect of this is that he needs to believe that the adult is right. 'So if I am being told I am as bad as all this, perhaps it is true,' is the process that takes place at some subterranean level. This becomes a seedbed for the confusion that shows in later life in the swing from, 'It's all your fault,' to, 'It's all my fault.' Most unhappy situations between two people arise because each of them is partly in the wrong. But if there has been unstable discipline in their roots they find it hard to disentangle the strands of right and wrong when the gut-level responses are swaying unsteadily, like a ship without ballast. Such people become ready prey for the Enemy's whispers of false guilt.

In this atmosphere a child not only absorbs confused messages about punishment, and about his own 'goodness and badness'. Any standards that he is being taught about the theory of right and wrong are being muddled by all that he observes and experiences. Is it wrong to be angry? He is told that it is. He is rebuked for it. He is punished for it – by angry parents! On other occasions there is complaint when he tells a white lie to save himself from fierce questions about an errand he has forgotten – and then, when he answers the telephone, dad says from his armchair, 'Tell them I'm out.' The inconsistencies are not necessarily as crude as these examples, but we are left asking ourselves what chance a child has of learning the truth about right and wrong.

Christian families are not exempt from a similar situation, and the inconsistency is likely to cause confusion – and aggravation. God's rules are emphasised, but not always lived. A biblical home, reading the gospels, standing with Jesus in

His rebuke of Pharisaical hypocrisy, may be interpreting Scripture as falsely as the Pharisees did. But the guilt that is felt about breaking some of these parental rules, or church rules, is enhanced by the deep impression that we are going against God Himself. It is difficult to help a client whose fear of God's judgment, coupled with his anger that has probably been wrongly directed against his own 'badness', makes it almost impossible to see past a barrier that has been set in concrete.

I look back at some of the 'Thou shalt nots' of command-ments numbers eleven to twenty that were the standard when I was first in an evangelical environment, and realise how much attitudes have changed. For a small example, 'Thou shalt not wear lipstick,' was the rule – until Ruth Graham arrived in England for Billy's first London crusade, and the taboos were lifted! What about our interpretation of keeping the sabbath? Or even of what we wear for Sunday worship? There are so many ways in which we say, 'This is God's way,' when really we are teaching our interpretation of God's way. What is more, we are often concentrating on behaviour and on what is seen by others rather than on inward attitudes. When Samuel had been told to go to Jesse's family to anoint one of his sons as the next king he had a surprise when God did not want the fine-looking oldest son. 'The Lord said to Samuel, "Do not consider his appearance or his height . . . The Lord does not look at the things a man looks at. Man looks at the outward appearance, but the Lord looks at the heart"' (1 Sam. 16:7).

One big topic of ethics and behaviour that I have not touched is that of sexuality. It is one of God's richest gifts to us, but it has become one of the areas of life in which we have made the biggest mess. It is hardly surprising that God's very good gift is one of the prime targets of the Enemy; if he can spoil the heart of marriage relationships and disrupt the core of society in stable families he rejoices to see damage in all directions. The number of different aspects of sexual distortion we may meet in counselling warrant a book of their own. For now, I have to be content with this one bare paragraph. In the climate of the permissive society in which we live, it is vital that clear guidelines are given about the rights and wrongs of sex. Overt sexual sin matters, but 'everybody does it' may cloud the godly rules. There are hidden distortions too. Much traditional Christian thinking has been restricted in attitudes to sex, and has talked about the wrongs, without being thrilled with the rights. This has led to suppression of the joy of sex, and then to underground sin, even among Christian leaders. All the principles of counselling I am advocating are relevant to the multitude of problems about sexuality we may face.

Social Development

God made us as social animals, and we need to learn how to relate to one another. The home is the foundation for this, but I see two prime weaknesses. The first is in a home where there is little real communication, and no foundations are laid for making relationships outside the home. Meals are often the best family time, but efforts need to be made to extend conversation beyond the bare bones of what different members of the family have been doing during the day.

Indeed, I stayed in one home recently where family meals scarcely appeared to exist! Breakfast was eaten in silence, each one with eyes glued to a page of the newspaper. The family scattered for the day, all in a rush. In the evening the two teenagers collected separate plates, and made a beeline for different television sets, leaving three adults to eat in semi-silence. Does that link with the fact that I felt that those two teenagers hardly seemed to acknowledge my existence? That is not intended as a complaint to my hosts, whose hospitality to me was more than adequate, and I do not know how things are when there are no prying visitors around. But there was a marked contrast with the easy acceptance from the children in the house I had just left, and it left me wondering what foundations are being laid for relationships outside the home.

A second weakness is found in a family that only looks

inside the home for all the needs in relationships. Such a family is too tight, sucking all emotional resources from one another. That, too, leads to difficulties in knowing how to mix freely with others.

I myself grew up with an intense dislike of visitors. When I was a child it was a major undertaking to entertain even a few people for afternoon tea. The whole day was taken up in the ritual preparations. Add to that my natural shyness, that my siblings were several years older than I was and that at school I was working alongside children who were two years my senior, and it is obvious that the recipe for social development was not a good one.

It is healthy to grow up in a family where there is more than one child, although it may not be peaceful. The rough and tumble of family life has both its joys and its tensions. I do not pretend to understand all the implications of the effect on each child of his position in the family, but some are clear. Each place has its own trap.

The oldest one carries an extra load of responsibility, and often suffers from being the experimental child. I reckon that parenting is the most important job in the world, yet it is the one for which we are given the least training. So the parents are unduly anxious for his success, and mother is so proud of his first tooth that you might think she had made it herself! The second child often reflects the parents' greater relaxation, while the middle one has no special place, and the youngest is either spoilt, or feels squashed by the pile on top of him. The number of years between each child, and miscarriages or infant deaths, also affect feelings and attitudes.

There are plenty of other relevant factors, but probably the most important aim for parents is to make each child feel special, in the same way that we are special to God. In a family or in a school class the adult probably has some favourites, but God is impartial. To Him each of us is 'favourite'. We are not down on the same level; we are up on the same level. That is how, as parents, we should try to love our children, despite our humanness with its natural tendency to prefer one child to another.

When our own four children were younger I rarely felt they were all nice at the same time, but they took it in turns to be difficult! If as a parent you want to minimise the jealousy between siblings that often leads in adulthood to jealousy between friends, seek that 'specialness'. And when as a counsellor you are listening to clients, one thing to explore with them is the quality of family relationships, and the feelings they had about their brothers and sisters.

Stability And Security

If there is solid love in a home the foundation is well laid for security. But there are often events which are outside anyone's control. There may be only one parent in evidence. A parent's death, mother's illness, father's absence at war, or his job that takes him away for long periods of time; all these diminish a child's security as he and his parents are separated. I grew up in a single-parent family – a phrase that has become all too common in the last decade – after my father was killed when I was six months old. At one level I accepted this as normal; it was the other children who were different. At another level I missed the absent father, and fantasised about his making a miraculous return.

What about a child being away from home? If he needs to be in hospital at a young age fear and loneliness easily set in. George was only two when his tonsils were removed. He remembers the feeling of being abandoned as he watched his parents' back view disappearing down the hospital corridor. He could not understand that the parting was probably as hard for them as it was for him. All he knew was that they were leaving him in a strange place.

William is aware of a combination of events in his childhood that have contributed to the deep loneliness he feels twenty years later:

I was about seven or eight when I had to be transferred to a hospital about 40 km from home, to pump out my colon which had hardened to the point of bursting. Afterwards the doctor told my parents that it had been a life-and-death struggle. If I had been operated on one to two hours later I probably would not have survived. The painful and frightening circumstances of the emergency, plus the delivery to a distant hospital, plus the 'abandonment' by my parents, plus the teasing by the nurses was the traumatic combination for me.

On the day he was due to go home his parents were late. The other children had gone, and the nurses teased him with, 'Perhaps they are not going to come.'

Another operation, on my eyes this time, when I was ten constituted one more trauma that I never forget. I was taken to a clinic even further away from home (about 100 km), and had to stay there for two weeks, with my parents visiting me only for one afternoon halfway through. My eyes were operated on consecutively, with both eyes being blindfolded for two days after each operation. I can still feel the sense of loneliness, sadness and abandonment of that incident. In the autumn of the same year I was put into boarding-school for eight years. The feelings I had during the stays in hospital became 'institutionalised' then; I was battling with constant homesickness and despair for years with nobody around that I could trust and confide in. Last year I started to allow old and painful feelings to emerge. They had always incapacitated me in living successfully, but now I consciously connected them with those experiences of the past and could start to deal with them, and I am still in the process of working on them.

Such memories leave deep scars in a person's feelings. I deliberately said then 'person', not 'child', for those emotional scars are carried down the years, as William expressed so clearly.

Frequent moves of house, even when the security of love travels with the family, cause disruption. Most adults moving house find it difficult; I have heard that the most common causes of reactive depression for a woman are a change of home and for a man a change of job. A child (who has had no choice in the matter) may be thoroughly upset at the loss of familiar bedroom, teacher, friends and pattern of life, or he may appear amazingly adaptable. I moved home little as a child, but I look at my strange over-reactions in moves during the last thirty years, and I can see how the combination of present change and deep-rooted insecurity caused those reactions.

Let me add a word of encouragement. Our last move, from England to Canada, was the biggest one I have ever made since we went from India to England when I was two months old. But the Lord's effective spring-cleaning process made the last move less traumatic than any of the previous ones! Perhaps that journey in 1932 contributed to my dislike of geographical change, augmented by my father's death in an accident soon after we left him in India. Is this irrelevant? No. I can say with assurance that I have known insecurity *and* I know God's healing from just the factors about which I have been writing.

There is one other big area of instability we must think about. That is the effect of strife between a child's parents, whether or not it leads to separation or divorce. Divorce is traumatic for all concerned, even if the disappearance from the home of one of the sources of argument may lead to more peace on the surface. But there are legal wrangles and resentments draining adult emotional resources, and children are often treated like ping-pong balls in the battle for custody or in their time being divided between two homes.

Do you know that it is normal for the offspring of divorced parents to take responsibility for the break-up? In God's providence a child has both parents. That is the right order of things. So when a child senses tension, hears mummy complain about daddy or lies in bed listening to arguments, she wants to do all in her power to keep them together. She hears comments that make her think that she is the cause of the trouble when they argue over her or try to buy her favour. So it is not surprising that when the split comes she interprets it like this, 'It's my fault. I have come between them, and

I have failed in my attempts to keep them together.' That message goes deep, and the oldest child in the family, or the only one, carries an augmented load of false guilt.

One summer afternoon I was out on the lawn, relaxing in the sun, convalescent after major surgery. Alan arrived, in a panic about his imminent wedding. He was the youngest by several years of three brothers. Their parents' marriage still survived, but it had gone through years of strain. As we talked and prayed, he realised that the aftermath for him was a gut-level belief that marriage was a bad thing. He wrote recently:

'You asked, "What was your parents' marriage like?" I said "It stunk." You then asked, "Do you believe marriage is a good thing?" I, from the depths of my being, said "No!" emphatically. "Marriage destroys good people!"'

The Christian adult in him affirmed that marriage was of God's making, but he was carrying the residue of years of trying to be the glue for his parents' relationship. As his marriage approached, with the normal fears that question the rightness of the commitment, his inner beliefs were screaming at him, 'Don't do it! It's no good!'

Alan remembers two things I asked him to do in prayer: first, to thank God for creating marriage, and then for creating it for our good. 'In faith I then went ahead with the ceremony, and since then I have NEVER questioned God's goodness in our marriage. Something changed in the core of my being.'

'The core of my being' – that shows how deeply the child absorbs the climate of life that surrounds him. Three years later, that marriage appears to be one of the happiest I know!

Spiritual Needs

God made us to be His children, related to Him as our Father. So there is in us a spiritual nature, that I like to describe as a God-shaped gap in the core of every human being. That gap has to be filled with something, even when no god is openly acknowledged in a life. The one right way for that gap to be filled is with the Spirit of Christ, and many are the wrong ways possible. Paul sums up those wrong ways as 'idolatry and witchcraft' (Gal. 5:20). Idolatry means that we are putting first any god, any person, anything other than Jesus. 'You shall have no other gods before me,' says the Lord in the first of the Ten Commandments (Deut. 5:7). 'Witchcraft' summarises opening ourselves to any spiritual force that is not of the Holy Spirit. That is a wide definition, and the spiritual nurture of a child should allow only for the one true God, without rivals and without imitations. That should be plain to any Christian.

There is something that may be less plain to many. At first sight it seems obvious to say that the Christian should demonstrate what is being verbally taught about God. But how often it does not happen! When I ask a client, 'What was your home like when you were growing up?' I am not wanting to hear first whether or not it was a Christian home, though obviously that is important. What I really want to be told is what relationships were like.

You see, parents are meant to be a visible demonstration of God. He does not want to be merely an idea to us, or a character study in a book. The essence of His wanting human beings at all is that we are to be people for Him to love, people to respond with our love. So human parents are meant to model God to their children, the God named Father who is really Father-Mother. Good relationships demonstrate Him even when no one talks about Him. Bad relationships also model God, but the image is distorted.

The Christian home may be as guilty as any of any of these failures; sometimes more so, in the expectations and standards of behaviour and of achievement that are often loaded on to a child. Add to the mistakes the confusion of mixed messages, and counselling may be very difficult, even if the offspring have not thrown overboard the faith of the older generation.

Here are some of the causes of confusion – and I am as guilty as many other Christian parents, particularly those

who are absorbed by the joy and the busy-ness of professional Christian ministry. 'Biblical' teaching about God
may be rigid, and over-emphasise high standards. Parents
may talk about grace and forgiveness – but never forgive.
Parents may talk about God the heavenly Father-Mother
being ever-present – yet they, the human father and mother,
are forever absent, busy doing 'God's work,' ignoring the
fact that their own children should be priority in the work
God has given them to do.

When we are counselling the adult offspring of such homes
we may find that their loyalty to their parents shouts so loudly
'they were Christians so they must have been all right' that it
becomes a block in the way of honest exploration of the fault
lines in personality or faith. We need to go delicately, for we
do not want to give the impression that we think that such
parents have been bad people. It is more that they have
been caught in the pressures of many demands, and they
succumb to the expectations that are imposed on them.

Homework

1) *Solo or with a group* In the last two chapters we have
thought about eight areas in which a child needs solidity.
There is the basic foundation of unconditional acceptance,
and seven strands in nurturing: good food for bodily needs;
mental stimulus; genuine love; ethical teaching; social interaction; security of environment; spiritual awareness. I have
written about some of the different ways in which depriva-
tion in each of these areas may cause blocks in an adult's
relationship with God. What further ways can you see?

2) We meet much fear in counselling. Think about this
statement. 'Fear is a God-given attribute for people living
in a fallen world. It is intended to steer us away from wrong
paths, but too often it is commandeered by the devil. He
uses it to inhibit us from going in the right direction.' a) Is
the statement true? b) What fears do you meet, in yourself
or in others, that probably have their roots in childhood
experiences?

10

THE INSECURE BUILDING

Who Am I?

Edward arrived at our church as a very depressed man. He had been for many years a respected teacher in a boys' preparatory school, but a charge against him of paedophilia had left him without a job. Newly aware of his own emptiness, he was ready to hear the Gospel, and he asked Christ into his life. One day I was showing him the diagram we have already seen, explaining to him how weaknesses in the basics of acceptance and nurture lead to a gap in the identity. He immediately said, 'That's me. I'm a nobody!' and he felt himself physically hit below the belt.

Basic human needs and fulfilment

He was not the only one. In a two-week period he was one of five people with an age range from nineteen to forty-six, who made similar comments. 'I'm not a real person,' and, 'I don't know who the real me is,' are two of the remarks I remember. If the foundations have not been well dug, and if the next layers of bricks in the walls are laid crooked, we expect the house to be insecure, liable to crash under pressure. This question of, 'Who am I?' is a common one and it appears in various guises. The client may feel worthless, or be unable to receive God's free forgiveness. There may just be no energy for living, and depression sets in. He may say, 'I'm not sure God really loves me,' or, 'I know He forgives – everybody else,' or even, 'I'm all bad.' If you hear comments like this, think of the diagram. You might draw it for your client, and then when he understands the general principle, you can start to explore his early life. One of the keys to Edward's crash was the traumatic experience of his mother's death when he was only four and all the changes in his home circumstances.

This is the way I do this. I start by explaining the ideal situation for conception and birth, and build up the picture step by step:

Unconditional love
and acceptance

Then I mention the different strands of nurturing: physical, mental, emotional, social, ethical, stable, spiritual (see over).

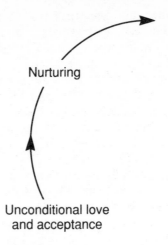

Nurturing

Unconditional love
and acceptance

That leads to a person having a core sense of, 'I know who I am.

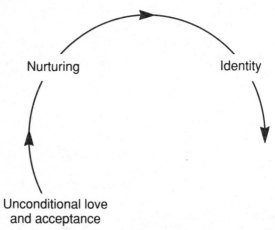

Nurturing

Identity

Unconditional love
and acceptance

But if we miss out on either of the first two stages (cross out ACCEPTANCE and NURTURE), then of course the third stage is incomplete. (Put a line through IDENTITY.) When all is well, when there is a good sense of 'I know who I am', the circle continues clockwise. Achievements of doing and loving and giving grow like sturdy plants from healthy roots. But if there is no confidence in 'who you are', then instead of someone being like this:

   he will be like this:

The trouble is that the circle only goes clockwise. However hard you try you cannot reverse its direction. So no achievement, even if it is marvellous, can make that inner core grow. But it's all right, God can rebuild, I promise.

It does not matter how primitive the drawings are. We often understand more easily by eye-gate than by ear-gate alone. That little person with a shell covering a vacuum is a helpful way of explaining what many people are like. If there is no core identity, then success in the world or in Christian busy-ness can become all-important – or the sense of failure may overwhelm any ability he has to recognise the value of his achievements. There may be intense swings from one extreme to the other. It is worth looking at Romans chapter 12 verse 3 in this context. 'I say to every one of you: Do not think of yourself more highly than you ought, but rather think of yourself with sober judgment, in accordance with the measure of faith God has given you.' Paul is aware how easily pride creeps in, but I wish he had written, 'Do not think of yourself more highly than you ought – or more lowly, either.' Perhaps the problem of low self-esteem was not around in his day!

The little man with a hole is helpful in another way. We can explain that his self-protective outer covering is like a house whose doors all swing inward. Hurts are easily felt, but the reactions are aggressive. There appears to be a concrete wall of pseudo-indifference, but any rebuke or confrontation penetrates to his core, where he interprets it as rejection.

There is also barbed wire fixed to that wall, and those who meet him wonder why on earth he is so prickly. If a friend or a client is giving you a double message of 'Come close, but keep your distance,' ask God for an extra dose of love to understand the roots of the ambivalence; pray for your own resilience when you are met with anger, and for special wisdom to know when to come close, and how to respect the need for distance.

The over-bearing person is usually a hurt person. Yesterday a young couple were with us for lunch. Tom was saying that he found it hard to understand his mother-in-law. She had been so domineering that both her children left home at the earliest opportunity, but now she was forever whining, 'Why don't you ever come to see me?' He found it helpful to understand this idea of the hurt core and the tough outer wall and he saw too that it was relevant to the way his wife swings. At one time she is over-dependent on him; then she moves the other way, afraid to trust him and wanting her independence.

This is a short chapter but an important one. I suggest that before you read further you spend some time quietly praying; ask God to show you clearly if your own feelings and behaviour resonate in any way with the 'hollow man'. If they do not, be thankful, and pray for sensitivity towards the many 'hollow ones' you meet. If they do, ask Him to excite you as you read further, so that you will not be overtaken by the feelings of inadequacy but will be able to trust the Lord to heal you. Then you will be better able to help others.

11

WHAT DO WE MEAN BY INNER HEALING?

Brian and Sarah Neufeld had a remarkable experience when they were house-hunting. God's guidance came as they prayed: to Sarah a 'spoken' thought in her mind; to Brian the picture of an unusual house, and a figure of £38,000 which was higher than they thought they could afford but less than they would expect for the house he could 'see'. They searched, with the estate agents and independently – and suddenly found FOR SALE outside a house that had all the characteristics in Brian's 'prayer-picture' of a house with a straight path, a hedge, long grass, tall trees, a firm dividing line at the side and unusual 'rooves coming down the walls.' A structural survey revealed extensive damage to the foundations and walls which would cost £19,000 to repair, and their offer of £38,000 was accepted despite the initial asking price of £55,000. They were sure that God was in charge, despite the upheaval and the expense they knew they faced.

Sarah wrote later about the repairs. 'The subsidence was corrected by removing sections of the wall, piece by piece, supporting the walls on jacks so that the house could be "levelled", digging out the old, inadequate crumbling foundations, digging holes at each of the twelve corners of the house to a depth of 4 metres at the front and 2.5 metres at the back. These holes were filled with concrete and a reinforced concrete beam set on top of the "pillars" and the walls of the house settled back on the beam. Internal doors which could not be shut were suddenly able to be closed. The external cracks were filled with mortar and are now nearly covered with roses!' The cost was £17,000; costly, but less costly than they had expected.

Inner healing is like that repair, although it does not always need to be as radical or as extensive, nor is there necessarily so much disruption to daily living. Bad symptoms disappear, gradually or suddenly, and years later the pain and inconvenience are forgotten as the 'roses' bloom. When the foundations of a life are weak cracks may appear unexpectedly or they may develop for a long time. The apparently irrational fears, the inexplicable over-reactions, the patterns of behaviour that we notice as we listen to clients; all these may be signs that inner healing is needed. But what do we really mean by that term? 'God's repair job' is a fair definition. To change the image from house to car, it is not merely stripping off the rust and re-painting the surface. It is decarbonising the engine first, and re-lining the brakes the following year. The Lord does a thorough repair, but it is not necessarily all at the same time.

We have already looked fairly extensively at some of the ways in which damage is caused to a personality during the formative years. God cannot alter the past events of our lives, but He can help us to change the feelings that we still carry from those events. It is often said that children are good observers, but poor interpreters. They watch, and they feel. Those feelings frequently hurt, but all a child can do is to bury them. He has no means of dealing with them. Like the bushy-tailed squirrels in the Walt Disney film of *Snow White*, you can sweep the dust under the carpet for quite a long time, but eventually the lumps will grow so big that you cannot help noticing when you walk over them! However, a Christian adult has tools to which the child did not have access, tools that he can use to sort out the damaging residue of feelings. The main tools are the Cross, the Bible, prayer, the Holy Spirit, and fellowship with other Christians. That is where we come in, as friends and as counsellors, when we show ourselves to be people whom others can risk trusting. We learn to use those tools, perhaps clumsily at first, but with increasing skill; we then share the joy of seeing God at work, making His repairs.

Our trustworthiness is a very important element. Often

trust in other people has been destroyed in a client early in life, making it hard to trust God. He feels that he is taking an enormous risk in asking God's help in exposing the fragile core of his life. The awful memories that have been stored away – what is going to emerge? But the Lord really is able to clear away the emotional junk that has been collected over the years. It clogs his freedom and spoils his harmony with God, with other people, or even with himself. We have already seen that the Cross is an enormous garbage tip, into which we can drop guilt, rejection, loneliness, pain, resentment, anger, and plenty else. We do not have to wait until we recognise all the rubbish. When we were clearing the accumulation of twelve years as we prepared to move house, we did not investigate it all before we started to use the dustbins!

It is not that all the negative experiences of the past will be totally forgotten, but they are seen from a new viewpoint. Have you ever returned as an adult to a place you have not visited since you were a child? It is amazing how perspectives change. The walk from my grandmother's house to the spring of drinking water seemed a very long way for small legs. Returning there many years later, I found the distance negligible. It is the same with memories that were overwhelmingly painful for a child. Faced with God's help the pain is not only bearable but it is opened up to His healing. Then trust grows, as good experience replaces bad memories of the past.

Is Inner Healing For Everyone?

More than you might think! Before you shoot me down in flames, let me explain. We usually think of inner healing as necessary only for the most scarred people, for those whose lives have had noticeable trauma. But no one has moved into adulthood from a perfect childhood (raise your counselling antennae suspiciously the moment you hear someone making that claim!), and rare are those with a happy home who dwell on any of the negative experiences. Even if the less happy moments are few they can leave small scars. How many

adults do you know – apart from yourself, of course! –
who appear to make wholly logical decisions all the time?
There are times when the apparent stupidity does not matter
one little bit, and we can laugh and forget it. But often
that illogical thinking, or the behaviour that accompanies
it, makes life more difficult for other people, or hinders
effectiveness in work. Matthew grew up in a loving home
where there was a mixture of generosity and poverty; as a
father his children were often hurt as he swung between
openhanded giving and suspicion of any lifestyle that was
more luxurious than he had known in his childhood home.
Do you see the connection?

One sentence from a counselling course many years ago
has stuck vividly with me. The speaker was talking about
stages in emotional development. 'You cannot move satisfac-
torily on to the next stage of life with incomplete agenda from
the previous stage.' Imagine a child building a tower with
wooden bricks. If a few bricks are out of line the tower may
grow tall without mishap, but it will still be less steady than
one built with bricks wholly in line. It is when the 'tower' of a
person's life is seen to be unsteady that we need to ask what
past experience is contributing to the present instability.

I used to be accused of wanting to delve into every detail of
the past and look for all the negative memories and emotions.
But not every past event is important in the present, and I
now prefer to ask the client to give the Lord permission to
bring to the fore the memories that *He* knows are relevant.
If the client is cautious and finds it hard to trust, my own faith
comes alongside to offer reassurance. In gardening terms,
we do not need to rake over the whole garden to look for
the roots of the weeds; rather we offer the rake to the Lord,
and let Him use it wherever He knows it is needed.

Inner Healing For Marriages

Already in this book you have met Margaret, Diana,
Matthew, Wai-Ling, Sisilia, Marlene, Peter, Charles,
Edward, Alan and others. Their stories have all touched

on the need for inner healing, or have shown a little of how God has been at work in their lives. Those are all individuals. What about married couples? It seems that most marriage counselling examines the years of the marriage relationship but ignores the moulding of a quarter of a century of life before the two individuals came together. Likewise, most pre-marital preparation – if there is any, other than plans for the actual day of the ceremony – considers the future relationship but ignores the feelings, the patterns of behaviour, the scars and the guilt that each may be carrying, heavily encumbered, into the marriage. We all know that fairy tales are not true. 'They got married, and lived happily ever after.'

It is only too easy for an engaged couple to go through a stormy courtship assuming that for *them*, so much in love, everything will be perfect as soon as they are married and can spend all their time together. Even physical violence is discounted. 'I thought it would be all right as soon as we got married,' is a typical comment, but realism quickly dispels false expectation. If either of the partners has been married before there is an extra layer of life experience to be considered. If the first marriage has been solid and rich it augurs well for the second one; but if the first marriage has ended in divorce there is likely to be a mound of pain and anger carried forward into the new relationship, however strong the determination that history should not be repeated.

The ways a married couple react to one another are largely determined by the models of lifestyle they have known. Their coping mechanisms, sufficient when they were single, rub thin in the intimacy of marriage. Differences of opinion lead to arguments, and they find pain rather than the joy they expected. Perhaps one explodes, and the other retreats behind steel walls. Both are reacting in the ways that they have learnt through life, often throwing out the anger that has been stored away over the years. One has grown up in a family where it was normal to argue loudly and then to let the storm blow over as if nothing had happened. The other has come from a home where problems were never aired, and tight lips were the norm. 'I want more from my marriage than this!' leads to, 'She's not giving me what I deserve.' Love that wants to give is replaced by, 'my rights to have'. Years of misery follow, and divorce may not be too far behind.

The 'ideal' couple come into marriage as whole mature people; they build their marriage like this:

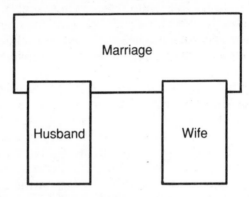

They bring secure personalities which give the marriage a solid foundation. But the ideal is rare, and the picture looks more like this:

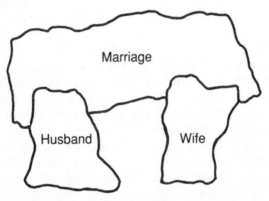

By the time they reach the marriage counsellor each finds it hard to see beyond the tensions there have been between them to recognise how much from the past is being projected on to the spouse. It is often easier for the counsellor than for the client to recognise when the anger that has been expressed is out of proportion to the immediate event. Whenever it appears to me that there has been over-reaction to a hurtful event I suspect that the feelings are resonating with pain from some earlier experience. 'You never . . . !' brings a build-up of years of resentment. 'Whenever you don't listen to me, you remind me of my father!' Unresolved anger against the parent is being thrown at the spouse.

One of the big difficulties in marriage counselling is that we are counselling three things at the same time: two individuals *and* the marriage relationship. There are times when we need to concentrate on the present state of the relationship or to examine the events and perceptions and feelings of the years of the marriage. We usually need to look, too, at the assumptions and emotions that each have carried into the partnership. We can talk together about the ways that upbringing have made each one presume that life happens in a certain way. Where possible I like to be together as a trio to focus on the inner healing that each may need. Sometimes fear or bitterness between the husband and wife is so strong that it will impede the healing process. But a couple is enriched when the experience of pain released and brought to the Cross can be shared, and each can understand more deeply *why* living with the other one has been so difficult.

William and Karen have been married for a year. His background has taught him to keep all emotions under strict control; I have likened him to a box screwed together so tightly that many applications of penetrating oil are needed to enable him to loosen up. Her home was one that caused, and modelled, deep anger. It is a joy to work with them, to see how they are finding it easier to talk together and to understand each other as we examine and pray over the past as well as the present.

Is Inner Healing Biblical?

This is a question that is often asked. 'Please give me chapter and verse.' We can easily point to Jesus meeting the paralysed man (Mark 2:1–12). Here was one who was brought to Jesus with an obvious physical complaint. Jesus saw past the paralysis to the guilt. He assured the man that he was forgiven, and strength immediately came to his limbs, evidence of the effectiveness of Jesus' ministry to the inner man.

We do not need specific chapter and verse for every counselling tool. Think back to the concept of a Christian counsellor as a channel of God's resources for all that is distorted by the world's sinfulness. We need to submit to biblical attitudes and to submit to God as authority in every way; we need to discover as much as we can of His purposes for mankind and His ways of fulfilling those purposes; we must avoid opening ourselves to any spiritual power that is not the power of the Holy Spirit. We fly in unbiblical aeroplanes, we keep our food fresh in unbiblical freezers and we are glad of unbiblical anaesthetics when we undergo unbiblical surgery! I have tried to show in this book that we ought to be soaked in Scripture, and in God Himself. When we are, we have no need to copy the Pharisees in nit-picking, while remaining on guard for biblical truth.

God's salvation is for the whole person. Isaiah 61:1–4 sheds light on the needs that are met by the process of inner healing. This is the passage that Jesus chose to read in the synagogue in Nazareth, when He made an outright claim to fulfil it (Luke 4:21). He was anointed:

> to preach good news to the poor . . .
> to bind up the broken-hearted . . .
> to proclaim freedom for the captives . . .
>   and release from darkness for the prisoners . . .
> to comfort all who mourn . . . (Isa. 61:1–2)

As the passage continues it tells us that those who grieve for sin will be given a 'crown of beauty' instead of the ashes of repentance; there will be 'gladness instead of mourning' and praise in the place of despair.

That is a pretty good message for the person with emotional pain! It is irrelevant whether the source of that pain is present or past, and Isaiah continues with a lovely image of trees. Even a person full of pain who feels like a wobbly sapling can grow into a sturdy oak.

The passage is not finished. A client who has lived with inner turmoil all her life, and sees that it comes from the inadequacies of parents, grandparents, or even great-grandparents, can take great comfort from verse 4:

> They will rebuild the ancient ruins and restore the places long devastated;
>   they will renew the ruined cities that have been devastated for generations.

These verses are marvellous ones to use to offer hope to a despairing client. 'With what words there do you identify?' She picks out a selection of the negative emotions. 'What does God promise to those people?' She gives the right answers from the verses. You could expect the reply to be joyful, and sometimes it is. It may be somewhat reluctant, when she sees that she is nearing the point when she will have to choose to face God, and she may not be too sure that she wants to change. We will think more about that later. For now, be assured that you need not be afraid that the idea of inner healing is in any way unbiblical.

What Do We Mean By Psychosomatic Illness?

The paralytic whom Jesus healed was clearly ill. His body was affected by the paralysis, and no one doubted it. But Jesus saw that the roots of his illness were not in his body, but in his awareness of guilt. We assume that his guilt was genuine, that he had broken God's laws; in what way we have no idea. It may have been false guilt, absorbing for himself guilt that was not his own. Jesus spoke to that inner need, and his body was healed.

There are many times when we see a simple relationship between our emotions and our body. After a bout of influenza, depression sets in. In excitement, the adrenalin flows. A time of tension in life sets up headaches, or backache; different individuals have their own weak spots which succumb most easily to the stress. David wrote this, soon after experiencing God's forgiveness:

> When I kept silent, my bones wasted away
>   through my groaning all day long.
> For day and night your hand was heavy upon me;
>   my strength was sapped as in the heat of summer
>
> (Ps. 32:3–4).

Here we find his body affected by his sin. Guilt and emotions sap energy, and it is not surprising when the body's functions are then put awry. Ruth, whose story I wrote about in chapter 6, was genuinely ill, but its underlying cause was the tension of years that she had kept inside, unrecognised.

A suggestion to a client that her backache is primarily caused by her strained relations with her family may produce fury. She thinks that you are ignoring her pain, or telling her that she is imagining it. No, psychosomatic pain is real enough. The body is indeed affected, but there is little hope of healing (indeed, of more than temporary alleviation) until the basic cause is treated. We sometimes wonder why God appears to be ignoring prayers for physical healing. Far from not paying any attention, He is trying to speak to us, to show us that all is not well in ways that we might otherwise ignore. Do you remember the thought about approaching the Cross with cupped hands, open to God, ready to receive what He knows we need? That is an attitude in prayer that He will always answer.

Another simple diagram helps to explain that bodily illness, emotional pain and our own sin affect one another. Each may contribute to either of the others. Psychiatric illness may have at its roots a chemical imbalance (needing drugs); emotional stress (needing therapy); or guilt (needing

God's forgiveness). All three means of help may be necessary, but without reaching the deepest cause there cannot be complete healing:

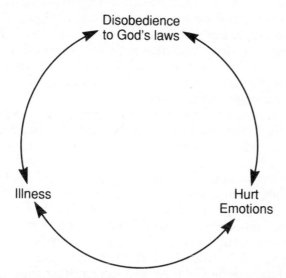

You could draw that diagram with a client on a large piece of paper. Explain how each strand may affect the others; for instance, physical pain may contribute to the anger and selfishness that makes life exceedingly unpleasant for care-givers. Then suggest that he thinks of himself putting that piece of paper in front of Jesus, saying that he is willing for Him to touch each area in whatever way God knows is best. Then ask him to write under each heading anything that comes to his mind that needs to be put right.

A Story Of Psychosomatic Healing – And More

Henry is in his mid-seventies. I met him when he came, with his wife, to ask for prayer when I was visiting his church. He was awaiting surgery for his prostate gland, and he was waking every hour or so in the night, needing to go to the toilet. He had recently been sent to the hospital for a scan, and he was pretty angry with his doctor for not having explained to him beforehand what this would be like. He asked us to pray for his sleep, but we explained that we could not do that unless he was willing to confess his anger and to pray forgiveness towards the doctor. It was amazing. He had simply not recognised how angry he was, but he was very ready to pray in that way. There was in him a lovely openness before God, although he looked at first sight like a stiff and formal churchman. Then we prayed for his sleep, and for the surgery to come.

At breakfast time next morning there was a phone call. Henry had only had to be up once during the night! It seems that his anger had been a bigger factor than the physical cause in his stress and wakefulness.

There is a sequel. I wrote to Henry to ask if I might use his story in this book. The permission was included in a five-page letter. He wrote about the way that God had opened up wartime memories, memories that included five days and nights in a cattle truck as a prisoner of war (a journey that was not good for the bladder). He re-read a precious diary, three inches thick, that he had kept during those years in a POW camp. 'There were details of all kinds of muck-ups both military and civilian. It contained photos that acted as reminders of some very deep inner hurts, along with what was for me almost unbelievable anger. I was simply seething.' He went to his garage, and ripped the diary to shreds, before telling his wife, 'I have totally destroyed the last physically visible reminders of very angry hurts that have never been dealt with . . . names that scourged my inner being – me, Henry P.'

The tailpiece of this story is also in his letter. 'I write a lot of letters, and my sweetheart always reads them back to me so that I can sense if I have said what I wanted to say. When she read this to me she said, "Has writing about these events hurt you?" I had to say "A non-event!"' '

Did Henry start that story, or did God start it? It is difficult to know. The Spirit worked. Henry responded. My companion and I in the church that day played a very small part, as we listened, confronted, and prayed. That is what inner healing is about.

To Do For Yourself

1) Go to Isaiah 61:1–4. Read it prayerfully in different ways.

a) The passage is first about the Messiah, so use it first for what He does for you. 'The Lord has anointed you to preach good news to me . . .'

b) The Spirit is given to you. So pray it as, 'Please help me to bring good news . . .'

c) Use it as a prayer for Christ to reach people you know who are in need. 'Lord, please take your good news to Philip . . .'

2) *On your own, or with a group where there is mutual trust* Think of some of the times when you realise that you over-react. Try to discover what events in the past are the roots of your behaviour.

12

STORIES ABOUT INNER HEALING

This chapter largely consists of stories. They have each been chosen to illustrate a different aspect of inner healing. So there is food for thought, even in the easy reading.

Loyalty To Parents

It is often hard for a client to admit that parents might not have been perfect. Her home was in general a happy one. So why does she feel uncomfortable? There was plenty of money – so why should she complain about lack of love? Or perhaps she knew there was little money; why does she still remember the embarrassment she always felt over her secondhand clothes? Perhaps she grew up in a middle income home, forever hearing about the sacrifices her parents had made so that she could go to a private school. She benefited from the school, she did well there, so why does she feel angry? She appreciates the good things her parents did for her; that is right. But her acknowledgment of the things they did well and her loyalty to them may cloak her underlying feelings.

I sometimes point to a half-drunk cup of tea. 'Would you call that half full or half empty?' Both are true. As she looks at the cup it becomes easier for her to see that, however many good things her parents did, even if they did the very best that was in their circumstances, they were unable to fill her 'cup'. Her head can make excuses for them, but that alone does not fill the empty space in the 'child' that is still inside her. Once she sees that it is perfectly acceptable to admit the force of the negative feelings she has started on the path of healing. One useful image is to think of opening the door of a roomful of childhood memories and invite Jesus to explore the room with her. That thought gives the client the safety of allowing the Holy Spirit to bring to the fore both good and bad memories.

Maureen was full of praise for her parents; her loyalty to them was strong. Her initial comments made me wonder how I could penetrate her defences. But they melted as she talked about being a child in a home where well-intentioned love and 'make do and mend' went hand in hand. One particular memory came to mind. She detested the old brown bag she took to school daily, but her parents repeatedly repaired it. One day she returned home triumphant, sure that the bag was past even their skill. She showed it to her father – who promptly gave her his black briefcase! She was diminutive, and the case was large, but she could not refuse because it was presented as such a 'special gift' and given with real love. She realised as we talked, sitting out in the sun, that her prayer needed to be, 'Father, I want to forgive them, for they did not know what they were doing.' Then I asked her if she could imagine herself standing in front of Jesus, holding her two bags, one in each hand. 'Yes. He is standing in front of the ocean, and He is smiling at me. I think He is amused to see such a small child with such big cases. It's a nice smile.'

Years later she wrote this: 'As I stood before Him with a case in each hand and my eyes downcast my expectation was that He would reprimand me (in a loving way) for making so much of such a small thing. It was such a marvellous surprise to see such a big smile on His face with a look of understanding that seemed to say, "How ridiculous can you get asking such a small person to carry such big cases! But we won't let on that it was so silly because it would hurt their feelings. The two of us can enjoy this as a joke together." It validated my own feelings from those years without demeaning my parents and left me with a real lightness of heart. I no longer felt like a "bad person" for detesting those gifts given so lovingly.'

'Can you give Him both bags?'

'Yes – and He is just throwing them into the sea behind Him!'

She saw that the whole matter was 'no big deal' to Jesus, so she could view it in the same light. She was able to thank Him that He was so decisive with the bags, and for His delightful sense of humour. And she saw this memory as a token, probably to cover many incidents when her parents either failed to understand how she felt, or knew there was nothing they could do to alter their situation.

Direct Connections

There are times when the link between the current event and the past feelings are blatant. Laura was suffering from mild post-natal depression after the birth of her third child. She could not understand why she was being so pulled down by this baby that both she and her husband wanted. In a time of prayer with her I suggested that she might imagine herself walking through the house in which she had lived as a child. Almost immediately she thought of the family room where she stood ironing. She was the oldest of six children, and internal anger was shouting at her about the chores and responsibilities that had robbed her of some of her childhood fun. The connection between past and present was clear. The hidden resentment from the past had infected her feelings in the present, and fear of the extra work and restrictions imposed by the advent of another child had outweighed the joy of the birth. It was good that the Holy Spirit uncovered the buried feelings, for now the adult Christian was able to forgive her parents for the burdens that had landed on her. Her reason had probably accepted that her busy mother needed her help, but her feelings had clung to the complaints of injustice. As she prayed forgiveness towards her mother the current depression lifted.

Heather's experience took her far further back in her life. She was a minister's wife in her thirties when she was involved in a minor car accident; she was thrown out of the car on to the road. She was not badly hurt, but the accident set up a phobia about emerging from confined spaces. She did not mind being inside a lift or an underground train, but she hated coming out from them. Each day when she drove her children to school they reached a place where her fear made her almost unsafe at the wheel. The road, after a long stretch where it was straight and narrow, branched out suddenly into very wide dual carriageway. At that point she panicked!

She was with a Christian therapy group one Thursday evening when she had an experience that sounds exceedingly strange when we first hear of it, rediscovering what it felt like to be born. It is as if our memory is stored in a tape library. Many of the tapes are out on the shelves, ready to be inspected, although most of them are partially damaged. Some of the tapes, the ones that belong to the pre-conscious period of our lives, are kept in a back room, very occasionally brought out and played. That is what happened with Heather. She felt herself thrust speedily into the world, a terrifying experience for herself as an infant. Later her mother confirmed that her birth had indeed been very quick. The baby had come out of the safety of the womb and suddenly found herself in the brightness and space of the delivery room.

That event set up a fear that remained latent for over thirty years until the car crash. Once she had 'remembered' the event as an adult and had been able to see it from a new perspective, the phobias cleared. Two days after her therapy group I was at a seminar entitled 'The effect of birth and early childhood on later life.' During the day the leader went to telephone her. He returned with the news that her Friday journey to her boys' school had been free from panic.

There were three parallel situations in the birth, the accident and the resultant phobias. In each one she was being thrust out from a confined place to an open space. She needed to cut the root of the fear in order to be free.

Fear

Heather's fear came to light suddenly. Diana's fear (p.40) had been with her from childhood days. Shirley's fear was different again. It had no apparent focus, which alerted me to the fact that there *might* be a spirit of fear around. Not all fear has a demonic element, but if FEAR seems to colour the whole attitude to life that possibility must be considered. So we explored the frightening events in her life, wondering whether there were any obvious entry points for an evil spirit. Various things came to light. As an eleven-year-old child she had joined her classmates in playing with a ouija board until her horrified Christian parents heard of it, and warned her of its dangers. Thereafter she merely acted as the watchman for the teacher's approach!

As a young woman she married a man who had a premonition that he would die before he was thirty. He was killed at the age of twenty-eight in a car crash in Kenya, a few months after their arrival there as missionaries, leaving her a widow with a small baby. Both incidents had fear, and both had many aspects that needed to be brought to the Cross. But neither of them, as we prayed, seemed to be infected by any dark force.

Then the key memory was uncovered. She was the daughter of missionaries in Zaire. She remembered with fear the sound of the drums at night, and then she mentioned the day when her curiosity took her into the witch doctor's house. That needed to be confessed and forgiven. When that was brought before Christ we took a firm stand against the fearful spirit, and were sure that he was beaten. Five years later Shirley comments happily, 'He was!' and she writes, 'I continue to look back at that time as pivotal to my growth and moving ahead without fear. Much of what God did at that time was foundational for what has happened since.'

Fear is prevalent, but the stories are not all as vivid as these. Fear appears in many forms. It has been given by God as a safeguard to deter us from doing wrong in a fallen world. That is part of 'the fear of God' which has a healthy respect for His rules; that fear is positive. But most of the time the devil commandeers fear for his own ends, and uses it to deter us from doing good; then it becomes negative. So we frequently find in the Bible the Lord saying to frightened people, 'Do not be afraid.' That encourages me; it shows that He knows how easily fear creeps up on us. He has two main themes. 'Fear not, for *I am with you*,' is one. The other can be summarised as, 'Do not be afraid, because *I have got everything under control*.' Isaiah 41:10 can be paraphrased as, 'Don't be afraid; I am with you and I am holding you firmly.'

Perhaps most encouraging of all is to see Jesus in Gethsemane. He knew fear. Part of him would have been glad to escape from the Cross. 'We do not have a high priest who is unable to sympathise with our weaknesses, but we have one who has been tempted in every way, just as we are – yet was without sin' (Heb. 4:15). 'Because he himself suffered when he was tempted, he is able to help those who are being tempted' (Heb. 2:18). Yes, Jesus' humanity is important for our fear. He understands. He identifies. So no one needs to be ashamed to admit fear and to look for His help.

What Is Primal Therapy?

Earlier in this chapter Heather's strange but logical story is an example of the way in which God can uncover deeply hidden memories in order to bring release. The principles of inner healing can be extended to the effects of memories carried from the earliest period of life, before we would expect any conscious memory to be operating; that is Christian primal therapy. In Psalm 139 we read the psalmist's confidence that God created him, knew him and loved him when he was in the womb; when the Holy Spirit is at work to uncover hidden feelings and memories it is only because He wants to pour the balm of that Spirit's love and truth over the infant and into a person's core.

Barbara's story goes back even earlier than Heather's.

She was born during the depression of the early 1930s, the second child in a home where money was short and food was scarce. As an adult Christian she had a short fuse; whenever she was in a situation that she could interpret as, 'I'm being rejected' she would be likely to flare in anger. One day when we were together she made some comment that I sensed was a flashback, similar to an earlier occasion when her statement, 'I'm hungry for love,' had been rooted in infantile experience of physical hunger. I sensed that this new comment had its roots even earlier. You might ask how I was aware of this. Was it through natural intuition? Through experience? Through the Holy Spirit? Through a combination of all of those? I do not know. If we proceed gently, not forcefully, with these 'hunches' the situation that develops will soon show whether or not the supposition is right.

So I began to pray for her during the nine months of pregnancy. I talked to the Lord about her parents' probable emotions as they awaited the baby's arrival in that situation, and of the preparations being made in the home. I talked to Him, too, about the child developing inside the womb, and how she might be affected by the atmosphere in the home. I prayed month by month, starting at full term and working earlier, gently bringing before the Lord, for herself and for her parents, the events and the probable feelings.

At three months she asked me to pause. She was shaking, aware that we were nearing the sensitive time. I continued cautiously; twelve weeks, ten weeks, eight weeks . . . suddenly there was an explosion. She told me afterwards that I had actually passed over the exact moment. The five-week-old foetus had felt herself rejected, and reacted in hurt and in righteous indignation.

What had happened to cause such trauma? At the time we could only surmise. There was already a three-year-old boy, and insufficient money for basic needs. Was her mother so shocked when she realised she was pregnant, that 'I don't want another!' reached the tiny infant? Was there an attempted abortion? We did not know, but she prayed forgivenesss towards her mother in so far as she could.

Many months later she was unexpectedly able to ask her eighty-two-year-old mother what had happened. There had indeed been shock, but no attempted abortion. 'I can't cope!' was not because of the poverty, but because Barbara's older brother had been such a handful that her mother did not know how she would manage another child.

It is not surprising that Barbara was a 'good baby', unconsciously wanting to earn her acceptance. There were several parallel tracks. The artificially good baby was on one track, and on another was a child who was genuinely certain that she was loved. At the same time there was a strong sense of, 'I'm never good enough,' and also deep underground anger from the foetus who sensed rejection. This was the anger that erupted so explosively in later life whenever Barbara felt rejected.

Can Our Parents Be Helped By Inner Healing?

No one is too old to be touched by God in special ways, if that is what you are asking. It is probably rare for the 'children' to minister directly to the older generation, but ministry can happen indirectly. There are three main stages of relationship between parents and children. When the children are young the parents are the primary care-givers. In the parents' old age roles are reversed; it is the offspring who look after their parents. In between there should be an adult to adult relationship which allows for reciprocal giving and receiving.

Young adults often come for counselling. Boyfriend-girlfriend problems; marriages; parenting; elderly parents; academic aims; uncertainty about careers; these are some of the pressures that open up the underlying cracks that have grown from their parents' failures. At first any suggestion that their own emotional healing might give them something new to offer to their parents comes as an unwelcome surprise; later it turns into an exciting possibility. Is God's love going to be made *real*? Is He really going to fill the internal gaps left by childhood experience? Suddenly light dawns about possibilities of the new levels of relationship – even with parents! I have mentioned earlier the awkward hump to be surmounted in the change from the first stage to the second. Bigger difficulties still arise in moving to the third stage, in parents' declining years, if the adult–adult stage has been omitted.

I recently met Monica, a tall, slightly uncertain young woman who is deeply committed to Christ. Over the years she had struggled over her relationship with her non-communicative father. Although things had improved, Fathers Day revived her hurt and anger. In our conversation together she told me some of the things that had troubled her about him; then I asked a question that I often ask in Canada. 'How long has your family been here?' That drew out the fact that her father had come from England during World War II. As a five-year-old boy he had been evacuated away from the bombing in London. It was a help to her to understand a little how that could have affected him, and she wrote to me a week later:

I never really thought of what it would be like for dad as a young boy to be sent off to the country not knowing where he was going – to whom he was going and not knowing when he would see his family again. It would have been *such* a traumatic experience!! As I ponder upon these things, I feel compassion for dad and his childhood – not knowing exactly how to pray but longing that he would also experience the healing hand of the Father. Sometimes I even feel like crying for dad. Thank you for challenging me to see things from dad's point of view. Now I feel the 'snail' [like the ant on the carpet on p.63] is reaching close to the other end of the table. I think that my feelings are finally aligning to my will and the desire to forgive dad . . . Truly I am grateful to God for how He is able to change seemingly impossible situations and a seemingly too hardened heart (mine) to bring hope for reconciliation in relationships.

A few weeks later she wrote again.

I have seen a big difference in how I react when any topics concerning dad come up in our family conversations. I used to be so critical and it was almost as if I couldn't stop myself to have more self-control. But God has really done something and I don't feel the anger that I did before. I am *very* thankful for that! . . . Haven't seen dad yet since we prayed – he is on his holiday still . . . I will see if he will talk about his evacuee experience. That is a good suggestion.

Now that her attitude to him has changed so much, I hope that he will find it easier to talk to her. As God roots out her resentment He will replace it with His love; she needs that love so that she will have the resilience to stay prayerfully seeking ways to reach out to him, even if he resists her first attempts to get closer to him. Her listening and understanding and prayer and patience can be used to bring healing to him.

For You To Do

1a) 'Do not be afraid.' Think of three verses you might use to encourage the fearful.

b) Work steadily through these references. Read them in their context, and write down the ones you find most helpful and would like to include in your counselling repertoire: Genesis 21:17; 50:19–21. Exodus 14:13. Numbers 14:9. Deuteronomy 3:22; 20:3–4. Joshua 1:9. 2 Kings 6:16. 2 Chronicles 20:17. Psalm 27:1–3; 46:2; 56:3–4; 118:6. Isaiah 41:10; 43:1–5; 44:8. Jeremiah 30:10. Zechariah 8:13, 15. Matthew 14:26–27. Timothy 1:7. 1 John 4:18.

2) Consider your reactions to the stories in this chapter. If there has been:

a) *Puzzlement and incredulity* Make a note of your questions and concerns, and look out for answers or further explanations later in the book. Your questions could be a topic for group discussion.

b) *Personal identification* If any of the stories in this chapter have rung bells with you spend a relaxed time with a friend to talk and to pray together about your situation.

13

THE SENSITIVE USE OF SCRIPTURE

You might by now be thinking that here is a mixture of some far-fetched stories and talk about the biblical base of counselling. Prayer is used freely – but what about actually using the Bible with a client? Yes, yes, yes. The more we stretch out in new directions, the more firmly rooted does our base need to be. Unquestionably, Scripture is that base. We have probably all known stories of people who thought they were listening to God, but their prayer has been utterly subjective, and it has led them, and other people, right off course. We do not want to follow them, like lemmings, into the sea.

Our Own Belief In The Bible

There is no point in talking about using Scripture as a tool if we are not fully convinced that it is a tool worth using. We can start with 2 Timothy 3:16 and 17. 'All Scripture is God-breathed and is useful for teaching, rebuking, correcting and training in righteousness, so that the man of God may be thoroughly equipped for every good work.'

For a start, 'all Scripture is God-breathed.' The Holy Spirit has breathed on it with His truth and with His life. So we must come to the Bible willing to submit to its authority. We too easily have our own ideas of God, what He is like and what we think He ought to be doing. If we read something that does not fit into our mould we reject it, rather than allowing ourselves to be re-shaped in our thinking or in our attitudes. Instead of rejecting what we do not easily understand we ought to ask that the Spirit stretches our comprehension. Then we can see that what we thought were contradictions are not contradictions at all, but part of God's truth, wider than our little minds had understood.

It 'is useful for teaching, rebuking, correcting and training in righteousness'. There are four strands, Paul says here, for which it is useful. The first strand is for our thinking, for our doctrine, for the way we understand God's truth. Then there are three strands for the way we live. I like to think of God's main road on which He wants us to travel; but we wander. 'For rebuking'; the Holy Spirit uses the Word to show us that we have strayed. 'For correcting'; He turns us round, to put us back on the right path. 'For training in righteousness'; He helps us to walk forward on the main road.

Then look at Hebrews chapter 4 verse 12. 'The word of God is living and active. Sharper than any double-edged sword, it penetrates even to dividing soul and spirit, joints and marrow; it judges the thoughts and attitudes of the heart.' Scripture has power. Do you really believe that? It is not always comfortable; far from it. But the Holy Spirit does not cause us discomfort for the sake of it, but only in order to push us to get straight with God. And when we have as sharp a sword as that in our hands, we must be responsible in the way that we use it, neither ignoring a powerful weapon, nor thrashing around wildly.

That thought takes us back to 2 Timothy: 'Do your best to present yourself as one approved, a workman who does not need to be ashamed and who correctly handles the word of truth' (2 Tim. 2:15). 'As one approved'; that makes us think of passing a test – and that involves study and practice! We do not want to be ashamed of the way that we use this tool that has been entrusted to us, God's workmen; nor do we need to be ashamed or apologetic about relying on its inherent truth. It is unnecessary to spend time and energy in a counselling session arguing about the infallibility of Scripture. Just use it! I hope it is superfluous to say that we cannot hope to use the Bible effectively to help others if we are not seeking to live our own lives by its truth. Then we will not only be people of God, 'thoroughly equipped for every good work' (2 Tim. 3:17), but we will be discipling others to be the same.

Our Own Grasp Of Scripture

As we read the Bible for ourselves and seek to obey it we become increasingly sure that we are teaching God's truth. But if we are really going to be able to use it as a tool in counselling we must be conversant with details. If a client is in floods of tears from guilt it is not very helpful to say, 'Well, I think it says somewhere something about God forgiving us,' nor to start looking for Psalms in the New Testament! It is not necessary to know the whole of the Bible from cover to cover, nor to be sure whether Obadiah is to be found before or after Jonah, nor do we need to be able to quote every verse that we might want in any situation. But it certainly *is* useful to start with a few verses and their references for basic pegs. It is not essential to be able to quote a verse if you can find it in your Bible; in fact, it is more use to be able to find it and to read with your client, than it is to quote it verbatim.

'Find it'; that is the sticking point. I recognise that many people have a real block about anything to do with numbers. If you are one of those, it is worth making it a specific matter for prayer if you find that the block inhibits your usefulness. For some, it is a matter of gift or no gift; for others, there may even be a block caused by a childhood memory of an angry mathematics teacher! It is not really wise to be dependent on knowing that the verse you want is highlighted in blue, nor that it is at the top right-hand corner of a page. You will not always have your own reference Bible to hand! (I do recommend carrying at least a New Testament with Psalms with you most of the time.) No, as you absorb Scripture, start to learn where to find passages about key topics. Do you know where to find the Sermon on the Mount? 'St Matthew's gospel,' you say. Quite right – but let me remind you that that gospel has twenty-eight chapters!

Do learn by heart, with their references, a few verses.
That is part of the psalmist's experience.

> I have hidden your word in my heart
>> that I might not sin against you (Psalm 119:11).

One useful way to learn by heart is to write each verse
out on a small card, with its reference. Carry some with
you, for the 'idle' moments of a day; waiting for a friend
to arrive, or travelling by train. I have seen the headboard
of a student's bed covered with 3″ × 5″ cards, each with
one verse written out.

But even more useful than being able to quote a few verses
word for word, with the exact chapter and verse, is to know
approximately what a verse says, and in what chapter you
will find it. If you can turn to the right page it is not too
hard to run your eyes down to find just what you want.
Train yourself on this. What did you read this morning – or
last evening? Where was it in the Bible? What was it about?
Did God speak to you in it? If you cannot remember, stop
reading this book for a moment. Find your Bible and look
for the passage. Think again about it. Pray that it becomes
real to you. It is amazing how often God speaks to me in my
private reading, and very soon afterwards I find the same
thought is utterly appropriate for a client.

Train yourself, too, with a friend, or in a small group.
Self-discipline is far easier if you are accountable to others.
Decide together what you are going to learn and check on
each other weekly. It will help you to become familiar with
your tools, to be a 'workman who does not need to be
ashamed'.

Do you remember this diagram from chapter 1?

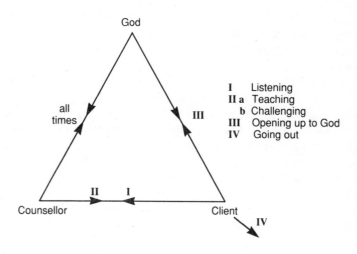

The Bible is used very differently in each of the four stages of counselling. In STAGE I, when I am listening, exploring, beginning to make a diagnosis, the Bible usually has no part to play. It remains shut, and often emerges for stage II. I find that I use it differently in each of the remaining stages, so we shall look at those separately.

The Bible For Teaching – Stage II

What is the difference between a preacher and the leader of a Bible-study group?

Both should be teaching from Scripture, making it clear and relevant to everyday life. The main difference is that the preacher does most of the work; the congregation is an audience, listening but not participating. The Bible-study leader, however, involves every member of the group. He has as good an understanding of the passage as the preacher does, but he asks questions to encourage each one to examine the book and find the answers for himself. I liken the group member to a farmyard hen scratching around to find her own food. Her eggs have more flavour than those of a battery chicken which has sat in a cage waiting for a carefully balanced supply of food to appear on a conveyor belt.

In the teaching stage of counselling I see myself like a group leader, working with a 'group' of one. I am there to teach by involving him, making him think what the Bible means and how it is relevant. It is sometimes good to ask him whether he knows any part of Scripture that he thinks is relevant. More often you will choose it, find it while he is still talking, and pass the Bible to him. Before reading it you may want to give a wee bit of background. Then ask him to read it aloud. The value in that is two-fold. One is that as he reads it he is to some extent affirming, even if he is going to question its truth, or – frequently – to admit that there is a discrepancy between his head and his heart in believing it. The other advantage is that, as he reads, you can sense how much of it he really understands. Then ask what he thinks of it, and what it is saying to him. That is a totally open question; do not guide him at all over the answer.

Then you can move on to drawing his attention to points he has ignored. Do this by asking questions, not by explaining it all yourself. His mind is fully involved as he seeks to understand what the verses are saying. Finally you can explain any remaining details, adding illustration, and brief testimony if that will help.

Try to avoid assuming that he knows more than he does. In fact, it is often easier if he does not know much, rather than finding that you are trampling over familiar territory. An adult who has head-knowledge of the Bible from his childhood, without the heart-knowledge with it, tests our ability to find Scripture that is not stale. I do my best to avoid jargon, which he probably does not understand even if he does not want to admit it. Who, for instance, readily understands the word 'grace'? It is so far outside everyday experience that it needs to be explained in a fresh way. Avoid, too, giving him mental indigestion by moving around too many parts of the Bible. Use one passage and extract all you can from it, rather than confusing him by showing off your extensive knowledge.

You may well reach a point when his head understands, but his heart is still fighting against absorbing it. Pages 53 to 57 will give you some suggestions. Here are some more strategies to use. You will find this section most help if you work through it slowly, with your Bible open.

1) *Personalise* Find Romans chapter 5. Verses 6 to 8 are among my regular repertoire.

> Question: 'What words do you identify with?'
> Answer: 'Powerless . . . ungodly . . . sinners.'
> Question: 'What did God do for the powerless and the ungodly and the sinners?'
> Answer: 'Christ died for them.'
> Question: 'What did He clearly show by that death?'
> Answer: 'God's love.'
> Question: 'Now will you try reading those verses, 6 and 8, in the first person. Put "I" where you can.'
> Answer: 'You see, at just the right time, when I was still powerless, Christ died for me, the ungodly . . . But God demonstrates his own love for me in this: While I was still a sinner, Christ died for me.'

Simple questions, simple logic. The client is led step by step to grasp that this truth is for *her*, not just for everyone else. 1 John 1:9 is another familiar verse that is particularly powerful when read in the first person singular by the client who does not believe in his guts that God forgives *him*. 'If I confess my sins, he is faithful and just and will forgive my sins and purify me from all unrighteousness.'

2) *Identify* I showed that a little on p.52 in Zechariah's vision of Joshua (Zech. 3:1–5). Isaiah chapter 61:1–4 is another passage where you can well ask your client to pick out the words which describe her. 'Broken-hearted

... captives ... despair ...' may be selected. Having identified with those negative feelings, she is ready to begin to see how the matching positive words are for her as well. This is a useful tool whenever you have a client who is almost determined to look on the dark side. Lamentations chapter 3, and several of the 'depressed' psalms (such as 64 or 77) can be well used in this way. There is usually a turning point when the writer chooses to look up to God instead of staying stuck in the gloom. Psalm 77 verse 10 is like that. From 'Has God forgotten . . .' in verse 9, he turns to, 'Then I thought . . .' in verse 10. Read that psalm, and find others in which he does the same.

I remember a day of emotional turmoil. A friend turned to Psalm 69. The turning point in that psalm comes in verse 13: 'But I pray to you . . .' I was unable to pray, even to listen to the words of the psalm, until she had read from the beginning: 'I sink in the miry depths . . .' (v.2). Only when she had read it through to verse 12, so that I allowed the psalmist to identify with me, was I ready to grasp verse 13 for myself. Later, having seen that psalm as one of depression, I found verse 9 quoted of Jesus (John 2:17). This was exciting, because it brought together the psalmist, myself, and Jesus. I noticed it one Sunday morning and used it that same afternoon with a depressed young woman. That is how our working knowledge of the Bible grows.

3) *Emphasise 'all'* Suppose you want to underline God's omnipotence. Turn to Matthew chapter 19 verse 26. The client reads it. 'With man this is impossible, but with God all things are possible.' Ask him to write it down, then open brackets, and write EXCEPT.

'. . . with God all things are possible (except . . .).' Into the space he is to write anything that he feels God is unable to do in his current situation.

'. . . with God all things are possible (except my marriage . . . my mother and her housing . . . my teenage son and his awful friends . . .).'

Then he has a choice to make. Is the see-saw of his faith

going to tip on the side of his feelings or his Bible? If he decides that he really wants the Bible to be his watchdog he can cross out EXCEPT and write instead INCLUDING EVEN. 'With God all things are possible (including even my marriage . . . my mother's housing . . . my son . . .).' The doubts will not disappear overnight, but an important choice has been made. 'Scripture is true.'

Any word that has an implication of totality can be treated in this way. I am reminded of the Gilbert and Sullivan song containing this exchange between two characters: 'What, never? No, never. What, never? Well, hardly ever.' It is a simple tool, not relevant for every client, but try it for Psalm 145, say. 'The Lord is good to all (except me . . . etc)' (Ps. 145:9). Or for, 'Do not be anxious for anything (except my finances . . . my . . .)' (Phil. 4:6). Then he can change it to, 'Do not be anxious for anything, not even for my finances.' Of course, this does not immediately sweep away all anxiety, let alone make a difference to the bank balance. But it puts him in a position to pray with greater openness and more faith.

The Bible For Ministry – In Stage III

When the client has understood what Scripture is saying about his current situation, he has to decide whether or not to obey it. In Stage II we are engaging his mind. From there we move to challenging his will (the topic of the next chapter). Then in Stage III (still using the concept of the triangular diagram) we ask him to open up to God himself in prayer. When he has turned to God with his situation and his feelings and his attitudes we use Scripture in quite a different way to nourish his soul.

At first we were teaching him, re-educating a mind full of misconceptions. Now we gently pour balm on to wounds that have been opened up to God; the picture is that of a nurse applying the ointment that the heavenly surgeon has ordered. So instead of asking the client to read aloud I read to him. I am not concerned about whether his mind is

active. Instead I allow his soul to absorb what God's word
is offering.

It is often appropriate to use the verses we have already
studied. Perhaps the problem was one of guilt, and he has
grasped 1 John 1:8 and 9 afresh. He has seen that God
really will forgive him when he confesses his sin. So he prays
a prayer of confession. After that confession I can read to
him the verses that we have already talked about. What
made sense to his mind now reaches his heart, whose doors
he has opened to the Lord in prayer. There are sometimes
audible deep breaths as the truth of Scripture is taken into
the soul's core.

Perhaps the problem has been one of worry over money,
and we have talked about his financial need and looked at
possible practical solutions. We have also talked together
about God, and whether He really is in control, whether He
is wholly trustworthy. Here is a marvellous verse to have in
your storehouse of Scripture:

> He is the Rock, his works are perfect,
>   and all his ways are just.
> A faithful God who does no wrong,
>   upright and just is he (Deut. 32:4).

When he prays, he can bring to God both the stress of
his finances and the half-heartedness of his faith. While he
is praying I am quietly praying alongside; at the same time
as my mind is underlining his spoken prayer I ask God to show
me what other parts of the Bible I might use. If the time of
prayer is a long one, I often find that various passages come
to mind. Some are retained, some are discarded along the
route, as his prayer moves. If he focuses on his need to trust
God more, I might repeat the verses from Deuteronomy,
or I could read to him Job's statement of faith after all his
anger and his struggles:

> I know that you can do all things;
>   no plan of yours can be thwarted (Job. 42:2).

(In turning to that verse to quote it here I find I have written in the margin of my Bible a cross-reference of my own to Isaiah 14:27. That reminds me of a verse that I noticed earlier, but had forgotten. I can look it up again and make a mental note of it. That is one way to increase the number of verses we are ready to use; we want to avoid the staleness that is bred by repetition.)

Even if his prayer has concentrated on his faith, rather than on the original question of the finances, we do not want to forget why he came in the beginning! We could move to the Sermon on the Mount, and read a whole paragraph, or even two. 'Therefore I tell you, do not worry about your life, what you will eat or drink . . .' (Matt. 6:25ff). At this stage over-feeding is not usually a problem, but he needs time and space to respond to God. It is just as important not to crowd him now, as at the very beginning of the counselling, when we were primarily listening to him.

In this stage, too, we do not necessarily read absolutely straight from the Bible. For instance, it is not being dishonest to turn a passage from a proclaimed truth into a prayer, or to alter its tense. Look at the beginning of Psalm 40. The psalmist is rejoicing in what God has done for him. 'I waited . . . he turned . . . and heard . . . He lifted . . . He set . . . and gave . . . He put . . .' We can read it like this:

I am waiting patiently for you;
    I believe you are turning to me and hearing my cry.
Please lift me out of my slimy pit,
    out of the mud and mire;
please set my feet on a rock
    and give me a firm place to stand.
Then I will have a new song in my mouth,
    a hymn of praise to you, my God

                                        (Ps. 40:1–3, adapted).

In doing this we are in no way altering the truth of Scripture. And if we are really tuned into the client and the place he has reached with God, we are not putting into his mind or mouth a prayer for which he is not ready. It is like catching up with someone who is cycling ahead of us, slowly and labouring. As we ride beside him, we go at his speed; but he goes faster because our presence alongside him is an encouragement. So I read slowly, and give him a chance to echo it, silently or whispering. As he absorbs it, he may again want to turn to God in his own words of thanksgiving.

The Bible For Homework

As he leaves it is good to give him some things to aim for in his life whether or not we are making arrangements for another meeting. It may be in his behaviour, in his relationships, in his lifestyle, in letters he needs to write or telephone calls to make, in practical steps over his finances. There is a wide range of possibilities.

Part of the 'homework' is to give him some specific Bible reading to do. If he is weak on his grasp of certain aspects of his faith, we can give him particular passages to read. If he is highly motivated, we can tell him to use a concordance, and give him some words or themes to trace through. It may be further nourishment he needs, rising out of the last part of our time together. We can jot down the passages we have used, suggest he re-reads those, and add some extra.

Many Christians use a note book or a journal to record personal experience and emotions and also the thoughts from Scripture that meet those feelings. We can offer some new ideas on ways to approach the Bible. This basic ingredient of Christian nourishment is often neglected, even by Christians of many years' standing. Bible reading has grown stale, and the Book is on the shelf.

We can suggest that one day he might make a note of just one verse he wants to remember; he can write it out on a scrap of paper, and have it accessible to learn by heart. On the dashboard of the car . . . above the kitchen sink . . . at the edge of the computer screen . . . wherever the client frequently glances. The next day he could mull over what he might write for a day's Scripture Union notes. After

that he could imagine that he had been asked to preach
from that passage; what would he want to say in his own
church? Occasionally he might think of himself as one of
the characters in a gospel narrative and then write from
that person's point of view. For example read Mark 2:1–12,
and write how the paralysed man might have written in his
journal at the end of the day. Instead of a story at a distance –
interesting history, but not quite pertinent to himself – he
finds himself feeling as a guilty man meeting Jesus.

Variety is one of the spices of Bible reading. If the
counselling time has stimulated his appetite for the Bible
we want to do all we can to keep that going. OXFAM has
a good saying: 'If you give a man a fish, you feed him for a
day. Teach him to fish, and you feed him for life.' Next time
we see the client, ask how he is getting on with his Bible.
If he fulfils his appointed task and then finds that it was
apparently not important after all he will be discouraged.
And if he has neglected it we need to know so that we can
help him further.

Back to where we started on Scripture. If we are thrilled
with the Bible we will be able to thrill others. Excitement
is infectious; so is boredom. If we are obeying it we will
be credible in asking others to obey it. So, to quote the
old Anglican prayer book, we should 'read, mark, learn and
inwardly digest it', so that we may model its truth and its
vitality.

For Your Own Work

1) *Put yourself into a gospel story* and write from one
character's perspective. Some suggestions:

Mark 1:40–45 The leper tells his wife about his healing

Mark 1:29–30 Peter and Andrew discuss the time in Peter's
house

Mark 2:1–12 The four friends converse on their way
home

Mark 7:24–30 The Syro-Phoenician woman writes in her
journal that evening.

What insight does this give you into yourself? Into Jesus and how you relate to Him?

2) *Start to make a list of passages* you might want to use in different situations. Keep a piece of paper inside your Bible with this list of topics, so that you can be ready to note a reference when it strikes you. If you are in a situation where a small group of you can work together the mutual stimulation will be helpful.

ANXIETY
FEAR
GOD AS FATHER
GOD AS JUDGE
GOD'S INFALLIBLE WISDOM
GUILT
LONELINESS
MARITAL DISHARMONY
NON-ACCEPTANCE AT BIRTH
RESENTMENT
SUFFERING

See Appendix II for some suggestions.

3) *Try some role play with a friend* Let one of you 'be' the client, with a simple imaginary problem and let the other one 'be' the counsellor. Get out your Bible, and see how well you can use it to explain something that is relevant to her 'problem'. Then ask her to give you some feedback. Was your choice of Scripture helpful? Were you dull? Did you explain it clearly, or were your words full of Christian jargon? Were you tongue-tied, or did you confuse her by your verbosity and by showing off your wide knowledge? Did you assume that she knew too much or too little? It is important that she is honest in her reply, and you can both learn from the experience.

14

CHALLENGING THE WILL

Anne and I had spent many hours together. The first time she came to see me she talked, almost without stopping, for two hours! Later there were tears and laughter as we talked and prayed about different areas of her life, past and present. One day she read aloud some verses I suggested from Hebrews chapter 12, them promptly slammed the Bible shut. I asked her to open it again. She refused. I told her that if she was not willing to see what God might be wanting to say to her, there was nothing I could do to help her. I then left the room, telling her she could find me in the kitchen if she wanted. Ten minutes later she came, and we continued with the counselling. Her initial anger had taken her as far as the front door before her desire for change conquered and she was ready to face the Lord, and whatever He wanted to say to her through those verses.

'You can take a horse to water, but you cannot make it drink!' In counselling, we can listen and love; we can teach the truth, and point to Scripture; we can pray fervently. But we cannot make the changes in another person's life. We cannot even persuade her to make the changes. God has given free will, and He respects it, because He looks for obedience to spring from love, not from coercion. We must do the same, however clearly we think we can see what is needed, however much we long for her to listen to God. He knows better than we do what she needs. He loves her far more than we ever shall, and He longs for her to know better things. But He does not force anyone along His path, although when we look at Jonah and at Job we realise that He sometimes allows some pretty drastic things to happen

in order to bring us face to face with Him. I remember a man
who was in tears under the burden of pastoring his church.
Those tears that broke through his shell were a crucial point
in his allowing God to change him.

'Do you want to get well?' Jesus asked the man at the
Bethesda Pool (John 5:6). On another occasion His question
was, 'What do you want?' (Matt. 20:32). Two blind men were
persistently shouting after Him; you would have thought it
was obvious what they wanted! But He still asked. He knew
it was good for the people in need to be sure what they
wanted, and to put it in words. The same is true today. It
is not that *He* needs to be informed of our heart's desire;
He knows it already. But *we* need to be as clear as we can
what we really want, and to express it.

There were other occasions when He either tested faith, or
specially commended it. You could read about the centurion
(Matt. 8:10–13), the lady who had been haemorrhaging for
twelve years (Matt. 9:20–22), or the Canaanite woman
(Matt. 15:21–28). Jesus did not make it easy for any of
them. I take great comfort from His encounter with the
rich ruler, which we read in Mark chapter 10. He loved the
young man. But when the standard seemed to be too high,
Jesus did not chase after him or change the conditions. He
let him go, as sad, I am sure, as the rich man was.

I take heart from that story on two accounts. One is
the example Jesus sets us in not pursuing him, in letting
him exercise his own choice. The other is for times of
disappointment, when I see my 'rich young ruler,' whom I
have loved, with whom I may have spent many hours, turn
away from whatever Jesus is asking. I can hide in Jesus,
who understands. He really knows what it is like, because
it is part of His human experience. That is a help to me. I
can bring Him my grief. I know that He shares it, and I can
leave it with Him. That is not being selfish, for it frees me
up to pray for the one who has turned away, without the
strings of my own expectations and disappointment. I can
ask what mistakes I made, and I do not have to beat my
breast with guilt. There is forgiveness for my own failures,

and I know that God is not totally dependent on me to do what He wants to in that individual.

Does the client really want to change? I see that question as the bridge between the second and third stages of counselling, when you have looked together at the situation, and have seen pointers to the way ahead. The teaching stage includes logical unravelling of the current situation, understanding some of the effects of past events, and shafts of light from the Bible. The time of prayer will ask for the release of God's power to change. Does she want it? It ought to be obvious. Things are uncomfortable. After all, if everything was fine she would not have come to see you. But change is scary. Change means moving out of the known, and the known seems safe.

I once received a telephone call from the Samaritans. A young woman was with them who was a Christian, and the Samaritan to whom she was talking knew that our church has a midweek group for people of her age. I said that she could come straight round to our house. Joan arrived about half an hour later, with one thigh bleeding. It was covered with light cuts, each an inch or so long, probably made with a razor blade. After we had bathed it, we talked. This habit of cutting herself did not appear to be suicidal, or even merely seeking attention, but a masochistic desire to hurt herself. I expressed that she was trapped in a ring, and the chance of freedom was waiting outside. Her reply was, 'It's safer to stay where I am.' Of course it was not safe for her to be compulsively slashing herself like that. But it was the familiar place, so it felt safe. It seemed that she did not want to change, so I could not help her.

It went differently with Lucy, a determined young Scots woman. She had originally come to see me because of her pain as she struggled with infertility after five years of marriage. We soon found that an even bigger issue was her anger with God, and her concept of Him and His apparent unreliability. One day she was in my sitting-room, with her friend Susan as co-counsellor. Lucy's Scottish stubbornness was in danger of winning the battle over her willingness to give in to God. I had suggested that she might pray. She did not want to face Him. So I told her that I would move up to the other end of the room, because I was going to pray anyway; she could join me if she chose. Poor Sue felt herself in a dilemma. Should she stay beside her friend, or should she join me in praying? She came almost at once, and we prayed side by side, in silence, while Lucy struggled.

Three years on, Lucy reflects on that time:

> When Rosemary moved, followed by Sue, I was left feeling very alone and even more stubborn! I wrestled with the decision to stand firm in my obstinacy or to give in and join the others. During those minutes, I came face to face with my strong lack of willingness to come back to God, yet deep down I knew that there was nowhere to go unless I changed my will. How I wished I could effect and affirm that change silently, alone before God! But here I was being asked to move physically to demonstrate my willingness. *That* became my next stumbling block. But only for a moment. Then followed a tremendously humbling experience. As I gradually moved towards the others who were praying at the table, I recognised that the physical distance between my friends and me was parallel to the spiritual distance between God and me. And God was waiting, like them, for me to take those first faltering steps towards Him.

I reckon that was a crucial point in Lucy's life. As she moved towards us, she moved towards deepened faith and renewed submission to God – and before three years were up she had not one but two children!

How Can We Challenge The Will?

Apart from the straight question, 'Do you want to be healed?' I have two main frameworks to use for this. One consists of three short – very short – questions. Can God do it? Do you want it? Will you let Him? They are innocuous looking questions at first sight; let us look more closely.

Can God do it?

'It' varies, of course, from one client to another. 'It' is whatever the hurdle is, the 'problem mountain' I wrote about earlier. There does not need to be an enthusiastic, whole-hearted YES in reply. The father of the epileptic boy told Jesus, 'I do believe; help me overcome my unbelief!' (Mark 9:24). There is honesty in that request. 'Lord, I think you can do it. I know that you are supposed to be able to do it. But my feelings are tugging in the other direction, and I'm not really sure that you can do anything – or that you actually want to. Please help me with this.' A little finger of faith pointed up is sufficient for Jesus to grasp – we do not need to reach up with both arms stretched wide and sure. When I make that comment in counselling I demonstrate, first wagging one finger, then stretching out my arms.

Do you want it?

Surely that is obvious, we might think; the client would not have come if she did not want 'it'. Not necessarily. She may have come looking for sympathy; she may have come just wanting her own attitudes to be reinforced. The conversation may have taken an unexpected turn of events. Her initial problem has turned out to be part of a much larger picture, and she is not sure that she wants the Lord to meddle with all of it. She would prefer to have a few potholes in her road mended, not the whole road dug up, even though its surface would be enormously improved by the end. The cost of the roadworks seems to be too great. No, she prefers to stay with the apparent safety of her present, uncomfortable position, as Joan did. She does not want 'it' enough.

Will you let Him?

'Yes, I suppose God can do it. Yes, I want Him to.' But there is still one hurdle. Do you want it enough to let Him do it in His way? Will you let Him take control? This may reach the roots of a person's being without her recognising it. A child's birthright is to live in an atmosphere of love and safety, where the ability to trust can grow naturally and firmly. But if the climate around is untrustworthy in any way, trust cannot develop. Instead she tries to be in charge of her own affairs and learns to take control of other people. So the manipulative person is born, who attempts to manage the world around her. She does this unconsciously, and with notable lack of success. So when we ask, 'Will you let Him?' we are asking her to do a very hard thing, to let go of her own flimsy pole, and to grasp the solid but invisible pillar of a God whose ways she does not fully understand. We are asking her to offer Him her long-term habit of planning her own life and of telling other people (subtly, of course!) what to do.

Again, only a tentative agreement is necessary. I reassure her that God understands, and that we can come to Him with all our uncertainties and fears. It is helpful to think about the problems as being in a tangle. Have you ever tried to unravel a bundle of pieces of string? Start with the right spare end, and it may loosen up easily; start in the wrong place, and it all becomes even more confused! We do not have to sort out our tangle of life, and then bring each strand, separate and tidy, to God. It is far safer to bring Him the whole tangle, and give Him permission to unravel it. After all, He does know best!

Do you remember Maureen, with her school bag and her father's briefcase? (p.149) That illustration of a tangle was useful for her as our conversation continued. She went back to her picture of Jesus standing by the ocean, and she handed to Him a 'tangled ball' of different areas in her life; she saw it as 'lots of colours of yarn.' She told me that He extracted a few of the strands and put them in the pocket of His long robe, and chucked the rest into the sea.

As she prayed I suddenly had a sense that the devil had his claws into this. Unusually for me I neither waited, nor even told her of my suspicions. I plunged in, telling the Enemy that if he had any hold on her fear, or on anything else, that he was to get out. Maureen told me afterwards that when I spoke in that way Jesus took those two strands from His pocket, black strands, and laid them on the palm of His hand; suddenly they burst into flames under His gaze and were completely consumed. If anything black appears in a prayer picture it is a sure sign of demonic activity. So here was a confirmation of my hunch that the devil should be rebuked. It was all a surprise – but then, if we give God permission to do what He wants, He is likely to take us by surprise!

God's Truth – And Confusion

Here is my second plan of approach for challenging a person's will. I start by drawing another rough diagram:

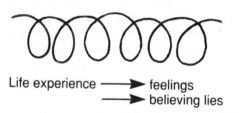

Life experience ⟶ feelings
⟶ believing lies

At the top is the GOD'S TRUTH layer. That includes Bible teaching about God and about His ways of looking at the world. For the client that may be merely head knowledge.

He may feel guilty that it is only theory, and not the reality that other Christians claim. But I am glad when he dares to be honest and to admit that it all seems very far away from his experience. The lower level includes those things that seem real. The experiences of life have left, and still leave, deep impressions on the emotions. The events and their accompanying feelings then lead to misconceptions about God, about ourselves and about other people. We believe lies. They are lies that contradict God's truth, yet they seem so much more 'real,' and the client is aware of the inner argument between the two layers. The lower layer shouts, while the top layer whispers.

I like this diagram, because it does not deny the source and the strength of the inward feelings. In the centre space there is the will to choose. The choice is a basic one: 'Which of those layers do you want to rule your life?' When the question is phrased in that way, I cannot remember a Christian who has not opted for the top layer, 'of course that is what I want.'

We know we cannot change course merely by will power. The New Year's resolutions that are broken by January 4th are evidence of that! The downward pull of the deeply embedded attitudes of the bottom layer is strong. But when we confess that we want to be ruled by God's truth, then we are allying ourselves with Him. When we pray, we are opening ourselves up to the power of the Holy Spirit. That puts a different complexion on things. So I express to the client (using my hands) that as we reach up to grasp God's ways, and then pray, our hands are opened up like a funnel. The Spirit can take from the 'God's truth' layer, and pour it into the layer of rubbish:

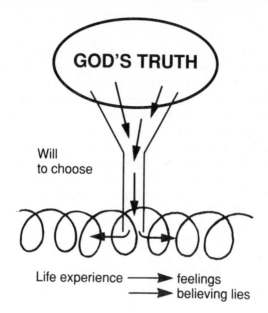

I encourage the client to expect changes in his attitudes, belief and behaviour. At the same time I point out that change is more often a process than a sudden transformation. We are more like ocean liners that turn in a large circle after the wheel has been rotated than nifty sailing dinghies that change course immediately the tiller is moved.

I can change the metaphor, and remind him that when a doctor prescribes a course of antibiotics he does not expect us to take one pill and throw the rest away. We can take that illustration further. Even if the pills are taken exactly according to orders the temperature graph will probably fluctuate, and improvement may not be steady. Often a client feels that he has tried in the past, and he has failed. We need to give him new courage to try again, if he is really wanting to live according to the truths that the Bible teaches.

Homework

1) Think of a time when you faced a crisis in your life. What were the issues? Did you really want to change? What were the particularly difficult things? How long did you stay stuck in the same place? What encouraged you to step forward? Did other people help or hinder?

As you reflect, consider whether there is any 'unfinished business' that needs your prayer or your action now.

2) *Discuss this situation with a partner* You can see that someone needs help but either does not recognise it or is unwilling to ask for help. Is there anything you can do?

15

THE IMPORTANCE OF PRAYER

Jesus said to the disciples, 'Apart from me you can do nothing' (John 15:5). We reckon that we are part of the vine, so all is well. But do we not merely pay lip service to that statement when we do not allow the sap to rise in us (or in our counselling) by prayer? We will not all pray in the same way. We do not all have the same gifts or temperaments, or the same patterns of praying. What matters is that we do pray. We prepare ourselves by prayer; we pray for our clients and with our clients; and what I hold as the most important of all, we enable our clients to pray for themselves.

Prayer For Ourselves

Our praying must not be confined to intercession for those whom we are seeking to help. The effectiveness, or otherwise, of our counselling comes out of the sort of people we are. 'Whenever anyone turns to the Lord, the veil is taken away . . . We, who with unveiled faces all reflect the Lord's glory, are being transformed into his likeness . . .' (2 Cor. 3:16, 18). So we need to spend time just being with Jesus, sitting at His feet, looking up at Him. Two people spending time together become more alike in their speech and behaviour. We can absorb Jesus' ways, and grow in sensitivity to His prompting.

Galatians chapter 5 (from verse 16 to the end of the chapter) is worth studying. Paul writes of the fruit of love, with its varied facets that the Spirit can ripen in our lives. But first he points out some of the weeds that must be

uprooted. They are the weeds of sexual impurity, of disharmony in relationships, of worship diverted from the true
God, of addictions and their destructiveness; all these hinder
Christ-like character from maturing in our lives. So the basis
of our praying will be for our own relationship with the
Lord. Neglect that, and our whole lives – including our
counselling – will be impoverished.

Prayer For Our Clients

Epaphras wrestled in prayer (Col. 4:12). Much of my praying
for clients is more like writing a name on a piece of paper
and showing that to the Lord, either in my regular times
of prayer, or in flash prayers as I move through the day. I
may pray for them in tongues or in English. I may pray in
silence, even without words, giving the Spirit space to bring
thoughts into my mind. Occasionally I know the dimension
of the 'groans that words cannot express' (Rom. 8:26), when
the prayer is deep inside and I am aware that the Spirit is
moving in an indefinable way.

We can pray at all sorts of odd times for our clients, and
we can ask other people to back us in prayer. We should
beware in this that we do not break confidentiality. Too
often requests for others to share in prayer become an
excuse to pass on Christian gossip. If another person has
opened up on his secret self it is vital that we do not
misplace that trust, yet that is desperately easy to do. It
may be an open secret that John is spending time with me.
I can ask faithful intercessors to pray for him, without my
having to divulge anything about what John is sharing with
me. Or I can ask for prayer at a particular time, without
needing to indicate who is coming to me for counselling.
Or I may be able to ask for prayerful backing for 'a man
with homosexual tendencies' without giving a single clue to
enable him to be identified.

A client who really wants to change is often surprisingly
willing to be identified. After speaking at a healing service
I have sometimes asked those coming forward for prayer

to tell me their Christian names, and also one or two words to describe their needs. These have been written up on the overhead projector, for the whole congregation to be able to see, and be able to join in prayer in a more informed way. I never insist on this, and some give just a name, or bypass me altogether while waiting for one of the pray-ers to be available. But I am surprised how many feel they can give a headline to their need as well as their name. They are given a choice, just as I am giving a choice to those who are being asked that their stories might be included in this book. That respect breeds trust, trust which enhances effective ministry.

Prayer With The Client

We are thinking about 'prayer counselling'. So it is not surprising when I say that the whole session can be steeped in prayer. At the start of our time together, I usually lead by suggesting that we commit to God the time we are spending together. In the first session I normally open with a simple prayer, asking the Lord to be in control. I may use words that convey an image, such as asking God to put a fence round us so that nothing unwanted invades our space – the space for the trio of counsellor, client and Jesus. I pause long enough to allow him to pray aloud as well, without embarrassing him by feeling that it is expected. If he wants to pray out loud, it is usually only a moment before I hear an intake of breath that indicates that words will follow. On our second or third meeting together, I may well suggest that he opens in prayer. Prayer is not my prerogative, after all!

During our time together I expect to keep one ear turned towards the Lord. That attitude does not need words to know that I am dependent on the Spirit to guide the speech between the two humans. Have you ever noticed Nehemiah's arrow prayer in chapter 2? The book starts when he received bad news from Jerusalem, and he spent an extended time of fasting, confession and intercession. Four months later he was with the king, who asked why he was sad, and what he would like the king to do. If the king had been recording the story I believe he would have written 'I asked Nehemiah what he wanted, and he answered . . .' But Nehemiah's perspective was different.

'The king said to me "What is it you want?" Then I prayed to the God of heaven, and I answered the king . . .' (Neh. 2:4–5).

Nehemiah's prayer for guidance was real, yet it did not interrupt the flow of the conversation. When I am praying in that way I am asking God to guide the flow of the client's speaking, and he sometimes includes things he had no intention of talking about; God knows they need to be said. At the same time, I am praying for myself. I need the ability to remember anything vital that he is saying; I need clarity of thought to connect together any relevant facts or to filter out the superfluous; I need insight to understand what lies behind his expressed thoughts and guidance to know how to move forward.

When I start to ask questions, or to make suggestions about what appears to be happening, we may hit a brick wall. How do we discover where to go? We pray together again. Not only are we expecting God to give some direction, but I am modelling an aspect of the Christian life that he may never have considered. *Everything* can be brought to God, at any time. Nothing is outside the scope of His interest and of His ability to affect.

Ron learnt this through a financial crisis. He was an adopted only son; his widowed mother was often depressed and manipulative, and was not very happy in her retirement home; his marriage to a lady from a different ethnic background had normal marital tensions, nothing startling; his second child had died within a day of his birth; his perfectionist tendencies pulled him into long hours of work in his private business. There was plenty to fuel a different topic for our talk and prayer each week.

One day he arrived loaded with the burden of pressing financial problems and heavy taxes to be paid. He mentioned that he tithed regularly, but it had never occurred to him that he might consult the Lord about the other 90% of his income. We prayed together about the finances, and he left considerably less stressed than he had arrived, without hearing a loud voice telling him how to pay his taxes. A week later he was able to tell me how another man whom he had feared had been unexpectedly co-operative, and he and his wife had been able to find a satisfactory solution together. Ron learnt more about prayer and more about the God to whom he prayed, as well as finding an answer to his immediate concerns.

Enabling The Client To Pray

It is vital that I am a prayerful person for this sort of ministry. Even more important, however, is that the client is helped to pray for himself. I suspect that in much prayer ministry, whether in the counselling room, after a church service, or in any unexpected venue, the person who is aware of his needs is allowed to sit back passively with his arms folded, and do nothing. After all, God is going to do the work, and the 'minister' is good at praying, so why has he got to bother? The prayer seems to float past him. He does not see change happening in his life, and he concludes that prayer does not make any difference, or that God has let him down, or the 'minister' did not ask for the right things. It becomes easy for him to evade responsibility.

But I am there to be a catalyst, to enable him to turn to God in prayer for himself. I expect that prayer to be on the spot, and aloud. Even if he has decided that he is not ready for the Spirit to move in and change anything, there is nothing to stop him from saying that to the Lord. Remember two things about the Lord. He looks for honesty and He respects the freedom of choice He has given us.

I am reminded of Matthew, an Oxford undergraduate. He arrived in my house one day saying that he had lost his joy in the Lord and was having to live behind a smiling mask as leader of the group of Christians in his college. I asked

the obvious question. 'Are you aware of anything to cause
your joy to leak out?'

His reply was somewhat shame-faced: impure sexual
thoughts were the trouble.

'Well, we had better deal with that first.' There was no
point in looking for any other causes of the leak, if we did
not first plug that hole. Time was limited, so I suggested that
he should pray. Knowing from a previous meeting with him
that he understood about using his imagination in prayer, I
asked him to imagine that he was sitting in front of Jesus.
His shame probably turned his eyes to the ground. I told
him to look up at the Saviour's face.

There was silence for about five minutes. Then Matthew
turned to me, beaming, and told me what had happened.
When he had looked at Jesus' face all he could see was
His eyes, wet with tears. Those tears melted Matthew; they
showed him how grieved the Lord was with his sin, and
drew out from him genuine confession. 'Then he picked
me up, like a little boy' – Matthew demonstrated, as if his
arms were hugging a child to his chest – 'and told me that
He forgave me. I started to say "But . . .", and Jesus replied
"No buts".'

'But I would like a word from Scripture.'

'It is finished.' Jesus' words were incisive. Matthew knew
it was true. He accepted the forgiveness, and we thanked
God joyfully together. Then he went off, committed to a
change in his thought life. When he first admitted his sin it
would have been easy for me to exhort him to repentance
or to pray for him. But he might have missed meeting God
for himself. As he faced Jesus, Jesus met him exactly as he
needed, simply and decisively.

Matthew was already accustomed to praying aloud. You
may wonder about the person who is utterly unused to
that. Do I force him? Well, not exactly! My approach goes
this way.

'You have been talking to me without any difficulty,
haven't you? It certainly seems so.' Assent from the client.
'It's as if Jesus has been sitting in that empty chair, listening

in to everything we have been saying. But He is really the person with the answers and with the means to help you carry them through. Wouldn't it be a good idea to draw Him in on the conversation? It hardly seems fair to leave Him out!' I have sometimes pulled the vacant chair nearer, and encouraged the client to turn, and start talking, thinking of Jesus sitting there. A matter-of-fact nudge of this sort may be all that is needed to start her praying.

If I use everyday language and a natural voice when I am praying, I defuse some of her fear that it is difficult, mystical or just plain odd, or that prayer out loud is only for the élite. If I am relaxed, and confident that she will be able to pray aloud, she is infected by that confidence, and is usually prepared to try. I may ask 'If you were going to say one thing to God, what would you want to say?' Her answer to that question can be her starting point. 'Right, say that to Him.'

Another opening is this: 'What do you want to ask Jesus to pray for you?' I think of Wendy, who felt that she was being persecuted in her office. She tried to be friendly, and to witness as a Christian, but she felt that everyone was ganging up against her. As we talked she saw that this was a repeated pattern in her life; there might be something in her that was out of place, not just in her fellow workers. 'What do you want to ask Jesus to pray for you?'

'Oh . . . That He will make other people nicer to me.'

I tried again. 'What do you want to ask Him to do for *you*?' She finally saw that I was implying that she needed to ask God to change something in her, not just in the other people or in her circumstances. But she did not know what to ask. She simply could not see anything that was wrong in her. The rest of the story of Wendy belongs to the next chapter, but remember that question. It is the question Jesus asked blind Bartimaeus, 'What do you want me to do for you?' (Mark 10:51).

A third way to help the reluctant pray-er is to appeal to her visual sense. 'If you were to draw a picture of yourself with Jesus, how would you draw it?' For someone who is finding it difficult to think that she might possibly be able to talk to God at all, let alone out loud, this may be a way in. Stella loved drawing, so this was just the question for her.

'I would be lying on the ground, flat on my face, with a dark blanket over me.' I asked where Jesus would be. 'He would be over the other side of the room.' I allowed a pause, and it was astonishing how quickly her imaginary rough drawing was taken by the Spirit, and used by Him. Stella found that Jesus moved and knelt down beside her. Then He lifted the blanket and picked her up. The picture was vivid and the Lord communicated to her heart truths that had previously been vague theory to her.

That evening she wrote in her journal, 'Jesus is no longer on the Cross. He is now with me in reality. Jesus knows where I am. He is close by and He sees me where I am now. He is not aloof because He sits with me. His face shines out stars of kindness and thoughtfulness. He humbles Himself to *come down to my level* in order to hear me better. He shows me by this *He cares* about me. I am for some reason amazed at His attitude because I had given up hope. In other words *He does not reflect my despair and weakness* but I can see in His eyes that He *knows* where I've been and where I'm coming from. He waits patiently for me to speak; all I can say is, "Help me".'

My need is to be helped
to be understood
to be listened to, thoughtfully.
God can and will meet this need
totally.

The simple picture gave her a concept of Jesus that was more real to her than my words could ever have been.

I used the same question with Nigel, who had been in Christian leadership for many years. Charming and able, he had recently crashed in depression; he was feeling that God was far away, and could not forgive him.

'If you were to draw a picture of yourself and Jesus, what would it be like?'

Nigel replied, 'There's a fire in the fireplace. He is sitting on one side, in an armchair, and I am on the other.'

God used this simple thought to make plain that He still accepted Nigel, that He was as relaxed with him as when everything was going fine. God's acceptance was not dependent on Nigel's success. This had been head knowledge to Nigel for many years, and it was a message that God knew he needed for his heart.

Here are some other suggestions for helping the tongue-tied to speak. One is simply to ask if you may ask God to free him up to pray aloud with you. Other ideas he can work on at home. First, suggest that he makes a habit of praying aloud when he is on his own, so that it is no longer awkward to verbalise his prayers, and he becomes accustomed to the sound of his own voice. The freedom of his own room, or a wide space outside, can be used to loosen feelings as well as words, and can help him to be more genuine before God. Second, he might try to put his thoughts on paper. I think again of Stella. The first day she wrote about four lines in her journal, in a great hurry before going out. Soon she was writing a full page or more, with her reflections on her Bible reading and her chatting with Jesus. She brought the book with her each week for me to read, allowing me to be a witness to the growth in her relationship with God.

'Allowing me to be a witness.' That is part of the value of the client praying out loud. The prime relationship is between the Lord and the individual. But if each of us lived in separate little boxes, with all communication private, there would be no real development of family relationship. I have known a client come saying, 'I have prayed about this a lot by myself, but I don't seem to be able to get through on it.' God has not been ignoring her prayer, but He knows her need to trust another member of the Christian family. So the apparent delay in her prayer being answered enables this to happen.

As I pray alongside, mostly silently, I am there to support. It may be taking a verse out of context to quote here Jesus' promise, 'Where two or three come together in my name, there am I with them' (Matt. 18:20), but there is no doubt that there is power in corporate prayer. It is not only my physical presence and my understanding that support. There is the spiritual undergirding of my prayer alongside hers. As she prays, it may well be that unexpected thoughts come to mind, and my presence is needed then to help her to think through their implications. Unexpected emotions surface, and the strength of my unshockable love is a pillar, as much as the relevant Scripture that I bring to bear. My experience of God at work in prayer together, aloud, has given me such a conviction in its value that I will urge a client in this direction pretty strongly, while also respecting her choice if she wants to wait.

A Pattern Of Praying

There is no set formula about how to pray. The most important thing is to allow plenty of time for the two-way prayer that gives the Lord a chance to 'speak'. If the talking has used most of the available time for today, pray briefly, and note that your next appointment must be spent mostly in prayer. This shortened prayer at the end reminds me of my mother (or myself!) with an untidy cupboard that has been partly sorted, but unfinished. The contents that are still strewn over the floor are pushed back in, and we know that we must return there later. In the same way we ask the Lord to hold a box, into which we push the unfinished business, and trust Him to look after it until our next meeting. Beware! It will be only too easy, in that next meeting, to continue to talk, and to talk, and to talk, and then to find that relaxed prayer has again been squeezed out.

Brian had been to see me several times, and we had prayed together on each occasion. One day, quite unexpectedly, he prayed for well over an hour, with me in silent support. It was as if the Holy Spirit was wielding a searchlight. Memories came to Brian's mind one at a time. They ranged from pre-school days at home, through primary school, through boarding school, and included some from his current time at university. He brought to the Lord each sin, each hurt, each fear. After every prayer there were several seconds of silence, while the searchlight roamed and then came to rest again. Some of the events he had already discussed with me; others were fresh reminders. This prayer cannot be rushed. This prayer goes deep.

'But how do I start?' may be the client's question when invited to pray. I like to be as nondirective as possible at this point – with two provisos. If sin has been acknowledged, or unforgiveness expressed, there is no escape from the need for that sin to be confessed; nor can anyone expect God's help unless he is willing to take at least one step forward on the path of forgiveness. How can we come to God and ask Him to help if we are deliberately ignoring His rules?

I think of a couple who approached me after a church service. They had a dilemma. He was divorced; she was single. The two of them had been sleeping together, and now she was pregnant. Medication that she was taking for a skin complaint would almost certainly mean that the baby would be severely deformed. Should they have the pregnancy terminated? Even before considering the question of taking a life there was another issue that could not be avoided. They had committed fornication. Unless that was confessed and forgiven there was a block in the path of their right to ask God for guidance about marriage and about the baby:

> I will instruct you and teach you in the way you should go;
> I will counsel you and watch over you (Psalm 32:8).

That is what God promises – in the context of:

> I said, 'I will confess my transgressions to the Lord' – and you forgave the guilt of my sin (Psalm 32:5).

Guilt and resentment are 'musts' for prayer. Apart from those the question, 'How do I start?' has an open answer.

So I suggest to the client that he spreads in front of the Lord all the assorted things we have talked about, and asks God to choose where to start. He may feel, 'Help! I don't know where to go.' There are times when I momentarily wonder whether he can cope with this lack of structure. But when I release to the Lord the responsibility for directing the prayer I give the Holy Spirit room to work, remembering that one of the Spirit's tasks is to help us to pray when we do not know how. If I try to control the proceedings I am actually hindering Him. When I recognised that it was His work, not mine, I became more effective in my counselling and less tired because of it.

As he keeps praying hitherto forgotten matters often come to mind, as they did with Brian. Often the client wants to stop and talk so that new factors the Spirit has brought to light can be unravelled. That is all part of God's work. Talk about them, and then take the new thoughts back into prayer. It is exciting; it is very exciting, to be allowed to be a junior partner with God, and to watch Him at work in this way.

Do not be afraid of silence, the silence that allows the searchlight to move. While he is praying, I pray quietly. My prayer has two main directions. My mind is following him, underlining his words and thoughts. At the same time I am seeking direction from God, asking whether there is any way in which I need to intervene, with Scripture, with a challenge, or with a supplementary prayer. I most often find that if I wait an extra moment, my possible suggestion becomes unnecessary, because his prayer goes in the same direction. That is confirmation that the Spirit is deeply at work.

Irene was walking with Jesus in a scene she could picture clearly. At one point she told me that she was standing by a huge waterfall, and I wondered whether I ought to suggest that she should step underneath it. I waited, and said nothing. A moment later I heard her say, 'I've stepped under it, and it is washing me clean.' Then she asked God for forgiveness, in 'ordinary' prayer; when she returned to her picture she found that she climbed a mountain towards a golden light.

Finishing The Time Of Prayer

When we are praying in this way there is a strong sense of God's presence. 'Praying in the Spirit' is a phrase that is often confined to the use of tongues. Define it instead as 'praying *open* to the Spirit', and you and your client will realise that in your openness to God you are indeed praying *in* the Spirit, even if English is the only language used. Incidentally, if I am counselling a client for whom English is his second language I like to give him the option of praying in his first language. That makes it harder for me to sustain my back-up prayer, but it may be easier for him; he is the person who matters. He can explain to me afterwards how God has met him.

I find it impossible to put into words how God makes His presence felt so strongly. His grip on the room is evident. We know when we should continue praying, and when to finish. When the client's conversation with the Lord seems to be ended I step in. This is the moment to use Scripture in a way that seals over the places in his heart that have been opened up and reinforces the ways that God has spoken. A true encounter with God is never anti-biblical, even if I cannot recall an exact verse in Scripture that ties in to it; but I am often surprised at the way that the Spirit brings a relevant passage to mind.

It may be right to resist Satan in a very definite way, telling him in Jesus' name that all these matters that have been brought to God are now holy territory, and the unholy spirit is utterly unwelcome. I pray, too, for the Holy Spirit to fill and to refill the client, asking for particular attributes of the Spirit's character and work. If doubt and fear have been admitted to God, I pray for the Spirit to give faith, to give the love that drives out fear and the power to be witnesses to Jesus. If anger and impatience have been confessed I can pray for the peace, gentleness and patience that are aspects of the Holy Spirit's fruit.

Then commit to God any of the unfinished business of which you are both aware, give thanks for what has happened and let him join in with a prayer such as this:

Send us out into the world in the power of your Spirit, to live and work to your praise and glory (Church of England ASB p. 173).

A song, sung or said together, makes a good close. Either start singing a song that you both know well, or use a hymn or song book if you have one nearby.

The Send Off

Do not let him leave thinking that this one time of prayer, however deep it has gone, has completed the work. Paul wrote to the Philippians, 'Work out your salvation with fear and trembling, for it is God who works in you to will and to act according to his good purpose' (Phil. 2:12–13). I like that. It speaks of co-operation between God and ourselves. We must work out what God is working in us. I am told that 'works in you' is literally, 'is energetic in you', with all the power that raised Jesus from the dead (see Eph. 1:19–20). That is invigorating, but not automatic. Think of an old house whose walls need to be stripped of the ivy that covers them. If you just try to pull the tendrils off the wall, it is hard work, and the ivy will grow again. You need to cut it decisively at the root. But even when the roots have been cut the shrivelling growth on the walls still needs to be pulled. So you must discuss with him how he expects the time of prayer to take effect in pulling the tendrils of the pattern of his reactions, and his behaviour. This is often a slow process, but he can expect change. He is unlikely to find that he is totally victorious, so remind him that he does not need to be too discouraged when he fails sometimes, and the old habits take over.

When that happens, he must not fear immediately that all is lost! Confess to God, apologise to other people, claim forgiveness, put matters straight, and go on. The point of failure is a vulnerable moment, when 'your enemy the devil prowls around like a roaring lion looking for someone to devour' (1 Pet. 5:8). He whispers in the ear, 'Look at the mess you are making of things. Nothing has really changed.' That voice must be ignored by listening instead to the one who says, 'There is no condemnation for those who are in Christ Jesus' (Rom. 8:1). That whole chapter in Romans is one to give him to meditate over and to absorb.

Another illustration comes to mind. I sometimes talk about climbing the spiral staircase in the turret of an old English church or castle. Its windows are narrow slits, all facing in the same direction. As you climb, looking out of each window as you go, the view scarcely changes at first, and you might think that your efforts are getting you nowhere. But gradually the view alters its perspective. Then a moment comes when you reach the top of the tower, and you emerge into the open. The view is no longer confined, but it is magnificently wide. Change has been achieved!

An Important Warning

The final caution is for the rest of the day. A time of prayer such as I have been describing may have gone deep into his emotions. That drains energy, so warn him that he may feel shattered before he revives. That is normal; nothing is wrong. Instead encourage him to relax as much as possible, confident that he will soon pick up and find himself renewed. After all, a surgical operation is followed by a period of convalescence. We do not expect complete fitness immediately after major surgery on our bodies, nor should we do so after emotional surgery.

I learnt that lesson from a young post-graduate student. Sarah spent nearly six hours with me one Tuesday afternoon. I expected her to leave after about two hours, when we had dealt with one major issue in her life, her father's academic expectations for her. But when she realised that she might have to go away with her enormous sense of deep loneliness untouched her tears started to flow. I had time free, so she stayed. Her sense of isolation had started when she was born. Panic over her mother's condition had left the infant lying untended for a time that felt like eternity. Her re-experiencing of that aloneness and the ministry that followed were extensive and effective. She realised that she was in no fit state to study at the moment and she went to stay with her parents.

A week later she wrote me a long letter:

I eventually reached home on Thursday having spent all Wednesday tying up loose ends. Not that I had much to do: a couple of things to type, some people to see, but I was so physically and emotionally drained that I could barely move! I was feeling quite apprehensive on the way home, wondering what my parents' reaction would be to my tale of woe, but when I saw them I was absolutely overwhelmed by their love and support. I had decided to discard my 'happy, successful Christian' image and show them exactly how I was feeling, and I'm glad that I did. The resentments and fears of childhood having been healed, I was able to realise their unconditional acceptance of me in the here and now! What they saw was a tired, weepy, fed-up daughter, bent on throwing up her career at Oxford, and they loved her. It was tremendous! For the first time since I can remember I felt I could lean on them completely; a little voice in my ear said frequently, 'You're not being a very good witness, are you?', to which I replied, 'If being a good witness means putting up a false front, I'd rather be a bad witness.' And the fact that I was showing them, 'the real Me' meant that there were no undercurrents of tension, not even with my father.

For the first few days I did nothing – I was so drained that I couldn't concentrate on a book, or muster up enough energy to pick up a pen. I simply, 'Let go, let God.' I resolutely ignored the little voice which whispered that I was wasting time and 'think of how many things you could be doing and making this week,' and simply got used to being Me, accepted by my parents, by other people and by God. I didn't even read the Bible or pray very much, which sounds dreadful doesn't it? But even that was too much activity for my poor little addled brain, and I just spent the time quietly thinking, or not thinking at all.

About yesterday, when my poached egg of a brain got round to functioning again I prayed a very important prayer which I'd like to share with you. I prayed it outside the library in the pouring rain with my umbrella up, but the location didn't seem to matter. I told God that He had destroyed my previous life, which was a good thing too since it was a very fragile edifice and hollow inside, and that He had in His mercy got to work on the cracks in the foundations, ready to build on, and I prayed that from that moment on the Lord would build *His* life on them.

You know, this all sounds very unscriptural! I firmly believe the teaching of the Word that our new resurrection life begins the moment we come to God through Jesus. But it seems that I have only just appropriated the reality of this, or rather that the Lord has brought me to a point when I see the emptiness and despair of life lived for Self and am very glad to have seen the back of it.

So here I am, the Real Me with a new life – all very exciting! If I told you that I was bubbling over with joy, however, I would be telling a lie. For the rest of last week I felt very miserable, although the worst of the depression had lifted, and longing for the joy of the Lord. I went to see a good Christian friend and shared with him something of what the Lord had been doing to me, but finished up by saying miserably, 'But I'm still not joyful.' 'You can never seek joy,' he said. 'It's a by-product, not an end-product. Seek the Lord and your feelings will look after themselves.' So I'm resting on the *Facts* of the new solid foundations of my life and letting *Feelings* take care of themselves. But like C.S. Lewis I'm being 'surprised by joy,' and every day finds me more peaceful and cheerful.

Sarah's 'surgery' had been fundamental. It is not surprising that she was so drained of energy, and it was good that she took the risk – or so it felt – of going home. Her convalescence was solid, and subsequent letters show how her new outlook began to work out in her life. From her perspective of fourteen years later she realises that her healing, 'was not a once-for-all completed event one afternoon, but rather a gradual process, no less wonderful and miraculous for that reason,' in which her husband's steadfast, unconditional love has been a major factor.

Rarely, of course, is there such extensive ministry at one time, and I would not normally recommend it. But the principle remains. Be open to God, and let Him control the whole of the counselling time. Tell the client she may feel utterly flattened before she is uplifted. Then she leaves, with a final prayer for God's keeping power and with agreement on when and how you connect together again.

Does God Only Work In The Counselling Sessions?

If I am giving the impression that God can only work when at least two Christians are together then I must deny it immediately. He is sovereign, and He is infinite. He has a multitude of ways and times and places when He meets people. I heard of one girl who knew almost nothing about Christianity, but submitted to Christ when she had a vision of Him in an empty Armenian cathedral.

Jane gave a testimony (during a counselling course) about the ways in which God met her on her own; here are some extracts:

Two years ago I was invited to join Rosemary in a co-counselling session when she was in Vancouver temporarily; I was to sit and observe. She invited the Holy Spirit to come and to shine His light in Raymond's heart and reveal certain things that would help during the counselling time. I sat watching and couldn't quite imagine that anything was going to happen. Suddenly things began to come from his past, things that he had not remembered for years and years, things which had terrific impact on why he was struggling the way he was.

So about a month later I decided it was time for me to begin spiritual heart surgery. Rosemary had gone back to England. I seemed to be left all on my own to work through this, so I made a covenant with the Lord. Every morning I would meet Him in my room, and spend a couple of hours in reading and praying and worshipping. So I began by asking the Holy Spirit to come and to reveal in my heart those things that needed to be changed. It was amazing. He did! I had a long list. You might think that this is navel gazing, but when it was brought before the light of the Lord I saw things that had held me back, things that had caused me to act the way I did, to treat my children the way I did, to speak to my husband the way I did, to have certain fears. There were many, many things. When it is brought to Him that way, then He can bring healing. The long-range goal is that I'll be conformed to be like Jesus. There were three prongs of things that might happen during these times with the Lord, the prongs of confession, forgiving and restitution. He graciously never brought more than one thing at a time. I'll use one simple example.

Our second son was fourteen at the time. He had done something to aggravate me early in the morning. I had given him quite an earful before he left for school, and we had parted that way. So when I sat down I asked the Lord, 'What are we going to do today?' The experience with Howard came so quickly to the surface that I knew that had to be dealt with. So as I sat and thought about it before the Lord I realised that even though he had done something that was uncalled for, my reaction was not fair. So I needed to ask the Lord to forgive me, and I needed to forgive Howard. The third part would be when he came in from school. I would have to go to him and bring up that painful situation. I told him what had happened in my room. He was most embarrassed by all this, but I didn't try to make him feel guilty. I said, 'Howard, I just have to ask you to forgive me.' He sort of shrugged his shoulders and went off. It was those kinds of things that I needed to forgive, or to be forgiven, and to do something about it afterwards.

Often during those times an awareness of something God wanted to show me would bring tears, tears of repentance and tears of hurt. They could all come, knowing that I was safe before the Cross. Then there were often tears of joy when I was forgiven and I felt lighter, and knew that my heart was cleaner and that God was just continuing the process. When I left my room I never felt dragged down by my weeping. Usually, if I go into my room, shut the door and cry because I'm angry about some situation in the family, when I come out I'm just as mad and as heavy as when I went in. But in these experiences it was a time of release to the Lord. He was bringing His forgiveness and healing into my heart. It was a refreshing time, and I could leave that room feeling uplifted.

Another thing happened a few days ago, after two years of new sensitivity to the Holy Spirit and of wanting to be exposed to the Lord. Last Monday evening I was sitting there in the model counselling session with Donald thinking, 'Don – angry with God?' Next morning I said, 'Lord, have I ever been angry with you?' And it came to me so fast I couldn't believe it. A few years ago we had a death in our family that I thought was totally unfair. My husband took the call, and I could tell what had happened by what he was saying. I began going through the house crying and screaming, 'God, it's not fair!' The Holy Spirit brought it back to me so quickly last Tuesday morning that I knew I had to deal with it.

It is rare to find a person who shares Jane's strength of character and depth of commitment to this process. Her vital experience of the Holy Spirit was very recent, but she had absorbed biblical teaching all her life, and she set herself purposefully to meet the Lord daily in this way. She committed herself to spending much time on her own with God, and God met her in deep and penetrating ways.

Although this book is on counselling, it is good to be reminded again that it is GOD's work. We are His agents, not His equal partners. Prayer is the biggest channel through which His love and power can flow.

For You To Do

1) *Meditate on Ephesians 1:17–23 and 3:14–21* Use these passages to pray first for yourself (e.g. 1:17 'I keep asking that . . . God . . . may give me the Spirit of wisdom . . .') and then for any others whom you are seeking to help. Use the verses, too, to lead you into worshipping 'the God of our Lord Jesus Christ, the glorious Father . . .' Allow unhurried time, more than once, to do this.

2) *Jesus at prayer* In Mark 1:35 we find Jesus up very early, praying. Read Mark 1:21–39, and then imagine how He might have been praying then. Use the insight from this experience to enrich your own prayers.

3) *A situation to discuss* At the end of a counselling session:

Counsellor: I will pray for you.

Client: Don't, it doesn't work.

The background is that initially the person was open to receive help, but later felt that God could not help, so she tried to help herself. The problem recurred and the cycle began again. What would you do now?

16

THE USE OF IMAGERY

Elaine was a medical student who came to talk with me occasionally. One day she suddenly blurted out that she was holding a small grudge against my husband. I assured her that he would not hold it against her but told her to pray about it immediately lest it was a block in our conversation. I suggested that she might imagine herself standing in front of Jesus. What did she want to say to Him? What did He then want to say to her? After a few seconds silence she blurted out in an amazed voice, 'He *wants* me to talk to Him!' Elaine had grown up in a Christian home, and I believe she had committed her life to Jesus as a child. But however many talks she had heard on prayer and however much she had prayed her heart had never grasped this simple truth. God actually wants our relationship with Him; it is an essential part of His nature.

Many of the living illustrations I have told have included pictures in prayer. This is a particularly powerful tool among the prayer counsellor's resources, one that I have come to value highly. But like a high-speed electric drill, it needs to be used with skill and sensitivity, brought out of the tool-box at the appropriate time, used with wisdom, not indiscriminately. Whenever I start to talk about this with a group of Christians there are some who are horrified. 'Surely that is New Age visualisation!' Others, quite rightly, ask for biblical validation for using such a method.

Imagination is part of our God-given make-up, along with all our artistic attributes and our appreciation of beauty and of music. Yes indeed, imagination often runs away with us. We mis-use it for escape from reality or for proud fantasy, and so we easily dismiss it as godless. We look on it as useless at its best, and positively harmful at its worst. But we need to be careful, for when we call ourselves biblical Christians we can easily be less than honest. The Bible is full of poetic language, of appeal to our senses; but we become hard-nosed, and our Christianity too cerebral. We dismiss emotions because they are unreliable, and accept only what our minds can understand and control. In our fear of opening ourselves up to wrong forces, we shut parts of ourselves off from God. If our imaginations are indeed part of the 'selves' that God made, surely we can submit those imaginations to God, and ask Him to use them for good. Paul wrote about 'taking captive every thought to make it obedient to Christ' (2 Cor. 10:5). There is the secret: *every* thought captive; every thought obedient to *Christ*. When our minds start to run riot in any way we need to rein them in and submit them to Christ.

If you are to ask me for chapter and verse that tells me I may dictate to a client what he is to see in his mind when he prays, I cannot give you one; in fact it is vital that we do not *dictate* to a client at all! If you want a particular reference for the way I do use imagery I still cannot give you one, any more than you can give me a verse for using a computer or an electric toaster or penicillin. But ask about God using the imagination, and we find the Bible full of it, in prophetic visions, in dreams, even in Jesus' vivid use of everyday illustrations in His teaching. General Booth, the founder of the Salvation Army, protested that the devil should not have all the best tunes. We can protest as vigorously that he does not have copyright on the imagination. If he has tried to steal it for his own ends why should we not claim it back?

Visualisation is, indeed, a powerful tool. I find God using it for three main ends. He often brings truth about Himself from theory into living experience. He also shows the client aspects of himself that were unrecognised. Sometimes He uses it to give a promise of better things to come than the client's present quality of life.

Safeguards

There are a number of safeguards for the wise use of this
tool of imagery.

a) *God's protection* I ask clearly that God will direct and
protect us. On one occasion I prayed publicly for God's
protection during a counselling seminar; one lady glanced
up – and saw two angels with drawn swords standing guard
over the door! It was very clear to her that the Lord was
indeed guarding us. That protection is needed because the
imagination is easily invaded by our human longings and
fears on the one hand and by Satan on the other. Satan
loves to play on our weaknesses – but those very weaknesses
need to be opened to the Lord, not shut away.

b) *The client at ease* A second safeguard is to do as much
as possible to help the client to relax. The thought of using
imagination for prayer may well be completely new to her;
she needs help in accepting that it is neither bizarre nor
impossible. Be relaxed and matter of fact. Emphasise that if
her mind stays blank, it does not matter. 'This may not be the
best way to help you, but we might as well try. You won't lose
anything by it.' And on the surprisingly rare occasions when
nothing at all happens, take the responsibility on yourself,
and apologise for suggesting this route. She may well be a
person who already reckons herself a failure; you do not want
to risk making her feel that she has failed yet again – even if
you suspect that the block is actually her own unwillingness
to face the truth God might reveal.

Explain as much as possible what may happen, and what
you want her to do. The picture may be in monochrome or
in colour; usually it starts as a still photograph, and then
turns into a movie. Like a film, the scene may switch from
one scene to another, without a sense of discontinuity.

I tell her that it will help if she can tell me a little about
what is happening, so that I can visualise the scene for
myself, and can pray more intelligently while it continues.
But I am not asking her to talk so much that it interferes

with whatever God is wanting to do. I explain that she will not get totally absorbed in the picture, but that she will still know that she is with me in the room. That, too, is like watching a film. However caught up we are in the drama we still know that we are living in the present. And just as she has the choice of walking out of the cinema, or of switching off the television, she can opt out of the picture at any time. All these preliminary comments aid relaxation before we move into the prayer.

c) *God's control* It is vital that God is the one in the lead, not the counsellor. The first time I read about 'faith-imagination' I was uncomfortable. There appeared to be too much of the counsellor saying what ought to happen and too little room for the Holy Spirit. I see no need to be in charge. It is much more exciting to be allowed to stand by, and to watch what God does with the situation! This means that if I suggest a rough outline of the picture to launch it I must not tell the client any details about how *I* think she ought to see it or how it should move. I can ask questions that help her to bring it into clearer focus, but these must be open questions, without any hint of my expectations for the answer.

d) *Avoid specific expectations for the outcome* Not only do we not know what route God will take; we do not know the destination of this time of prayer. Often the picture includes a challenge to her will, as real as the challenge to Moses when the Lord met him in the desert, and told him that he would head up the rescue of the Israelites from Egypt. (Was that a bush burning or a vision?)

At times the picture is vivid but its meaning is obscure. I have sometimes felt defeated when the client is looking at a blank wall. The temptation then is to take charge and tell the client how to find a way through. But remember that you are *not* the leader; even if you have to leave a picture without any clear understanding, do not worry. Before you meet again the Lord may very well bring some new event or new thought into her life that will give a clue about the way forward. Counselling is often like doing a jigsaw. Some of the pieces fit together in an obvious way; others have to be left on one side for the time being, until things become more clear.

How Do We Start?

First pray for the Holy Spirit to be in charge. Then the simplest way is to think of offering the client a roughly drawn pencil sketch, or asking her how she might draw one. There is no paper, no pencil. Words draw the picture, without elaborate detail. The starting point is varied.

a) *The client in front of the Cross, or in front of Jesus.* Suppose I suggest that she imagines herself in front of the Cross. Some simple questions will help her to focus.

Look at the Cross. What does it look like? Is Jesus on it, or is it empty? (The client usually 'sees' the Cross with Jesus crucified.) How tall is it? Do you see anything special about Jesus? Is there anything else you notice?

Now look at yourself. How near to the Cross are you? Are you standing or sitting, or what are you doing? What are you wearing? Are you carrying anything? How old do you think you are?

As you ask these questions, pray for God's leading. If she is carrying a bag or a box, whatever it is, pray that you know how to ask the next question. What do you think Jesus wants you to do with your box? The more vivid the picture becomes, the less you need to ask.

b) *A picture given to client or to counsellor.* Even if the counsellor's picture is vivid, instead of asking together, 'What does that mean?' try to describe it to the client and let her make it her own.

Fiona arrived one evening in tears over her boyfriend. Should they continue together? What was happening? She admitted that the Lord had been squeezed into second place by the relationship, and her tears of uncertainty rolled freely. Suddenly I – who rarely have pictures myself, although I am often instrumental in other people receiving them – 'saw' the rough outline of the girl, crying in desolation, standing on a rutted farm track. About a hundred yards down the road there was the figure of a man. I offered Fiona this simple outline, and asked her to visualise it. I gave her several seconds of quiet before I asked if the man (whom I sensed was Jesus) was looking at her, or away from her. A question like this shows whether the scene is clear for her, as well as describing it. There was no hesitation in her reply:

Fiona: He is facing me.
Me: Is he moving?
Fiona: No.
Me: Or you?
Fiona: No.
Me: What do you want to do?
Fiona: I can't move towards him. (Pause.) Well, perhaps I can try.

There was a short silence. Then she told me what happened. As soon as she took one step Jesus ran down the road to her. While she hugged Him with both arms He stroked her forehead and her hair with one hand. Love, gentleness and understanding are all communicated by that caress. With His other hand Jesus was holding on to someone who was behind His back. It was evident to both Fiona and me that the only person that could be was her boyfriend, and the message was clear. Jesus had tight hold of the situation, but He must be in the centre of the relationship. She responded to Him in 'ordinary' prayer, thanking God for His love, and committing the friendship to Him. When she left she was no clearer about what would happen to the relationship, but at peace about it.

c) *An illustration used by either the client or the counsellor* may start a picture. When I was talking with Wai-Ling (ch. 5) I likened her anger to a black lake in which she must plant the Cross. The imagery of the words immediately gave her a picture she could see vividly.

Audrey was another old friend. She had been a Christian for a long time and she used charismatic gifts, prophecy and others. One afternoon, however, after a country walk, she confessed that her spiritual life had run dry. She expressed it like this. 'Whenever I try to have a Quiet Time again there is a little bubble of life, and then a net closes over me.' She agreed that we should pray together, and that the net made a good start for a picture. I allowed a long enough silence for the scene to be set, and then asked about the colour of the net. The answer came at once. 'It's light grey.' The picture was clear. She could see a pair of hands which she knew to be the hands of Jesus, coming through the net. To her surprise she found she was shrinking away, not wanting to be rescued from the net after all. She was afraid of being cold and naked. Who would have expected that the net was not a trap but a refuge?

She was so reluctant to be lifted out that we stopped to talk. The core question was this: Could she trust the hands of Jesus to be safe? This longtime Christian could not – or would not. I faced her with the truth of God's reliability, and she realised that she had to make a choice. Reluctantly she admitted that God was probably reliable, and she returned to the prayer picture. Immediately she found herself outside the net, being held by strong, cupped hands. She could physically feel herself being warmed all over, and she was almost overwhelmed by the power of the experience.

Normally I end a time like this with ordinary prayer, earthed in the normalities of life. On this occasion I was already late, and I had to leave in a hurry, with Audrey breathing, 'Wow! That was powerful!' When I was next in touch with her I asked how things were. 'Yes, fine.' After I had left she had the wisdom to record the experience fully in her journal, and to pray over it by herself. The extract from her journal is in Appendix III. You can see that the perspectives of the client and the counsellor are not identical but they mesh together.

d) *Ask the client to return to a remembered place from the past* I asked one client to wander through the childhood home. Her mother went out to work and she remembered being a latchkey kid; she could feel the weight of the heavy front-door key on a string round her neck as she played skipping games in the school playground. Later, when she was a young teenager, she had to cook supper for her young brothers when she returned from school.

The memories were sad and resentful; they showed her need to pray forgiveness towards her mother so that she could be free of the hidden resentment she was carrying.

The prayer picture may not bring specific memories to mind, but impressions – an empty room, or father retreating behind a newspaper. But they still unlock thoughts and feelings that guide the direction that prayer needs to go.

e) *The scene may be entirely imaginary* Carol was stuck; the inside of a fortress was a good image for her. She wanted to be freed, but she was not too pleased when it was Jesus, not her heavenly Father, she could see standing in the hole where the walls were partly broken down. She too was faced with a choice. But once she decided to go the way that God was offering her the scene changed; she found herself running over the fields with Jesus. 'It used to be like this a lot, but it hasn't been for a long time,' she admitted. She realised that she had not been keeping in touch with the Lord as well as she thought. Repentance, surrender and a change in her relationships were needed.

Anthea went into an imaginary house. She found herself walking up the stairs into the library, telling a white lie to the old man who was the owner. She had already been talking about her poor relationship with her parents. The picture faced her with an uncomfortable truth; the relationship was marred partly because of the half-truths she was telling them.

Another picture I use is to ask the client to imagine that she is standing by the front door of a house, looking out. 'Look around, to see the view, the weather, what people are there. Then look for Jesus in front of you, beckoning you to go out to Him. Are you free to go where He is asking you, or are you stuck? If you find you are holding on to the doorposts, see if you can discover what they are that you need their support.'

Once I used this picture with the whole congregation after preaching in my home church. After the service Maisie came to talk. She was in her late twenties; since her late teens she had suffered from intermittent depression. She had a surprise in her picture. She could see Jesus asking her to go to join Him, but she was clutching the doorposts. Then she realised that the doorposts 'were' her psychiatric illness, and she knew she had a choice to make. She could either continue to use her illness as a refuge or she could pray for the courage to step out. She prayed firmly that she might stop using her illness to evade responsibility.

Soon I missed her face from the choir, and it was months before I remembered to ask the music director what had happened to her. 'Oh, she left to go back home to Canada.' Nearly two years later I was greeted by a young woman after a day conference near Vancouver. It was Maisie, assuring me that God's picture for her and her response had been a turning point in her attitude to life, although she is still not healed from the illness.

f) *A scene from the Bible can suggest a picture* Wendy had described the situation in her office, where it seemed that everyone was against her. She felt like the woman caught in the act of adultery, standing with Jesus in the centre of a ring of people all wanting to throw stones at her. I suggested she might prayerfully imagine a scene like that – not that I was implying adultery in her life! She could 'see' the threatening circle of bystanders; in the centre of the ring she was sitting on the ground, looking at Jesus, who seemed excessively tall to her. He was standing with outstretched arms, a position in which He is frequently seen.

Me: What does that say to you?

Wendy: He wants me to come to Him.

Me: Can you do that?

Wendy: No . . . Well, I'll try . . . No, I can't.

Then Jesus was typically gracious. He bent down towards her. To her astonishment she found herself turning away from Him. 'Scrabbling in the ground like a cat,' was her expression. It was a shock to the 'good' Christian to recognise that she was not really wanting Him. Her pride took a severe knock. Jesus gently but firmly picked her up, and she found herself in His arms. At first she was resistant, like a squirming child. As she calmed down and nestled into His arms, she could look down at the others in the ring. From the height of His arms they appeared tiny and she felt a new security with Him.

The leader of Wendy's house group was with us, and she read Psalm 131:

> My heart is not proud, O Lord,
>   my eyes are not haughty . . .
>   . . . I have stilled and quietened my soul;
>   like a weaned child with its mother . . .

Wendy found she could now pray in a fresh way, more honest than she had been before. Her own unexpected resistance to her Master's way; His love and persistence; the new perspective on her 'enemies'; all these were the subject of her repentance, her gratitude, her intercession, her request for guidance and for new joy in her work and relationships. She left us strengthened to face the next day in the office, a more humble person than she had been.

g) *A client's dreams* can also be used to initiate a prayer picture. I have only rarely done this. The scene that stands out the most clearly is a dream in which Ruth was lying in bed, her face turned to the wall for fear of an evil presence in the room. We talked about Jesus' promise to be with her *always*; then we prayed, with her picturing the bedroom of her dream. The dark presence was real, but so was Jesus. As we prayed the evil disappeared ('The light shines in the darkness, and the darkness has not overcome it'), and Jesus came and knelt by her bed. He caressed her forehead, just as He did for Fiona. He showed her the reality of His love which drives out fear (1 John 4:18).

Making Use Of The Picture

In Old and New Testaments alike, we find visions being given so that God could bring home a truth. He wanted to reveal something new, or to underline a principle for His people.

The examples I have given show how God uses the image to shine a spotlight on the client, to challenge her, to reveal Himself in a way she has not understood, or to encourage her to persevere. The image is a tool, and we can move in and out of it, weaving together imagery prayer, 'straight' prayer, and talk between ourselves.

One picture started with a sailing boat that needed to be cast off from the shore, with Jesus at the tiller. After Val had landed on the shore she had to walk through a field of cows – and she eventually arrived in a Golden City. There were many sections of that 'movie' that we needed to explore, one piece at a time. The Golden City was the incentive she needed to encourage her, to boost her slim faith that this part of her healing would not be an endless process.

When the picture has been a starting point to open up the counselling process it is often useful to return to it at the end of the session. I met Kathleen at a conference. In a small group where we could share personal needs for prayer she asked us to pray for her in the loss she still felt five years after they had moved from settled parish ministry into an itinerant job. Half an hour later, after the coffee break, she was in the counselling workshop. With that group of fifteen people I led them into an imaginary scene. 'Imagine you are walking down a road. Look around to find out whether you are in the town or the country . . . what time of year it is . . . whether you recognise where you are . . . You will come to a house, and I would like you to go inside . . .'

Notice that I did not fill in any of the details. That is for the Spirit to do. Kathleen wrote, four years later, 'You gave us a bare minimum for our picture, as I remember it. Just "walk down a path; you will come to a house" – not much more. When I found myself on the path behind the vicarage I thought it wouldn't lead to a house (because it doesn't) but sure enough there was the house.'

We waited in silence for each one to pray. Next day I asked who would be willing to be a guinea-pig in sharing the scene.

Kathleen was willing. She told us about the familiar road and the unknown house. The familiar road gave the context of the need God wanted to meet; the unknown house showed that the Spirit was in charge. It was dark inside and she could not see at all plainly. The feelings she had shared in the earlier group gave a clue. God wanted to help her to stop grieving. She remembers, 'Some gathered round and prayed; you read some verses from Isaiah. I cried; it was almost as if something was being uprooted from within me.'

At the end of the corporate counselling-cum-teaching-cum-prayer session I suggested that she might return in prayer to the house. That is often a useful thing to do, as it brings reassurance that God *is* at work. Kathleen felt dismayed for a moment at the suggestion, for fear of the embarrassment if nothing had developed. But she found that it was lighter and she could see the table spread for a meal and a way through beyond the window towards the view. 'It led somewhere after all.' She was encouraged to know that God was changing her outlook, bringing light into the 'new' job which the house represented.

Her final comment is this. 'Strangely, it seems now, I would never have sought help. It did not occur to me that I had a problem/burden that my Father wanted to take from me. It was just, to me, the Way Life WAS! Afterwards I have thought that if help is available for *me* – comparatively undamaged, stable, secure, non-desperate – how many other *normal* folk is He waiting to release from what they are bearing?'

The Surprised Picture-Maker

There are many people who are surprised at the way God works for them once they open themselves up to Him in a new way. Anna described herself like this. 'I'm not a person who has a naturally vivid imagination. I'm much more the rational type who likes to know what is going to come next, and how God is going to do things.' You could call her a thoroughly well-ordered person, who likes to be in control. But God surprised her. She told us about it during a counselling course:

> I was, and still am, trying to work through some of the things from my family background and my upbringing that have affected the way I view God. I realised that I had a problem in grasping that God forgives *me*, not just everyone else. I was told to read Psalm 103, about God's character, but it still seemed to be just head-knowledge. My understanding of His forgiveness did not honestly reach down to the place where I was feeling guilty.
>
> I left one session feeling utterly stuck. I seemed to be unhelpable. I felt that there must be something wrong with me, or that I wasn't performing the right way. Our next session began thinking about false guilt. During the week my friend Sandy had used an image of loads of guilt weighing down on top of me. Rosemary suggested that to find the root of that guilt I could either just pray that God would show me or I could use that image. I chose the image because it was more concrete, but I was afraid that nothing would happen. She assured me that I didn't need to perform, and it would not matter if nothing did happen.
>
> I might have thought I was inventing a picture, if God had not surprised me by doing things I would never have thought of by myself. The picture formed a wooden cart loaded with bundles of false guilt, some labelled, some unlabelled, from different situations in my life. I was trying to pull the cart up a hill that had a Cross at the top, but the cart was too heavy and I couldn't even get it to the Cross. That's where the first surprise came, because Jesus came alongside and helped me pull the cart. I didn't invent that. As it happened I thought, 'Oh, He's not on the Cross; He's beside me, helping to pull it up.' So we pulled it together, and I realised that was important. It meant I didn't have to get it right all by myself. He was there, working with me. Once we were at the top we unloaded bundles of guilt, and piled them

all up next to the Cross. Then I knew that I needed to go away.

Sandy was with me in the session, and we talked for a bit. Then I allowed the picture to form again. It was clearer this time, but it had changed. Instead of the bundles being piled up next to the Cross, they were not there any more. There was no clutter – just a Cross, and Jesus, and me. The disappearance of the bundles is a mystery, but somehow it didn't need an explanation. It was clear and pure; there was something different about it. I talked to Jesus again, and thanked Him that the bundles were gone, and that we could walk away for ever.

As I reflected on that image over the course of the week I thought at times, 'You know; it was kind of a simple picture.' It wasn't in bright colour, or on a big screen. It was just a picture which I took to Him, but even in its simplicity God has spoken to me in a very deep way. It surprised me in the fact that Jesus came alongside, and also when the bundles disappeared. But He surprised me even more by using a method of talking to me that I thought wasn't for me. As I prepared this for tonight I was drawn back to Psalm 103, and I suddenly realised that God had spoken its truth to me through the image. Now I can read it more as my own:

> Praise the Lord, O my soul;
>   all my inmost being, praise his holy name.
> For as high as the heavens are above the earth,
>   so great is his love for those who fear him;
> as far as the east is from the west,
>   so far has he removed our transgressions from us
>   (Ps. 103:1; 11–12).

Conclusion

This is not a tool that is essential to counselling, but do not be afraid to take the risk of trying something new. Anna was surprised; as may you be.

Try It Out

1) Prayerfully imagine yourself going into the house (or one of them) in which you lived as a child. Roam round the house, letting God bring into your mind any memories, good or bad that He wants. Notice what emotions are aroused, and use this to stimulate prayers of thanksgiving, confession or forgiveness towards others.

2) *With a partner* First pray that God will work in your lives. Then let one of you imagine himself standing in front of Jesus, holding some kind of container. Describe the scene to the other; the two people, the container (a box? a suitcase? a plastic bag?), the surroundings. Then offer the container to Jesus – if you want to – and see what He does with it. Talk together about the scene and what it is showing you. Then pray about those things. If nothing is clear, ask the Lord to do something in the next few days that links with your scene.

Reverse the roles, but leave that for a later time if God works strongly for the first person.

17

USING SPIRITUAL GIFTS

Two years ago I met a delightful young minister who told me how his Christian experience was being enlarged. During a communion service one day he was in the pew, waiting to take the bread and the cup. A stranger was sitting next to him in tears. Suddenly he found God saying to him, 'That woman is committing adultery.' John was unused to this sort of experience. Indeed, he did not even know that it happened outside the pages of the Bible. These matters were not part of Christian education in *his* church circles. He wondered what to do, and after a time he moved over, and gently prayed for her, without divulging the unexpected revelation.

The next day she came to see him in his office. This seemed to be the time to ask her whether there was sin in her life. She denied it. Only after a third meeting was she willing to confess it to him, and he was then able to help her. We met him soon after this, and were able to assure him that his experience was not unique.

John's experiences continued. Here is an extract from a letter he wrote only a few weeks later:

My walk with the Lord continues to be exciting, and I have had other occasions of receiving a word from Him. On one occasion I had a woman come into my office from off the street. She *had* to speak to one of the ministers. When she walked into the room I had the immediate sensation that I must be very cautious – for my very life. She talked a mile a minute and when I interrupted her to ask a question of clarification she became instantly angry. She told me never to interrupt her again. I laughed, and told her it was my job to interrupt her. She didn't think this was funny, and stood up glaring into my eyes. I asked her what her name was, to which she replied with a name. Then the Lord said softly to me, 'That's not her name.' I said to her, 'That's not your name. Tell me your real name.' She looked absolutely stunned, stood back, and sheepishly gave me a completely different name. Once more the Lord said, 'That's not her name.' I again told her that this was not her name, and I demanded that she tell me the truth. She had now risen and was about to flee from my office when she gave me yet another name. I thanked her, and told her that I would be happy to help her if she would covenant with me to be truthful. She fled.

In recounting the incident with a police officer later, I found that the last name she gave me was correct, and that she had eleven aliases with which she operated. She came back again, and I referred to her by her real name, and let her know that Jesus wants to help her with her life. We have had ongoing contact since, and I believe that for the first time in her life she actually believes that there is a possibility of her receiving help with the mess of her life.

These are two occasions when God gave John a surprising bit of knowledge. This was not to make him feel clever, so that he might be 'one up' on the ladies. It was the Holy Spirit at work, making those two women feel uncomfortable in order that they might be open to recognising where they could find power to help.

God Imparts A Variety Of Gifts

Before we go on to consider how the 'supernatural' gifts are used in counselling it is worth thinking about the variety of gifts that God gives. We must be careful not to categorise gifts as first and second class. All gifts come from God, so all come with a First Class label on them. All are given for communal use, not for the private enjoyment or pride of an individual. There are various places in the New Testament where assorted gifts are named, and I have the feeling that on each occasion Paul or Peter haphazardly picks a few, without considering which are of prime importance. One gift that Paul rates high is the gift of prophecy. 'Follow the way of love and eagerly desire spiritual gifts, especially the gift of prophecy' (1 Cor. 14:1). But the biggest gift of all is love. That is the one thing that shouts aloud. Every list of gifts is found in the context of love. Paul is emphatic, though at the beginning of 1 Corinthians chapter 13 I wonder if he has also slightly got his tongue in his cheek! Even if the tongues were the languages of angels as well as all the languages of the world; even if gifts of prophecy and knowledge were given that would enable a person to fathom *all* God's mysteries; and even if there was faith to demolish Mount Everest, then none of these impossible standards for those gifts would be of any use unless they were encased in love. About that Paul is certainly not joking. He is absolutely sure. It is love that binds the body of believers together, and frees us up to serve one another in humility. Love 'does not boast, it is not proud . . . it is not self-seeking' (1 Cor. 13:4–5). Pride causes us to say 'my gift' and brings competition and division.

Look at some of the gifts that we find mixed up in the assorted lists. We find them jostling side by side: prophecy, serving, generosity, wisdom, encouraging, teaching, administration, leadership, showing mercy, knowledge, tongues, interpretation of tongues, faith, healing, helping, discernment of spirits, miraculous powers, evangelism, pastoring, hospitality. All are given by God for the common good. All will be used at some time in a counselling ministry.

It is not that all the gifts are used all the time. In fact, we should never say that we *have* any gift, even though we find that there are some which we are using regularly. If we claim that we 'have' a gift we will be in danger of coming to think that we own it, that we have a right to it; even that we start to think we can do it by ourselves. It is better to imagine coming to Him with empty, open hands, to be given a fresh gift for each occasion.

I frequently use tongues when I am counselling, and I must admit that I normally say that I have that gift. But whenever I move from praying in tongues under my breath to praying aloud, I stop for a moment, and ask God to use them however He wants to, just for this one time. That keeps them fresh, submitted to Him each time. When Michael was first ordained he worked under a clergyman who reckoned that once only in his life had he been given a gift of healing, to pray for his own seriously ill son – long before the current wave of charismatic renewal and interest in supernatural gifts. There are some people who are so hospitable that we are likely to say that they *have* a gift of hospitality. How easy it becomes for others to assume that the home will always be open, and how hard it then is for the home owners to say no! Tiredness and staleness set in, because they have presumed on a gift, and have stopped consulting the Lord.

Spiritual Or Supernatural?

At the same time as recognising that God is the giver of all good gifts, we also see that there are some very distinctive ways in which He communicates with us, and equips us. 'To one there is given through the Spirit the message of wisdom, to another the message of knowledge by means of the same Spirit, to another faith by the same Spirit, to another gifts of healing by that one Spirit, to another miraculous powers, to another prophecy, to another distinguishing between spirits, to another speaking in different kinds of tongues, and to still another the interpretation of tongues. All these are the work of one and the same Spirit' (1 Cor. 12:8–11).

We must be watchful, for all these gifts can be aped by the unholy spirit. Think, for instance, of the slave girl at Philippi, 'who had a spirit by which she predicted the future' (Acts 16:16). Her 'prophetic gift' enabled her to shout constantly, 'These men are servants of the Most High God, who are telling you the way to be saved' (Acts 16:17). That was indeed true, but she was a menace to Paul and Silas until Paul used the gifts of 'distinguishing between spirits' and of 'miraculous power' to command the spirit to leave (v.18).

Demonic tongues have an exceedingly ugly sound. I have only once had a conversation, in tongues, with a woman who was speaking in tongues inspired by Satan. It was an utterly unfruitful battle. On another occasion a teenage girl started to shake violently during a meeting for praise and prayer. She had recently been for treatment by a Hindu osteopath, and in the course of our ministry to her she was contorting herself in the weird shape of a Hindu god. Faith healers may be used to bring physical healing at the cost of bondage to an unknown spiritual force.

I do not want to major on this unholy topic, but we need to be aware that the supernatural gifts all have their demonic counterpart. Moses discovered that. Moses and Aaron turned their staffs into snakes by the Lord's power. The Egyptian magicians did the same by their secret arts. The difference was that God's power was stronger. 'Aaron's staff swallowed up their staffs' (Exodus 7:11–12). The same is true today. Jesus is the victor, but that does not mean that we should deliberately make ourselves vulnerable to Satan's clutches.

Are The Supernatural Gifts Essential?

I like to use the phrase 'hot-line' when thinking about the renowned spiritual gifts. Insight or power are given in a way that could only come direct from the Lord. Think of the illumination that John (about whom I wrote at the start of this chapter) was given, totally unexpectedly. God communicated with him, and he was able to reach past the defences of both those women. But the way that John heard from God is unlikely to be identical with the way that another person hears, and we cannot be entirely specific about how each of the gifts is recognised or used. God sees us as individuals, and there is individuality in the ways we receive and use supernatural gifts. For example, one friend of mine is sure when God is giving her a picture because she sees it framed inside a Gothic arch! Another can distinguish easily between a God-inspired picture and one that the devil has slipped in because the first is sharp and the second is fuzzy.

There are various ways in which these gifts have been brought into disrepute. Rigidity in describing them is one. They are outside the normal scope of life, so they are hard to define; but we want to understand them so we try to confine them in a formula. However, we cannot box God in a formula, nor His gifts. We might even say that they come individually giftwrapped – and in uneven shaped packages, at that! When I am counselling I often have a 'hunch'. Is the source of that hunch my experience? Is it my natural sensitivity in listening and observing the client? Has it come direct from God? Or is it a combination of all of those things! It is hard to be sure, even when the hunch is proved to be right.

The reputation of spiritual gifts has been tarnished, too, by the way that they have been used to distinguish between first and second class citizens in God's kingdom. Tongues is a particular culprit here, the gift that has often been looked on as the badge of membership of the Spiritual Club. At the end of 1 Corinthians chapter 12, Paul asks a number of rhetorical questions: 'Are all apostles? Are all prophets? Are all teachers? Do all work miracles? Do all have gifts of healing? Do all speak in tongues?' (1 Cor. 12:29–30). The Greek is even more clear than the English that the answer is definitely NO. Many Christians are struggling because they have been made to feel that they are useless, or that God has let them down, when their repeated prayer for this gift has not yet been answered.

And Paul moves from there to the 'most excellent way' of love. Christ-likeness of character and awareness of God are the marks of spirituality. We can be wholly open to the Spirit of God without having any of the hot-line gifts. One sentence stands out to me from a sermon given at a confirmation service by a bishop who would certainly be described as a card-carrying charismatic. 'Charismatic renewal is compulsory for all Christians, but the charismatic movement is not.' He was talking about the essential quality of spiritual life and the spectacular trappings. We can eat bread without jam!

Misunderstandings about God's gifts have frequently caused pride on the one hand and disappointment on the other. Some Christians go overboard on spiritual gifts, and others deny them altogether. Both attitudes are sadly wrong. These gifts are not essential to spiritual life, but they are given by God to enhance it, and they can be a big asset to our counselling ministry.

How Are The Hot-line Gifts Used In Counselling?

It is helpful to think of the gifts under the three headings of gifts of knowing (wisdom, knowledge, discernment and faith); gifts of speaking (tongues, interpretation and prophecy); gifts of doing (healing and miraculous powers). We can see Jesus using many of these in His ministry; not surprising, when we remember that the Holy Spirit is the Spirit of Christ.

Gifts of knowing

Wisdom is often a combination of maturity, experience and sensitivity to God. It is one of the easiest gifts to define, for we all know what we mean by 'a wise person'. Yet there are times when we suddenly find a person, even a young person, making a comment that is far beyond his normal understanding. We react with 'That's it!' because we recognise a solution to a problem has been given by God. At the start of Jesus' ministry we find that, 'the people were amazed at his teaching, because he taught them as one who had authority, not as the teachers of the law' (Mark 1:22). We remember Him, too, countering the

Pharisees with their questions designed to trap Him. When they queried His authority He silenced them by asking them a question in return. Their lame reply was 'We don't know' (Matt. 21:27).

A friend talked about the wisdom she saw one day in her young adult son:

> It was only a few weeks till my youngest son, Peter, was to take his final exams, and as a former school-teacher I was aware of the amount of effort needed after a rather 'laid-back' academic year. Yet as a mother I have tried to rear my children without nagging, and whenever I raised the issue of work it was interpreted as pressurising him, with the negative response that brings.
>
> It had become a very sensitive area for me as well as for Peter, when his brother James, two years older, came home from university for a weekend. It didn't take James long to recognise the difficulty I was having in trying to encourage Peter and to offer such academic assistance as I could without pressurising him. James came to me, took me by the hand and said, 'Would you like to sit down and we can talk about it?'
>
> Then he led me into a time of sharing and unburdening; he let me get rid of some pent-up emotions and tears and I left feeling really 'heard'; then he prayed with me, bringing real peace and a feeling of acceptance. All this was done with maturity far beyond his years. To me that was a real gift of wisdom.

Knowledge is usually interpreted as knowing something, often about another person, that we could not know by any normal means. We find Nathanael's surprise when Jesus knew him (John 1:47), and we see Peter confronting Ananias and Sapphira over their lies (Acts 5:3) or Simon over his bitterness (Acts 8:23). John, mentioned earlier in the chapter, was given clear knowledge by God; one woman was hiding her adultery, and the other was lying over her name.

I once asked a friend to pray with me about a strange

picture I had about myself, a picture of a huge black parsnip with a curly tail. I wanted that whole root to be pulled out; I assumed from that tail that it referred to something very early in my life. As we prayed, she said confidently, 'It is to do with when you were two.' I did not believe her; that did not seem early enough in my life. She held firm. 'It is to do with when you were two.' I stopped arguing, and immediately God reminded me that I had been told that at that age I had fallen into a goldfish pond in the garden. I prayed round that incident as well as I could – asking forgiveness for a wilful child, and forgiveness towards a careless adult. 'Inspired guesswork' is the phrase for such a situation. That led us to a whole theme about drowning which led us right back to an incident in 1916. I do not need to go into all the strange details, but her 'knowledge' for the two year old did indeed lead us back to the curly tail of the parsnip.

Knowledge may be given in pictures. One counsellor had a picture of a thorn bush as he prayed. 'Does this mean anything to you?' he asked the client. That question evoked a memory that was pertinent to her immediate need. The same counsellor would sometimes be given a biblical reference, perhaps to an obscure part of the Old Testament of which he was ignorant; that verse often proved a key to the situation.

These examples show that the 'knowledge' given does not have to be complete; it may be partial, but enough to lead the counselling process forward. Marlene did not tell me about her twin being miscarried until I observed her curling up with a cushion, 'sensed' it as a foetal position, and prayed gently for any fear she might have had in the womb (p.108).

Distinguishing between spirits   Does Sally have a psychic gift from the Enemy, or a gift of knowledge from God? Is the anger that Robert habitually displays merely his longterm reaction to deep pain, or is it infected by a spirit from his family background? The answer to such questions is often

not immediately clear, but failure to get the answer right
can cause much damage in ministry. Recognition of satanic
forces comes in a variety of ways, sometimes with absolute
clarity, sometimes merely as a possibility. Jesus frequently
exercised this gift. With the Gadarene demoniac it was
not hard for Him to understand the signs that the man
was heavily influenced by demons – although nowadays
he would probably be diagnosed as having schizophrenia
(Mark 5:1–8). But Jesus certainly knew when a man needed
only to be physically healed, or whether there was a spirit
in the illness. Sometimes He commanded healing, and at
other times He rebuked a spirit. (See the two incidents in
Matt. 9:27–33.)

As with the gift of knowledge, there is a wide range
in recognising the presence of evil; the recognition comes
in different ways and with different levels of clarity. If
there is *active* evil around Michael he knows it clearly
and uncomfortably. His gift of discernment comes as an
unpleasant tingling, in his hands, at the back of his neck,
or even all over his body. That is usually aroused only when
he has challenged the spirits. Often he makes that challenge
after I have sensed, in the steady course of counselling, that
some weakness in a person's life has a stronger grip than
even the background circumstances can explain. A 'hunch'
is born out of a mixture of clues that have alerted me to the
possibility of the presence of dark forces.

One of the most bizarre experiences we have had occurred
when we were with a married couple, Mark and Gillian.
During that meeting we saw different clues being fitted
together, clues that we had already been given about Gillian.
One discerning person had 'seen a spirit of witchcraft on her
head', to use the phrase that was reported to us. Another
person's tongues had been used to indicate that her deceased
mother, who in her life had been strongly dominant over her
daughter, had some significance in the present situation.
A few months before this meeting she had suffered an
unexpected stroke, when she was only thirty-five. She had
recovered from this, but they knew that it had left her

different in some way. When the four of us were praying together a thought came to me, a thought that seemed so crazy that I hardly dared to say anything.

I took the risk. 'This seems absolutely mad. I am wondering whether a spirit that affected Gillian's mother somehow got hold of her, in those three days after the stroke when she was so vulnerable.' Even now, I am not sure about the theology of that remark. But I am sure about the sequel. I glanced up from praying. There was Gillian sitting bolt upright on the edge of her easy chair; her eyes were bulging as she glared at Michael. It seemed that my crazy idea was not so crazy after all. I tapped him on the knees to attract his attention, and motioned that it was time for him to take charge; he could follow my gift of discernment by using his gift of miraculous power!

What do we learn from that astonishing story? The biggest lesson is our need to be continually open to the Lord and to His surprises. Our tidy formulae will never be complete. There is no end to the surprises. We live in a mighty ocean of spirituality, in which we are merely paddling most of the time. Every Christian is in the water, but it seems safer to keep our feet on the bottom than to move out into the deep water. God is always calling us to swim in deeper water, and we must not be too astonished when we hit submerged rocks or an evil undercurrent as we explore the ocean.

Faith must be present in some measure in every meeting between Christians, even if the faith is only as big as a mustard seed. It is likely that my trust, with forty years of Christian experience, is likely to seem stronger than the client's faith. After all, mine is not being tested by the circumstances that are bringing the client for counselling, and it is always easier to have faith for another's problems than for our own. But faith as a gift seems to have an extra dimension, like the centurion whose servant was healed at a distance. 'I tell you the truth,' said Jesus. 'I have not found anyone in Israel with such great faith' (Matt. 8:10).

There is a quality of faith which grows over the years from the study of Scripture and from experience. There is another dimension of faith that comes as a gift from God. We saw that very clearly some years ago. Doreen was a musical girl whose mind was not always on the immediate facts of life. She emerged from a side turning, and cycled straight into the path of a double-decker bus. Her head injuries were such that she was expected to die, or at best to survive as a mental cabbage. Late one afternoon Michael went, with one of his colleagues (who was an enthusiast about healing), to pray for her. She was in a restless coma. Michael suddenly stopped praying, and said confidently to John, 'She's going to be all right.' God had just given him a gift of faith that went against the evidence and the medical prognosis. As they left the ward he faced her non-Christian parents, who were waiting in the ante-room, and said, 'She's going to be all right.' John had been surprised, but they just smiled at Michael with unbelieving smiles.

By next morning Doreen was sitting up to eat breakfast. At lunchtime she was out of bed on a chair. Within two weeks she was out of hospital. She had some temporary and mild epilepsy, but no permanent after-effects. The last I heard of her she was working overseas with a missionary society, but her parents had still not turned to Christ. It is sad that the faith given to Michael for her recovery was not matched by their making a conscious choice to trust God.

Gifts of speaking

Let us start with some definitions. *Tongues* – a language given by God, which we first see clearly on the Day of Pentecost in Acts chapter 2. *Interpretation* – the words given by God to enable the tongues to be comprehensible. *Prophecy* – the direct message given by God: 'Thus says the Lord.' Allowing for the fact that these things take us out of the normal realms of life they sound reasonably simple. Unfortunately it is not all quite so straightforward as those first few sentences make out. Those basic definitions are not wrong, but they are too neat and organised. We need to examine these gifts further to see how they interlock and to have a glimpse of the variety of ways in which they can be expressed.

Tongues are indeed a language given by God, and I find them an invaluable tool in counselling. They have two main directions. Sometimes they are messages from God; at other times they express the heart of an individual. On the Day of Pentecost they were both, simultaneously. The Christians, newly flooded by the Spirit of God, were overflowing with praise. The visitors to Jerusalem heard them, 'declaring the wonders of God', and were amazed and perplexed at the events.

I find both these directions of tongues being used in my counselling. First of all, I pray in tongues quietly when the client is talking, tongues that are seeking the Lord's guidance for the session. Then, when he is praying aloud, those quiet tongues continue, while my mind endorses his prayer. I see his words, with which my mind agrees, like the bricks in a wall; the tongues are like the mortar, filling in the cracks.

Then comes a moment when my tongues can no longer keep quiet. The Lord seems to push them out loud. At that point I consciously (often aloud) ask Him to use them in whatever way He wants. Then I let the words flow freely; they emerge with astonishing variety in their tone. I do not understand what I am saying, but the tone of voice often gives a clue. Some of the tongues reflect the heart of the client. They are like God's penetrating laser beam; they reach into the inner place that God alone understands. Then the voice changes completely, and I sense that God is speaking to the client. Again I know only the general import of the message, from a voice that is loving or stern, encouraging or angry. When there is anger, it is not usually directed at the person, but at the devil's infiltration into his life. How do I know that? As I submit my mind to Christ I trust that my 'hunch' is a gift of knowledge.

All this can easily be subjective. It can also come from a heart that is striving more for personal success than for God's way with the client. That is when my 'flesh', my 'self', is in charge, not the Spirit at all. Much damage can be done to a person when we 'misuse the name of the Lord our God' and break the third of the Ten Commandments by claiming spiritual knowledge for human desire.

Here are two examples of tongues used in counselling. The first time I ever ventured to use tongues aloud I was with Joanna, a chronically depressed young woman. I asked her if she would mind my praying for her in tongues. 'All right. I don't mind if you do. I don't suppose it will do much good' was her resigned reply. After we had prayed she said, 'That was marvellous. I felt as if God Himself was praying for me. I have never before really believed that He bothered about me.' In her diary that evening she wrote, 'The strange language I heard Rosemary speak is so tangible, solid, now I know that God is on my side.' That was what she needed.

I have already written in this chapter about Gillian, and the strange time when a demonic spirit connected with her mother was affecting her. One of the clues had come when I was with her alone. As I prayed for her, in tongues out loud, my voice sounded like that of some other woman. I stopped to ask her if she recognised the voice. 'It is either me or my mother,' she told me. That afternoon her husband came to my house straight from work; the identical voice came in my tongues. I asked him the same question. 'Do you know that voice?' Without hesitation he replied, 'That is Gillian's mother.' Although we had not yet put all the clues together, here were my tongues being used to identify one of the hidden aspects of Gillian's problem.

Interpretation is God's gift to clarify the mysterious tongues. On the Day of Pentecost 'each one heard them speaking in his own language' (Acts 2:6). Does this mean that the disciples were speaking in the languages of the visitors who came from many places? Or does it mean that each of the hearers was given a gift of interpretation, in order to be able to understand? We cannot be sure. What we do know is that they were able to understand in their own languages the Christians 'declaring the wonders of God' (v.11). Even then they did not understand what it all meant. They needed Peter's evangelistic gift in his sermon and the work of the Holy Spirit to convict them of sin (v.37) to make any sense of the strange speech.

There is huge variety in the ways in which the Spirit interprets the tongues. Interpretation is rarely a direct translation. It can come through words, through pictures, or through an undefined 'sense'. I usually find that it is the client who interprets the tongues, although that interpretation may be just one step forward, not complete understanding. When I used tongues with Joanna she became aware in a real way of God's personal care for her. Mark and Gillian did not understand the words, but they recognised the voice of Gillian's mother. Patricia (in chapter 7) was given three successive pictures, each one after prayer in tongues. When I was exploring my picture of a black parsnip my friend's 'knowledge' came at a point when my tongues had whimpered like a baby and then faded away. Different kinds of tongues are partnered by different interpretations to help many different people.

Prophecy   is God's direct message, given to an individual to pass on to others. In the Old Testament prophecy came by speech and by vision; it came directly as 'the word of the Lord came to me' and it came as a story. Jeremiah visited the potter's house, and the Lord gave him a message for the Jews. God sent Nathan with a story to rebuke David for his adultery with Bathsheba and his disguised murder of Uriah. Jacob spoke prophetically when he blessed Joseph's sons, the younger one first. Ezekiel was given a vision of a valley full of dry bones being brought to life. God spoke messages of encouragement and of warning, to individuals and to a nation, through Joseph's dreams.

God is active through those same streams of prophecy nowadays. He speaks a direct message into a situation. It is not a *new* message; it does not add to Scripture truth. It is a *now* message, highlighting God's truth for the immediate situation. As with other gifts, it often does not stand alone. We could sometimes write an equation like this:

$$\text{Tongues} + \text{Interpretation} = \text{Prophecy}$$

and we do not need to waste energy by asking, 'Do I label this insight as prophecy or as knowledge?' We do better to ask for a gift of wisdom, to know how to use the insight we have been given. Right knowledge, prophecy or discernment is easily spoilt by misuse, in the way or the time in which it is passed on. These gifts from God are powerful tools; they need to be handled with dexterity, with love and gentleness if they are to be used for God's good purposes.

Jeremiah has a strong warning from the Lord against false prophets. 'They say, "I had a dream! I had a dream!" How long will this continue in the hearts of these lying prophets, who prophesy the delusions of their own minds? . . . Let the prophet who has a dream tell his dream, but let the one who has my word speak it faithfully' (Jer. 23:25–28).

Such prophets are still active today. I was once given about forty typed pages of words and dreams, from one woman with a prophetic gift. I am sure that there were many occasions when God did indeed speak through her, in words and dreams. Did it go awry when she assumed that she *had* this gift, infallibly? When she assumed that *every* dream was a message from God about another person, and never from the stirrings in her own mind and emotions? It is ironic that she was the person who drew my attention to those words of Jeremiah's, when I believe that she should have taken them for herself! She was politely angry with my refusal to accept her ministry, when I had honestly tried to ask God which of her many 'words' and dreams were truly ones to which I had to pay attention. I do not know how she looks back on that time. I am glad to have had such a clear warning about the misuse of prophecy in heavy-handed counselling.

What about the right use of this gift? I will tell you one story. I wrote in chapter 14 about Lucy, who originally came to see me because of her distress and her anger over her infertility. During the counselling some basic attitudes in her relationship with God changed. Soon after that a married couple, Eric and Nicola, told me that God had given them a message for Lucy, that she would conceive. They hardly knew her; they did not know about her struggle; they had no idea that I had been counselling her. They prayed, and they asked me to help them know how they should use this 'information' that God had unexpectedly given them.

There are good lessons here. When we are given insight about another person we should first of all use it to pray for that other one with greater understanding. We pray as well for the wisdom to know whether, how and when we are to pass it on. Eric and Nicola waited. They communicated with Lucy just after she and her husband had helped to lead a weekend for childless couples, during which a prophetic prayer assured them that they would have a child. Eric and Nicola knew nothing of this, but when they met with Lucy and Ned and prayed with them they received another word of reassurance about a child – not knowing that Lucy was already pregnant! Here is an example of a genuine word from God, humbly submitted to Him for its right use.

Gifts of doing

There are two gifts in Paul's list in verses 8 to 10 of 1 Corinthians chapter 12 that we have not yet considered.

Healing   is the most ecclesiastically respectable of the spiritual gifts. Clergymen with little interest in charismatic gifts hold healing services and pray for those who are ill. I do not know whether miracles are expected in many of these services; if miraculous healing happens does it take the leader or the patient by surprise?

All can pray for the sick, and the more we see God active

in healing, the more our faith is nourished to expect God to do big things. But we can never demand that He does what we think He should. Expectancy in His power to heal needs to be partnered by trust in His unerring wisdom.

Sickness of body, mind and emotion are frequently inter-twined. If one aspect of our lives is using an undue amount of energy there is less energy left to fight assaults from other directions. And Satan may have caused illness or depression, or he may have invaded any cracks in the immune system of the whole person. 'Holistic medicine' has become fashion-able; unfortunately those who practise it are often drawing on power from spirits that are not the Holy Spirit.

Miraculous powers   have already been mentioned. Every Christian is told to resist the devil, and God gives us authority over him, as Jesus did for His disciples when He sent them out on mission (Matt. 10:1). But when we encounter active evil we know that we are indeed up against Enemy strongholds, and God gives this gift to some to banish evil spirits in Jesus' name.

The first time we encountered a woman who was deep into witchcraft I was scared to meet such evil power. Michael clearly knew how to counter her – or rather, how to counter the demons – although he too was a novice in this sort of ministry. He was given a gift of 'miraculous power'. He rather wishes that God would pass him over with this particular gift, but he cannot argue! Over the years since then his skill and his experience have grown, but the power needs to be given fresh for every encounter. There will be more about this aspect of counselling in the next chapter.

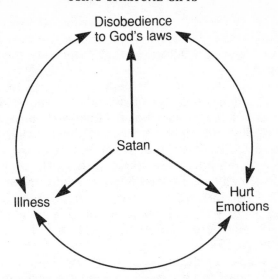

That diagram tries to express how each aspect of 'sickness' leads to another, and how Satan can invade each area. So we are reminded that if we are going to pray for healing we need to ask as well for gifts of faith, discernment, or miraculous powers. In fact, we need to be open to whatever *God* knows we need in the circumstances.

Jesus was not locked into any one method of healing. Careful reading of the gospels shows Him healing young and old; men, women and children; healing the sick of all kinds of illness and deformity. Usually He healed those who were present; sometimes they were far away. He used touch, He used words, He used mud and spittle. Usually His healing was immediate; on at least one occasion it was gradual. He rebuked a demon if He knew that a demon was the real problem. He assured the paralysed man that he was forgiven before He gave vigour to limbs.

Jesus had a gift to heal, a gift that was used in many ways. He was a channel of His Father's power to bring healing in a variety of ways. That same gift is given today to Christians who find that through them God's power is released to heal in ways that are beyond normal medical channels. Often a

person recognises his gift because of the sensation of heat
he experiences in his hands when he prays, but we must not
think that God is confined to that particular manifestation
of the gift.

There are sometimes clear parallels between the healings
of Jesus and the healings of nowadays. One sabbath day
Jesus met in the synagogue in Israel a woman who had
been crippled for eighteen years. Others saw her just as
deformed. Jesus knew that she was bound by a demon,
a 'spirit of infirmity'. He spoke to her, He touched her,
and He silently confronted Satan. 'When Jesus saw her,
he called her forward and said to her, "Woman, you are
set free from your infirmity." Then he put his hands on
her, and immediately she straightened up and praised God'
(Luke 13:10–13).

One Sunday I met, in a church in New Zealand, a woman
who was reacting to her medication after recent surgery. We
saw a lady in her seventies, radiant with her Christian faith.
Doug, the clergyman with me, was given discernment by the
Spirit that she was similarly infected by a demon, a 'spirit
of infirmity'. We touched her and prayed for her, and in
the name of Jesus he confronted Satan, aloud. We saw the
spirit show itself in her shaking, and she was set free, and
praised God.

God is never tired of giving us surprises. The clergyman
commented afterwards that he had never before met a spirit
of infirmity in a person of that age, and he was amazed.
The sequel came a few weeks later. His own mother, in her
eighties, had been deteriorating for years with Parkinson's
disease. He confronted a spirit in her, and she was immediately more lucid than she had been for years, despite her
husband's death.

Here is the last surprise about God at work through
spiritual gifts. Mrs King was a crusty old lady in our congregation, always complaining, never happy. I occasionally
visited her at home; there were many grumbles and no joy.
One day her husband phoned to say that she was in hospital
with severe bronchitis, and next day Michael went to visit

her. She was in a coma. He prayed over her in tongues and left, expecting her to die. Not a bit of it! Not only did she recover; she was a transformed character. Her crustiness disappeared and visits to her became a delight instead of a drudge.

Homework

Examine each of the supernatural gifts in turn (p.225ff). Consider three questions about each one: a) Can I see an example of it in the book of Acts? b) Have I seen an example of it in use, in my own ministry or that of another? c) Am I willing to be given that gift or to work without it, according to the Lord's choice?

18

MINISTERING TO THE DEMONISED

Several times in this book I have referred to the presence of evil forces in a client's life. Our counselling will be weak if we ignore the reality of demons, but it will also be unbalanced if we search for them in every corner of every client's life. 'All the world's mad save thee and me, and even thee's a bit mad' is a saying that is more true of this aspect of our faith than any other!

The Reality Of Demons

Renewed awareness of Holy Spirit power has brought a new recognition of the reality of the unholy spirit. Jesus knew it. He encountered Satan face to face in the wilderness, and He and His disciples challenged many demons. Often it was the demons themselves who recognised who Jesus was, while the humans did not (Mark 1:23–24). Modern thought has tended to dismiss these incidents as 'primitive ignorance', but demons are as real in twentieth-century western life as in places where paganism, polytheism and animism are rife.

For years I dismissed evil spirits altogether. Then my outlook changed, one step at a time. First I thought it might be possible for people to be possessed by evil spirits in countries in the Orient where they were actively worshipped. That would be safely the other side of the world. But not in civilised Britain. Then I read a book, the biography of an English woman who had been a witch, who was freed from the evil spirits that had taken over in her life. I had to admit that they could be active even in my own country.

Then the surprise came. We had an urgent request one
evening to go to the home of our assistant minister. He
met us on the doorstep saying a woman who might be
possessed was in his house. We saw her shrink back as
we entered the room, and we had no doubt that John was
right. I was frightened as I looked at those dark eyes. She
seemed to be Evil personified. I had never seen how strong
was the power of evil. With shaking knees I said to myself,
'I s-s-suppose that Jesus is stronger.' I was far from certain.
Three hours later we left that home, having just begun to
see the power of Christ triumph over the power of evil in
that woman's life. Then I was SURE. Jesus is indeed the
victor.

Since then we have been in some pretty dramatic situations,
but there has only been one occasion, in a nasty moment at
2.00 a.m., when I have again been frightened. I learnt more
about the power of Christ through our encounters with
that woman than I have through any other experience.
I learnt too of the power of God's love to overcome
evil.

Can A Christian Be Possessed?

This question is often asked. This is partly a matter of
language. If by 'possession' you mean the rare state when a
person's life is wholly invaded by evil, then the answer must
be NO. The Spirit of Christ is resident in the life of a real
believer, so he cannot be wholly overtaken by evil forces; a
Christian cannot be *possessed*. But if you are asking whether
it is possible for a Christian to be *affected* by evil spirits, to
be demonised (the literal word from the New Testament) or
oppressed, then the answer is YES. No Christian is totally
free from sin and its effect. So one in whom the Holy Spirit
lives can be vulnerable to the influence of satanic forces. Any
areas of our lives which are not taken over by the Holy Spirit
may be invaded by dark forces. I am not saying that they
necessarily are.

We can think of it like this. If a person who has not had

measles is in contact with the disease he is likely to catch it, but infection is not inevitable. The greater his exposure to the germs, the greater the chance of his contracting measles. Some cases of measles are worse than others – and so are some cases of demonisation. There are plenty of parallels. But there is one big weakness in this illustration. Most measles patients would recover even without any medical care. However sufferers from evil spirits rarely get free without some measure of ministry from another Christian although it is God's power, and His alone, that brings release.

We can look at it another way. Our lives are like houses. Jesus knocks at the front door, and waits for an invitation to step inside. He then asks us to hand over the keys to every door and cupboard in the house so that He can take full control. But sometimes there are already squatters in the house, and when the rightful owner of the house comes a fuss starts. Until then they had been living there reasonably peacefully. Even if no intruders were there already a thief can sneak in when we leave the back door or a window open and unguarded.

Does Any Occult Involvement Matter?

The answer is unquestionably YES. The Old Testament is very clear on this. 'When you enter the land the Lord your God is giving you, do not learn to imitate the detestable ways of the nations there. Let no-one be found among you who sacrifices his son or daughter in the fire, who practises divination or sorcery, interprets omens, engages in witchcraft, or casts spells, or who is a medium or spiritist or who consults the dead. Anyone who does these things is detestable to the Lord . . . You must be blameless before the Lord your God' (Deut. 18:9–13). Have you ever noticed in the Ten Commandments that it is the commandment that tells us not to worship idols that warns us that future generations may be affected by this wrong worship? (Deut. 5:8–10). Jesus calls us to love God with our whole being, and we should not deliberately expose ourselves to Satan and his forces.

What Are The Possible Points Of Entry Of Evil Forces?

There are four main ways. God brought us into this ministry right at the deep end, with the woman of whom I have written. As our experience grew, so did our sensitivity to the subtlety of Satan's infiltration. The times when my cracks of resentment were invaded by 'Nasties' (as the spirits became known in our family) were a small part of our education; so was the spirit of infirmity in a saintly Christian lady. The main gates of entry of evil forces are personal involvement with the occult; personal sin; any sort of sickness – physical or emotional; inheritance from past generations.

1) Personal involvement with the occult

Here is a warning; it is inclusive.

WE ARE EXPOSED TO ENEMY FORCES WHEN
WE TAKE PART IN or SUBMIT TO or TAKE AN UNDUE INTEREST IN
ANYTHING THAT INVOLVES SPIRITUAL POWERS
THAT ARE NOT SUBJECT TO THE TRINITARIAN GOD

You may complain, 'Is Rosemary not being unduly fussy?' This has come out of fifteen years of counselling when I have grown more and more aware of how pervasive Satan is. If there has been such participation (however slight; voluntary or involuntary; recent or in the past; with knowledge or in ignorance) the person needs to repent and to renounce the involvement. To use the measles illustration: he might pray, 'I'm sorry I went into the room where the germs were, even though I didn't know that anyone had measles, and I have not actually come out in spots.'

Here are some of the things to be avoided:

Occult   Fortune telling; horoscopes; automatic writing; spirititualism; faith-healing; astrology; astral projection;

hypnotism; tarot; ouija; black or white magic; I Ching; therapeutic touch; Satan worship; clairvoyance; yoga; levitation; ESP; teacup reading; palmistry.

Cults and false religions   Transcendental meditation; Buddhism; Hare Krishna; Jehovah's Witnesses; Christian Science; Mormons; Children of God; Bahai; Scientology; Moonies; Freemasonry; Eastern Star; Daughters of Job; theosophy; New Age Movement . . . and many others.

Films, books and games   Films like *The Exorcist*; books such as by Denis Wheatley; games such as Dungeons and Dragons.

They come into three categories: gaining power, gaining knowledge, and communication with the spirit world.

Even committed Christians sometimes argue with the list. One afternoon during a counselling course there were forty people in a large circle. I had just handed out the summary of my lecture, and one gentleman, who was in training for the ministry, confronted me from the other end of the room. 'Rosemary, there is one thing you have down on this list that ought not to be there. It is Freemasonry. I am a mason, and so are eight others in my church. You are wrong.'

There was an electric atmosphere in the room. I do not pretend to know all the ins and outs of Freemasonry – after all, it is a secret society, which is one of the charges we lay against it. But I was sure enough to be able to say quietly but firmly to him, 'Bob, I'm sorry, but you're wrong.' It was not the time to argue further and we continued with the class.

We do not need or want to know the details of every aberration. There are two comprehensive tests to use of any expression of faith. Here is the first:

IF ANY HUMAN LEADER IS AS IMPORTANT AS JESUS	THE FAITH IS NOT CHRISTIAN
IF ANY SACRED BOOK IS RECKONED AS IMPORTANT AS THE BIBLE	

Years ago I saw a leaflet put out by the Mormons. It showed three almost identical pictures of black leather-bound books. One was labelled *Old Testament*, one was *New Testament*, and the third was *Book of Mormon*. The message was clear. They acknowledged the Bible, but the *Book of Mormon* (with its very dubious history) was reckoned to be as important. That makes it unacceptable to the Christian.

Here is the second test:

OUR LIST OF FORBIDDEN TEACHINGS INCLUDES ANY THAT DO NOT ACKNOWLEDGE JESUS AS LORD OR THAT ADVOCATE A MEANS OF SALVATION THAT OMITS THE CROSS.

John has a severe warning against other spirits. 'This is how you can recognise the Spirit of God: Every spirit that acknowledges that Jesus Christ has come in the flesh is from God, but every spirit that does not acknowledge Jesus is not from God' (1 John 4:2–3). I am convinced that we cannot be too particular in our tests.

Amazingly, God sometimes uses one of these errors in a person's search for Him, but this does not make them right. One woman told me a strange tale of how she became a Christian. She was using I Ching (an ancient Chinese system of divination) during her search for God. An apparently chance meeting took her to a Christian conference centre where people believed in the Bible and in Satan. She was not impressed and wanted to leave – but her I Ching said she should stay; the teaching she was being offered was the source of life and she needed to humble herself and listen. Six weeks later she committed her life to Jesus, and thereafter the I Ching stopped working and she discarded it.

This is not a recommendation for occult practices. It emphasises the power of the God who is sovereign even over Satan, who can work in any way He chooses, with or without human agency.

2) Personal sin

Not all sin leaves us infected by satanic forces, but it may leave a weak spot. After all, a burglar does not need the front door of a house to be left wide open in order to gain entrance. He can sneak in at the back, through one tiny window left unlatched! The areas of sin that most often lead to demonisation are sexual impurity of all sorts; anger, bitterness and unforgiveness; and drugs and other addictions. Paul has an uncomfortable list of 'the acts of the sinful nature' which he says are 'obvious', before he lists the qualities of character that are the fruit of the Spirit in our lives. These sinful acts are in four categories: sexual sins; misdirected worship; unloving relationships; wrong use of alcohol. He warns us that, 'Those who live like this will not inherit the kingdom of God' (Gal. 5:19–21). His tough words are a valid warning.

3) Emotional, physical or mental sickness

Negative infantile experiences such as fear and rejection may be the weak spots that allow a person to be demonised. A voice once growled at me, 'I am Bernice,' naming the client. I refused to be deceived by that claim; it was patently a lie. A 'familiar spirit' had been resident in her life for a very long time; such spirits are exceedingly reluctant to leave. We have earlier recognised that spirits can infect a physical disability. They can also invade, or cause, mental illnesses, like the Gadarene demoniac.

On one occasion I was in a house with a woman who was manifesting the evil spirits that affected her. We were joined by an occupational therapy student who was working at the time in a psychiatric hospital. Afterwards she commented that she now understood the prickly sensation she experienced in the presence of some of the patients. She felt similar sensations in the room with the demonised woman, and she realised that their source was the same.

4) Family history

The genes and emotions, the spirituality and habits that we inherit from our parents and from previous generations make a thick rope of many strands. Among them may be some inherited demonic streak. We are in no way responsible if we have been affected by an evil power from the family, but we are responsible for asking to be freed from it. The lives of many Christians are like cars that are being driven with the handbrake on; they wonder why they do not know the joy and freedom they expect. One possible cause is that a dark force has troubled their family, perhaps unrecognised for generations. We can ask if there is any known involvement by parents or grandparents in spiritualism, or witchcraft, or Freemasonry, or in any item of the extensive list above. If the client has a psychic gift, that seems to be a sign that there has been some occult involvement in past generations.

Suicides in the family frequently leave their mark, particularly on grandchildren. Why grandchildren? I presume this is akin to the special bond that often exists between children and their grandparents. It does not mean that all the grandchildren will be oppressed, any more than all children have that special tie with their grandparents. I do not pretend to understand it all. But I am sure it happens. It is not too difficult to ask about family history without chasing after every straw or being too specific about the reason for these explorations. I heard of one woman who had received extensive help for her longterm depression. The final clearance came with the cutting of her link with her great-grandmother who had committed suicide.

Mary's friend phoned one morning. Mary had been in a prayer counselling session with another couple a day or two earlier; there had been a strange picture of arrows flying through the air, which seemed to be connected with the Norman Conquest in 1066; there had been some deliverance ministry. Mary was still feeling raw. Please could she and her friend come round? The picture seemed odd but I thought we would have a short and gentle time of prayer for Mary to be refilled with the Holy Spirit. My simple expectations were not fulfilled!

As we talked, Mary mentioned that she became depressed each autumn, so I asked whether any autumnal event might have started this.

'My best friend Meg committed suicide seven years ago, soon after she became a Christian.'

My alarm bells started to ring. She told me that she and Meg came from families that had belonged to the 'New Age church' thirty years earlier.

'Have you ever prayed about that New Age church?' I had never heard of it, but its very name was suspicious; I sensed from the Holy Spirit's nudge that it was wrong; although this was before the current New Age Movement, with which there is no apparent connection, had received any prominence.

I am uncertain exactly what happened next. As I prayed in tongues with my eyes shut, the coffee-table was overturned, and a mug landed in a far corner of the room. Help was needed! As I went in search of Michael, who was in the room below, I met him bounding up the stairs, already responding to the crash! Two short sentences were enough to explain the situation and he came into the room, gently singing a Christian song that started with the name of Jesus. Mary growled, and crawled into a corner.

After she was persuaded to emerge the three of us talked further. There were four strands in her life which needed release from Satan's touch. The New Age church; Meg's suicide; Mary's brother slightly active in the occult; all these were leaving their mark on her. There was also the picture of the arrows. Mary's family prided itself that they could trace their family tree back to Saxon times. Whether it was the pride, or whether there were occult practices somewhere down the line, we did not know; some evil power had touched her. At the end of the time of prayer, she was lying exhausted but rejoicing on the sofa, confident that the Spirit's power had set her free from any of these strands that had tied her.

How Do We Discern When There Is A Need For Deliverance?

There are many ways in which discernment comes, and much of it is as individual as the other supernatural gifts. There are different ways in which the Holy Spirit communicates

this. Some people know that there is evil present, without
even knowing how they know. For others there is a physical
sensation, tingling or a smell. For my own part, I have learnt
to distinguish three different physical reactions. If the dark
force is present in myself my limbs grow heavy. If it is
in another person my breathing is constricted when I am
praying with her. If an inanimate place or object is infected
I feel, 'Yuk! I want to get out of here!' and almost vomit.
That does not sound very specific – but I can assure you
that I know it! There is much subjectivity in recognising
the presence of active evil, and it is a mistake to rely on
one piece of evidence alone. Enormous damage is done,
usually to vulnerable people, by charging in on deliverance
ministry too soon or when none is needed.

When we first found ourselves called to combat evil spirits,
we tended to respond immediately and allowed the urgent
demands to take priority. That was a mistake, and we learnt
to be far more ordered in our approach; then Satan was no
longer able to rub his hands with glee as he diverted us by
his tricks from other priorities in regular ministry.

I learnt an important lesson from one particular incident.
A couple in our congregation, now in their thirties, had
both been Christians since they were in their teens. Their
zeal was limited and their church involvement was confined
to bringing their four children to the short Family Service
on Sunday morning. Then they came to a week's church
holiday, and on the same evening David and Linda were
both decisively filled with the Holy Spirit. He received a
call to full-time Christian ministry, and she started to speak
in tongues.

About two years later she remembered an event from a
quarter of a century earlier. As an elementary school child,
playing with a friend, she had made a plasticine model of
her friend's mother, and stuck pins into it. Four months later
the lady died. This incident had left its mark on Linda. She
needed to confess it and the dark force that had been an
unseen cloud over her was rebuked and banished.

I remember her saying to me later: 'If I had remembered

that any earlier, I would not have been able to cope with the guilt of it.' She needed those two years of new experience of God and of new assurance about the reality of His forgiveness in order to face that memory. God knew that, as well as He knew about the dark cloud in one corner of her life. He was not in a hurry to deal with that darkness, and we do not need to be any more impatient than the holy God is. I have learnt that right timing is a vital part of effective ministry, and I can look back at many mistakes. I pray for God's forgiveness over my misplaced haste or my rash 'discernment', and am thankful that He is able to pick up on my failures.

I classify in two ways the signs we are given that evil forces are present, whether they are signs that we see and hear with our natural senses or those that are conveyed in supernatural ways. Some signs are pointers and some are definitive. It is the difference between circumstantial and conclusive evidence. If your suspicions start to be aroused ask God to give you signs that either confirm or deny the correctness of your hunch. Here are some of the signals that we are given; the list is far from exhaustive.

1) Reactions to holy things   If someone shrinks from a cross or can only see it blurred, you can be sure that a demonic force in her does not want to admit its defeat at the Cross (Col. 2:15). Revulsion to the bread and the cup at communion indicates satanic influence. A lady who had once taken part in the spiritist equivalent of communion 'saw' a hideous face sitting on the cup. Once that whole incident had been fully confessed and forgiven and the Enemy had been confronted and rebuked, she could take the cup freely; the ugly vision had gone. I have also known real difficulty in taking communion often associated with suicide or murder in the family.

The demons hate the Bible. A young woman who had recently asked Christ into her life, used to talk a lot, rather enigmatically, about light and darkness. So I read to her, 'The god of this age has blinded the minds of unbelievers, so that they cannot see the light of the gospel of the glory of Christ, who is the image of God . . . For God, who said "Let light shine out of darkness," made his light shine in our hearts to give us the light of the knowledge of the glory of God in the face of Christ' (2 Cor. 4:4–6). She immediately said, 'I can't hear.' This was my first clue that she was troubled by evil spirits. Another young woman, a Christian who had previously been into both drugs and the occult, knew a sure sign when evil spirits had touched her again. The words in her Bible were blurred while the type of any other book was perfectly clear.

If prayer for a particular area of life (or prayer in tongues) brings heaviness or sharp reaction we can reckon that the Enemy has a grip that he is reluctant to release. A client sometimes gets worse, rather than better, after being anointed with oil, or after definite prayer for healing. At those times we strongly suspect that the 'Nasties' are in residence.

2) Psychic powers   or spiritual gifts not used in the name of Christ show that the unholy spirit has infiltrated. These gifts can be inherited; think, for instance, of the families of fortune-telling gypsies. It is not essential for effective ministry to know what occult practices there have been in previous generations. God knows.

3) Black in a prayer picture   If the client tells me that he has seen something black or very dark in a picture when he has been praying I am sure that there is some demonic streak. Whether or not I tell him this immediately depends on the maturity of his faith.

4) A selection of the circumstantial evidence   Nightmares; enormous fear; suicide attempts; confusion over life and death; denial of previous deliverance; inability to repeat the Lord's Prayer or baptismal vows; a strange look in the eyes; abnormal strength; amnesia; bondage to compulsive habits; holding on to objects which have been used in other religions;

a change of voice in speech, or in strange laughter; or if I find myself unnaturally tired after a counselling session; religiosity; compulsive anger.

This is a mixed and incomplete list. We store the pointers away in a mental pigeonhole, in no hurry to take action. If our suspicions are correct we can expect to see other signs. Meanwhile we can pray more specifically and intelligently.

What Do I Do If I Sense Evil Present?

First of all, there is no need to panic. God is in control, and we can pray for wisdom to know how to proceed, and for love for the person even while we hate the Nasties. Even when I see that active evil is present I prefer to leave it on one side and proceed along the normal path of counselling. Think of those four strands of the Cross we considered earlier: the two directions of forgiveness, healing and victory over Satan.

It is helpful to move in that order. I can draw a pin-man picture of a Christian standing at a distance from the Cross; he has a bag of sin and resentment and he is unguarded from attack by the black figure nearby. If the pin-man is standing under the arms of the Cross, he is safe and the Prowler cannot reach him; if he is away from the Cross he is unprotected.

If I can help a Christian to reach the point where he wants to put things right, any deliverance ministry that is necessary is comparatively easy. We want to pull together; his will, my will and, above all, the power of Christ. But if the client does not really want to change, the demon has a comfortable niche in which he can continue to hide, and he is not lying when he claims, 'I'm wanted here, so I'm not leaving.' During the counselling we can talk about fears about Satan and about the possible course of ministry, and the whole situation can be soaked in prayer. Then you can plan a time of prayer with a more experienced counsellor or ordained minister.

The Deliverance Ministry

A novice counsellor should always link up with someone
with more experience; an experienced one should not work
alone. So I am only going to suggest a brief framework. Find
a place where there will not be interruptions and allow plenty
of time. Either your regular meeting place or a church are
the obvious places. Brief the minister beforehand as fully as
you can and then trust him. He will probably want to make
his own relationship with the client and decide for himself
how to proceed. You have moved from being the leader
into being the assistant and your main job will be to pray
quietly. Remember that you do not have a monopoly on
discernment, and the minister may well notice something
that you have missed, however many hours you have spent
with the client!

1) Pray together   for the fulfilment of God's purposes for
this time together. You are working together in love; *with*
the client *against* a common enemy.

2) Anyone present needs to confess any known sin   This
is followed by repentance and renunciation. 'Renounce' is
a strong word which I use at other times in counselling. It
says firmly, 'I do NOT want any more of this in my life.
I refuse to be ruled by it any longer. I push it away from
me.' Renunciation is not followed by immediate perfection,
but it expresses a determination of the will. Forgiveness can
then be claimed.

3) The minister then tells the demons to leave   He gives
clear, confident commands in the name of Jesus. No argument is tolerated. They are expected to do what they are
told. This does not mean shouting at them. Calm strength
is as relevant here as it is with a child. Protestant though
we are, we have found the value of holding a small wooden
cross or of making the sign of the Cross.

Even more surprising to our evangelical heritage was to

discover the power in consecrated water when it is used in faith. We found this almost by accident. A deeply demonised woman made some reference to holy water (in the demon's voice.) Michael turned on the tap in our host's kitchen and put some water in a cup. We heard a scornful voice. 'That's not holy water; that's just *tap* water.' But as soon as the water was prayed over in the name of the Trinity she shrank from it when it was sprinkled on her head.

Oil is another scriptural element to use. An eye to eye meeting between the minister and the client often becomes an eye to eye encounter between the Holy Spirit and the demon; the minister must make it clear when he is talking with the client, and when he is being tough with the recalcitrant demon. The client is more likely than anyone else present to know when the demons have all departed. He may sense them in various ways; for instance as a physical block in his chest or a battle raging in his head. He knows when they are there and when they have left.

If there is no apparent headway do not keep fighting when you are all exhausted. Commit the client into God's hands and arrange another meeting in a few days. Often he will realise what has been either ignored or forgotten altogether.

4) Pray for the infilling of the Holy Spirit   Give thanks and praise together. Perhaps share a simple, informal communion service. Fix a follow-up session soon afterwards; remember, the client has had major surgery, and needs tender aftercare.

5) Encourage him to go off to live obediently   That includes destruction of any articles in his possession that are associated with the occult. Things as well as people can be infected, and the vulnerable person can be reinfected if he leaves himself in the pathway of germs. But reassure him that we are on the winning side in the heavenly battle. HUMBLE CONFIDENCE is to be our watchword.

Homework

1) *Luke 4:1–13. Ephesians 6:10–18* What can we learn from these two passages a) about the reality of the devil; b) how to fight him?

2) *Turn to p.244* As you pray over the list of forbidden practices ask God to remind you if there is anything you need to confess. If anything comes to mind commit it to the Lord. Then go to your minister or to a trusted friend to confess it and to pray together.

19

MISTAKES AND FAILURES

One man's death was on my conscience for years. He was an intelligent man who had received psychiatric help intermittently since his late teens, and I cannot remember how I came to be trying to help him. One day a letter arrived, a letter couched in unusual language that seemed to be saying that he had recommitted his life to Christ. I rejoiced, and was a little surprised when soon afterwards he told me of his new plans to set up a support group under a long-standing clergyman friend instead of me. I was disappointed, but he talked of his hopes to visit a Christian psychiatrist who had an unusual prayer ministry, and I thought he would be in safe hands.

Some months later I visited him to see how things were going. There did not seem to be much progress. I urged him not to let matters lie fallow, and at some point in the conversation we spoke about the reality of demonic spirits. Within forty-eight hours he had committed suicide; a carefully planned overdose, taken in a ditch at the edge of a field, where he would not easily be found.

Had that conversation disturbed him? Were there evil spirits active in his life that had been stirred up? Or was it a coincidence? I shall not know until I get to heaven. But I do know that I was deeply troubled for a long time by the fear that I had contributed to his death. Even if there were no connection between my visit and his suicide, I realised that I had been exceedingly unwise to mention demonic spirits to one who was so unstable whom I was not even counselling at the time. My intentions were good but my words were foolish.

This chapter is going to be a difficult one to write, not only because it is painful to remember such incidents. It is often hard to know what has actually been a mistake, and even harder to define the failures. Mercifully I am not aware of other mistakes that have been fatal to life, though some have proved fatal to relationships.

What Mistakes Do We Make?

Mistakes are of various kinds. There are mistakes of ignorance; of wrong diagnosis; of relationship; of over-eagerness. Underlying most of them is pride.

Mistakes of ignorance and inexperience   I am appalled to remember how, with a client who had a phobia of vomiting, two of us tried to induce her to vomit by tickling her throat with a feather! Or how I assumed in the early days of my counselling that the few methods I had been taught were appropriate for every person in every situation. I am shocked to remember how quickly I jumped to diagnose the source of difficulties or to prescribe remedies.

Nowadays I sometimes warn a client not to expect perfection. I tell her that I will do my best to understand, but ask in advance that she will forgive me when I get things wrong. I try to be alert if she hesitates; I can then be quick to comment, 'I'm sorry; you don't look very happy about that. What is wrong?' If a good relationship has been built up between us even a 'good child' client who tries to conform can have the courage to voice her concern and to tell me where she thinks I am wrong. Then mistakes due to my ignorance or lack of discernment can be covered by love and humility, by sensitivity and apology.

Mistakes in diagnosis   are often the fruit of assumptions. *Every* client is an individual. Many cases are similar but none are identical. I think of a young lawyer who came to talk about his homosexual tendencies. I assumed the roots of this were in the relationships in his family of origin and spent considerable time digging around; all exploration seemed to lead to dead ends. Finally the novice co-counsellor suggested I might be on the wrong path. Apology and prayer followed – and then God's shaft of light put us straight.

One of the most sensitive areas of wrong diagnosis is the demonic. Demons are real – but they are not to be found under every bush, and real damage may be done to a client if demon-hunting is a daily sport.

Mistakes in relationship   Perseverance is good; 'love never ends.' But perseverance can lose perspective; there have been times when I have failed to notice that my perseverance has stopped being helpful to the client and instead has fed her dependence on me. This is not real love. Love is always concerned for the well-being of the other person, and the client's growth will be inhibited if I continue to allow her dependence on me to control the relationship.

What should I do if I recognise that this is happening? First I must look at myself. Is my own need to be needed uppermost? Is her dependence feeding my pride or my sense of power? If it is, the first thing I must do is to confess it to God and to repent. I should then go and talk over the situation with a wise friend who can observe what is happening in the relationship and advise me on the best steps to take.

Then I must put it right with the client. Explain what has been noticed; that treats her as an adult – even though she will probably not agree because it is the 'child' in her that is dependent! A gentle withdrawal can follow; not total – just one or two steps back. A firmer hand is applied; perhaps an abrupt end to sessions is needed instead of the extra fifteen minutes that has become the order of the day (or night).

This may arouse anger. I was shocked the first time a client turned round and vented her anger on me. I did not see immediately that she was loading on to me the anger that belonged to a parent or to some other authority figure earlier in her life. But if I can stand firm, wise, loving in the face of the onslaught the mistake can be turned to good if the true source of the anger can be explored.

Mistakes of over-eagerness   I long to see progress; I long to see the client growing in confidence in God and in herself. These are right desires, so long as they are governed by love for the client rather than by a subtle desire for my own success.

Over-eagerness includes impatience. I can think of occasions when my discernment has been right but my timing has been wrong. I have been too quick to speak or to act, unwilling to wait and pray. I can think of other times when my high standards have not been matched by the depth of my compassion; or when my desire to see a person move towards wholeness has been according to *my* agenda or for *my* success without respect for her choices or for the Lord's agenda.

A friend challenged me not long ago. We were talking about the difficulty of writing this chapter; a snatch of the conversation went like this:

Her: I'm one of your failures . . .
Me: Why do you call yourself a failure?
Her: I wasn't calling myself a failure. Why can't you bear to think that it might be you who failed?

I was silenced! I had to stop and consider whether my need for success was paramount and why I had assumed that she was the one who had failed. I saw that I had tried to foist on her my own agenda for her change. I believe my hopes for her were in accord with biblical standards; but my plans were not hers, and I cannot even be sure that they were God's plans for her at that time. His priorities do not always tally with our ideas! He is a patient Master sculptor carving beautiful figures out of granite; the sculpture takes a lifetime. Our job in counselling is to work as apprentices to the Sculptor, not carving the hands when He wants to work on the feet.

What Do We Do When We Recognise The Mistake?

It is good that we have a God who is a redeemer! He is an amazing God who can actually bring good out of bad. His good outcome tempts us to believe that the bad might not have been bad after all. No, bad is still bad; wrong is still wrong. We must rectify what we can.

When we recognise that we have made a mistake the first need is humble apology. We apologise to the client and to God and ask forgiveness from both. The Lord accepts the apology, and we can count on Him to forgive us. The client, on the other hand, may either be overtly angry or may express polite words of forgiveness which mask anger. In neither case do we keep apologising until we are sure that the apology has been genuinely accepted, nor do we match anger with anger. Rather we turn to Jesus who knew disappointment and misunderstanding when He was on earth and ask for heavenly grace and wisdom to know how to proceed.

What Is A Failure?

'It is harder to define the failures,' was my earlier comment. Is it the counsellor's failure in being too hard or too gentle? In making wrong assumptions or in leading in the wrong direction? Is it the client's failure in evading change? In allowing old patterns of thought and behaviour to dominate? When there appears to be failure there are questions of 'Whose failure?' and 'Why?'

But first there is a more fundamental query. Is it really failure at all? Growth in the Christian life is like reading a book. We may read it all at one stretch; more often we stop at the end of a chapter; less satisfactory but sometimes necessary is to pause in the middle of a chapter until we can pick it up again. There are times when we express, 'This book's no good!' That may be true, or it may disguise our own inability to understand it or to accept its teaching. We can throw it to the other side of the room exclaiming, 'Never again!' or we can say we intend to continue it some time in the future.

Stuart was a student whom I was counselling in Oxford some six years ago, and we have exchanged letters intermittently since then. My initial reaction when I heard that he had been seeing a therapist recently for some of the old problems was one of disappointment – and wondering where I had failed. I looked at two letters from the Oxford days. 'The fear is broken, gone. I find myself rejoicing that God knows all of me, and has forgiven me . . . I can't believe how stable I have become emotionally. Occasionally I have ups and downs, but honestly that's worlds away from the semi-permanent depression/elation I used to experience . . .' It is exciting to receive letters like that. What was missing in my counselling with him? What went wrong later?

He has written again recently. It is clear that the work we did together in his student days was one chapter in his healing. Now he has moved further forward, and has understood more of the effects of his early family life:

Basically, my troubles stem from growing up in an alcoholic family and being sexually abused by at least one of my parents. I have had all the usual reaction to this: depression, anxiety and a feeling that I can never do anything well enough. I've also been pretty bad at relating to the opposite sex . . . Over the years the Lord has shown me ways out of this. I am not out of the woods yet, but I am immensely better . . . None of this would have been possible without the counselling I had with you.

I had very little experience or knowledge at that time of the effects of either alcoholism or sexual abuse. My ignorance could not teach him all he needed to understand about the denial of the problem of alcoholism or the false guilt caused by the abuse:

My mother abused me when I was eleven years old, and I did not mention it until I was twenty-one and talking

to you. This was my awful secret . . . the environment of
prayer and counselling enabled me to remember something of what happened, and to experience the acceptance of God for these events. I cannot exaggerate how
important that was.

That letter has given me helpful perspective. I am sure that
I did not do things perfectly, but the Lord did what was
necessary for him at that stage of his life. Our failures are
hard to define.

God has a bird's-eye view of our lives. He looks down
on the whole pattern, while we have a worm's-eye view of
limited perspective. So what appears to be FAILURE may
only be PAUSE or TEMPORARY SETBACK. There are
times when *my* expectations for a client are not realised;
perhaps my hopes were mis-directed or my mistakes were
big; perhaps she could not, or would not, face the challenge
of change. But even if the book of her progress has been
put aside at present, even if relationship is broken and there
appears to be deterioration in the quality of life, even if
God is left aside, we do not know what the future may
bring.

Some perceptive comments on failure reached me recently
from a Christian friend who is taking a secular counselling
course:

When I started to think about 'failure in counselling' –
that of the client or the counsellor – I found that first of
all I had to think out the aims and objectives of both. I
then realised that I must look at the differences between
the Christian and the secular situation, as the Christian
has the added dimension of evangelism in the motivation
and the resources of God in the healing.

Failure is not so apparent in secular counselling because
without the God-dimension, failure is less tangible. Christian counselling is directed towards a healing that will
bring the client into peace with self, others and God.
This involves breaking down barriers and healing the

hurts revealed. Failure occurs when a client does not move Godwards. Whose failure is it?

The client will feel guilty at not moving in the expected direction and so has let God down as well as the counsellor and can end up with more problems than there were at the beginning. The counsellor will feel to have failed because, with all the resources of God at hand, the client does not appear to have moved forward to the expected goal or even to have moved off into the opposite direction.

Secular counselling does not have the God-dimension and so failure is not so apparent. If the client has not moved in the expected direction (if there is one) then that is the client's choice. The counsellor's task is not to bring the client nearer to God but to enable a developing wholeness and integration for that person. In Christian counselling the work overlaps with evangelism and is confined by the counsellor's understanding of God as revealed in the Bible. As God's representative the counsellor acts for God in all humility, honesty and sincerity. God can and must be bigger than our human understanding or He is not God. When the outcome seemingly is failure, in God's hands and in His time it may turn out quite the opposite.

Any work done, either with or without God, which enables the client to have a greater understanding of self and so grow into wholeness cannot be a failure. As Christians we expect miracles. God still provides them but not always within the confines of our time limits – He is bigger than that.

Those comments challenged me. They challenged me to consider the times when I have laid my own expectations on a client, thinking they were the Lord's expectations. They challenged me again to respect the client's freedom of choice given by God. They challenged me to pray for those with whom my work has been obviously unfinished. They challenged me to continued growth in my own Christ-likeness and in understanding. They challenged me to trust God for His work. But they did not shake my confidence that 'wholeness' in this world cannot ignore the Creator and His unique salvation. They did not shake my conviction that God will judge the world by His own holy and merciful standards.

What is a failure? Only He can judge.

20

A CLIENT'S RESPONSE

I am going to finish with some extracts from a letter from Marlene (pp. 108, 112, 227). My first session with her lasted four hours; there have been others since. Healing is a process, not a matter of instant completion. Her struggles are not finished, but eighteen months after this letter was written her academic studies were going well and she was being used in counselling others. Marlene has a testimony that offers hope to those who feel locked in with their turmoil. Healing and wholeness are possible.

I am including her own description of what it was like for her to receive the sort of ministry I have been describing, not to boost my own ego but that you might feel and experience with her. She wrote this just two days after Alice, a pastor at her church, brought her to me. She describes some of her experience of those first four hours and she also reflects on what it was about the approach that was helpful to her. From time to time I have added my own comments on her letter in [NOTES].

Marlene says:

> I wanted to write, simply to let you know how much I appreciated your time, your energy, your love and your gentle firmness with me. I was reminded of the story of Jesus healing the ten lepers and only one of them came back to give thanks. How discouraging that must have been to their Healer.
>
> I've had a couple of days simply to absorb what happened in our time together. I am still very tired and can only guess at the incredible exhaustion you yourself must

experience after such a session as ours. [NOTE: Since I have learnt to expect God to carry the load, my energy is drained surprisingly little.]

There is a new quietness about my being. An emptiness in the sense that something is missing. Praise the Lord! The beast is out there now, lingering and raging yet, planning a new attack, but outside my skin. I know now that with the power of the Cross and the sword it cannot get back in me.

Marlene's out-of-the-body experiences as a child, in an attempt to escape from the awfulness of her brother's sexual abuse, and the ritual abuse to which she had been subjected in her teens, left their mark on her in a variety of ways. Among these was a hairy beast half-human, half-animal, with many heads, which she has 'seen' on previous occasions. It appeared to her vividly during our time together.

Marlene goes on to tell how vivid the experience was for her. This helps to explain how important it is for the counsellor to be loving and sympathetic, yet like a rock, throughout. During the session she told me that in her image MORMOT was outside the circle of light around the Cross. I had no idea of the intensity of her struggle until she wrote like this:

'Name the evil,' you said. My mind was screaming; I experienced blinding pain in my brain and incredible chest pain. I could no longer hear your voice; I could not even hear my own thoughts. Imprinted on my mind was the word MORMOT. Does that make any sense to you at all? It would not go past my vocal chords, but what it consists of I can verbalise. It is everything that is immoral, all that is blackness, all that is negative. Its nature is evident in the faces of the beast. Anger, wildness, destructiveness, vengefulness; mean to the core. [NOTE: I have not made any investigation into that name. We knew a Christian who noticed one word being repeated several times in her tongues. On investigation, this proved to be the name of a murderous prostitute in the Apocrypha; this gave us clues needed to be able to help her. We can never know everything about the spiritual world; there will always be surprises.]

My imagery was switched on full tilt. I was seeing, hearing, smelling and feeling; experiencing with all my senses. The physical pain was coming in ever intensifying waves, threatening to distract me. My counsellor back home taught me to breathe through the pain and that enabled me to stay with the process. [NOTE: Marlene had recently moved to Vancouver, accepted as a candidate to start training for full-time pastoral ministry.]

Incredible terror gripped me, immobilising me. I was lost to it at one point; I could neither hear, feel or see anything external to myself. My very being was a confused racket. I know myself well and found myself screaming out, 'Don't panic, Marlene. Don't panic. You are safe. I know it doesn't feel like it, but you are safe. Don't panic. Breathe.' Then Jesus was there with me and I could hear you again, telling me to remember the Cross; letting me know that the power I needed to get the beast to back off was in the Cross, telling me I only had to use it and that it was my choice. You couldn't choose for me; I had to make that move on my own. I remember thinking, 'Listen to Rosemary, Marlene. Listen to her.' Your voice was firm and commanding. I listened.

You were telling me, 'The Cross is like a sword, Marlene. It can cut off the beast's many heads. Take your hands away from your ears, Marlene . . . Take at least one hand away and hang on to this Cross.' Your voice was firm and confident, expecting that I could and would find the strength to reach beyond the absolute blinding force of my terror, past the beast. I wondered, 'Can I?' [NOTE: I believe it is a valid use of imagery to pick up the Cross and use it as a sword. I keep a small wooden cross, only about five inches tall, in the room where I often counsel.]

The beast is screaming at me, 'Touch it and you die'.

I know my MORMOT's incredible power; I believe it; I have seen it destroy a friend just four months ago. [NOTE: Marlene is referring to a friend who committed suicide.]

Then MORMOT made its fatal error. 'I am not going to let you ever hold that Cross.' Won't let me?

Won't LET me?
WON'T let me?
WON'T LET ME?!

I choose for me, not you, or anyone else! I realise that my damned fierce independence is now a gift. [NOTE: How important that I had not trespassed on her will.] I told MORMOT that I was prepared to take my chances with death, that I was listening to Jesus and you Rosemary not it any more.

MORMOT had me immobilised. It knew that now it was fighting for its very existence. All of a sudden so was I. A surge of determination got my eyes open and I saw that wooden cross. In my visualisation I saw myself standing close to the Cross. MORMOT had me enveloped in its clutches; the circle of light extended to about three feet from where we were. I fought and struggled and wriggled. We entered the light. MORMOT recoiled. One arm came free. I grabbed the Cross. Agonising, searing pain ripped through my body. I chose to endure and hold on. I remembered you telling me this might involve a real struggle. I remembered you were out there. I started to register your arms holding me tight. My attention came back into the room.

This is all too weird! I remember wondering where the cross came from that I was holding in my hand. I sensed that you knew that something significant was happening to me, Rosemary. You were praying in tongues, patiently waiting for me to return. You discerned when I was with you again and we carried on.

Marlene goes on to explain her return to the womb experience. This was after I noticed her clutching the cushion tightly. In my prayer about her fear I touched on the fact that it might have started before the remembered events of her life. I believe that this was insight from God coupled with my counselling experience. She then told me that her twin brother had been miscarried, six months through the pregnancy.

You encouraged me to let Jesus show what was distressing me and when the fear had begun to affect my life. I actually went back in time and was in the womb, foetus size; seeing Mark's eyes registering fear and knowing it was too soon and we were not ready to come out. I was reaching to him, holding him, feeling my own connection tearing away under the strain. I let go to save myself!

I can't actually remember this part of my life, can I? Maybe it was a matter of, 'If you remembered what it would have been like?' No! It's real all right.

I felt the emptiness in there.

I was so frightened.

It was so lonely on my own.

He was gone.

It was my fault.

When we talked about this you said to me, 'Here is one more place where you can choose to believe your reason, your rationality, your intellect. They tell you it was *not* your fault. The engine of your train must be the knowledge; that is where the power is, not in the guard's van or feelings.

We paused often to summarise in prayer; your ability to discern the real issues kept me on track. They were healing cleansing prayers for everything I remembered.

Your use of Scripture was very healing to the process. I especially remember when you read to me:

'Peter, do you love me?'

I responded 'Yes.'

You immediately changed to Marlene.

'Marlene, do you love me?'

It's God and me together now.

The third time God asks it registers.

Like Peter I had denied God in the face of my fear.

Oh, what have I done?

I remember my prayer. 'O God, forgive me in my humanness for denying You. I feared for my life. I believed MORMOT. I chose to survive, meaning that I chose bondage to Satan. Help me to be strong in Your power and go on to accept the challenge to feed your sheep.' [NOTE: It appears to me that the Enemy first got into Marlene's life when, in the womb, she believed the lies about her responsibility for her brother's death.]

It was important for me to pray to be an active participant in speaking with God, to ask for forgiveness where my actions and attitudes needed to be forgiven. I am grateful for the new understanding that came to me that day on the importance and the power of renunciation. [NOTE: A reminder that renunciation is expressing firmly to God 'I do NOT want to be stuck any longer with . . .']

I have some questions. I'd like to talk about the issue of suicide, and how a devout Christian who has a close friend could kill himself recently? How could my pastor friend blow his own head off seven years ago? Does God allow? Where is the issue of choice?

What about my beast MORMOT? I have a strange sense that I haven't seen the end of it yet. I am disconcerted by its desperation, the intensity of its fury as it hissed it was coming back and then I would see. How do I maintain my watchfulness? How do I make sure it doesn't come back in through the cracks when I'm not paying attention? [NOTE: Marlene was indeed right. MORMOT has not yet let her go. But she has worked on her relationships within her family, overtly forgiving and asking forgiveness, where this has been appropriate. Most recently she has drawn her family tree, as far as she knows it, three generations back. On both sides there is a history of accident, violence, suicide, sexual and substance abuse, as well as some dark spiritual overtones. We are taking time to pray through the effect this has had on Marlene and on others in her family.]

What about false guilt? I had close friends die at the age of eight, twelve and sixteen. My feelings tell me I am responsible for all of those deaths. Best friends, relationships, even friendships have been next to impossible for me since then.

I have already mentioned some things that were helpful to me during the process of that morning; I am sure you must wonder if you are getting through and what is helpful about the methods you use. For me it was a lot of things that made the time effective:

1) The issue of the length of time. I didn't feel rushed or put on hold or shuffled off to some other 'expert'. My pain was important enough for *you* to spend several hours with me, struggling with me, praying with me, teaching and guiding me; most importantly facilitating my taking that pain and confusion directly to God. The intensity of my pain could never be adequately expressed in a pastoral visit an hour or two long.

2) Taking it as the Spirit directed and not necessarily in chronological order.

3) Interspersing the entire session with prayer and Scripture, and more prayer and Scripture.

4) The atmosphere of simple trust happening between us. You knew me not, and yet trusted me implicitly. That, I tell you, is a unique gift. Other counsellors and pastors have been guarded and even sceptical with me. Your trust and respect freed me to be completely honest with you and with myself.

5) Your non-judgmental attitude allowed me to be wholly Christian and confused and sinful at the same time. This allowed me to get beyond protecting my own sense of integrity and reacting in self-defence. My own maturing spirit was free really to examine my heart and my attitudes. [NOTE: The phrase 'It's all right', at a time when things are clearly not good at all, conveys both acceptance and hope.]

6) Your empathy and compassion; your ability to allow my experience to hurt your own heart. I felt an incredible understanding of my pain and struggle which was somehow very validating. Finally here is someone who understands, who can register the intensity of my pain, hurt, agony, grief, struggle, fear, anger etc. That somehow freed me to address it without getting strung up in trying to express it adequately. [NOTE: I remember that I started to take notes at the beginning of our time together, but as Marlene moved into the awfulness of the ritual sexual abuse I felt as if taking notes was intruding on the pain of her story. I put my paper on one side, and just listened, trusting that I would remember anything that was necessary.]

7) The affirmations you poured on me. 'I know this is difficult, Marlene . . . I know the sharing is painful . . . I appreciate your being honest about that . . . you are doing very well, Marlene.' All of these gave me the courage to continue.

8) The touch. When you and Alice both came to hold me very tight and did not let go when part of me tried to pull away. [NOTE: How do you know when to hold and when to let go? Keep prayerfully listening.]

9) Your sense of humour and your appreciation of mine were essential to the process.

10) Your experience and knowledge around the topic of abuse, both the victim and offender parts of me, and around the early life in the womb. [NOTE: As with many she, the abused, had become an abuser.]

11) Alice sitting tender and gentle at my feet ministering, praying, encouraging; resting against my legs, willing me to hang in there; watching and waiting with me, attentive and alert; her tears. [NOTE: Alice knew that she was out of her depth with Marlene, but she contributed enormously through her sensitivity, her love and her perception. She has learnt and grown through being part of the ministry.]

12) Your constant teaching at each stage. 'This is what is happening . . . This is where we are going . . . Do you

understand? . . . I'm going to ask you to . . .' These all gave me a sense of actually participating with understanding and informed consent. [NOTE: Respect for her spirituality, for her intelligence, for herself as a person; all these were vital in enabling her to assent and to move forward.]

13) Most important was your ability to deal effectively with the incredible power of evil that existed in and around me. I remember your amazing calmness in walking right up to evil and saying, 'Okay turkey, remember! Jesus took the keys back and has control, so GET LOST!' (Sorry, my slightly irreverent style shows; your words would have been more eloquent.) I have never witnessed such confidence and calm assurance. [NOTE: Christ says, 'I hold the keys of death and Hades' (Rev. 1:18.)]

14) Your use of tongues and your ability to discern the appropriate exercise of that gift. My Presbyterianism is baffled by it, but I cannot deny the reality and validity when it echoes the sounds I have heard myself utter in prayer, and when it gave me a real sense of the Spirit's presence and ministry.

15) Your ability to challenge what I was saying without attacking my sense of integrity in the process.

16) The gift you have to facilitate process, to move my gut and my intellect to a meeting place, and gently but firmly make me decide which was going to rule my life.

Marlene finished her letter with an offer to be alongside in ministry to listen to someone else's pain, to offer her love, to go with someone to hospital or to court. I have never called on her for those things, for others in pain are coming to her.

She also said, 'Feel free to use my story and your experience of me as a teaching tool.' Thank you, Marlene, for your willingness to share your story. Thank you as well to the many people who have allowed me to tell something of their stories in this book so that they might help others. For the final Homework in this book use this chapter as a basis for discussion. Make your own comments and questions about her experience and about my approach. Think how you might answer her questions on p.270. Then pray that you continue to grow in your knowledge of Him and in your ability to be used to help others.

For we do not preach ourselves,
but Christ Jesus as Lord,
and ourselves as your servants for Jesus' sake.
For God, who said, 'Let light shine out of darkness,'
made his light shine in our hearts
to give us the light of the knowledge of the glory of God
in the face of Christ
(2 Cor. 4:5–6).

Appendix I

GOD'S RESOURCES

In question 1 of the Homework in Chapter 1, the reader was asked to list the resources for counselling that are uniquely available for the Christian.

1) The Bible gives us the Creator's perspective on mankind as we are meant to be and on the sin that has spoilt us. It gives us a norm for our doctrine, so that we are not dependent on the ideas of people for our beliefs. Used sensitively, the word of God is a powerful weapon of truth.

2) Jesus is the unique source of our salvation. The Cross is solid evidence for God's love for us. It gives us a place to deal with guilt (both real and false), to discover how to forgive others, to find healing and to know victory over Satan.

3) The norm of God's standards for ethical and moral behaviour.

4) The Holy Spirit not only illumines God's truth and character, but also opens us up to the power of the Godhead through prayer and spiritual gifts. Much Christian counselling is subservient to biblical standards of doctrine and behaviour but fails to draw on all the resources of His power.

5) The fruit of the Spirit in our lives enhances good natural characteristics to enable us to demonstrate, as well as to speak, about God and what He is like.

Appendix II

SUGGESTED BIBLE REFERENCES

Here are some references for question 2 of Homework for chapter 13. These verses are suggestions to supplement those you have already found for yourself. Build up your repertoire gradually, especially as you read the Bible on your own, and through sermons and study groups. Selwyn Hughes' small book *The Christian Counsellor's Pocket Guide* is a useful resource.

ANXIETY	Matt. 6:25–34; Phil. 4:6,7
FEAR	Isa. 41:10; Isa. 43:1–5; Matt. 14:27
GOD AS FATHER	Ps. 103:8–14; Matt. 6:9–15
GOD AS JUDGE	Heb. 10:30, 31; Gen. 18:25
GOD'S INFALLIBLE WISDOM	Ps. 18:30; Deut. 32:4
GUILT	Jas. 2:10; Lev. 4:27; 1 John 1:8,9
LONELINESS	Heb. 13:5; Deut. 31:6; Josh. 1:9; Matt. 28:20
MARITAL DISHARMONY	Col. 3:12–14
NON-ACCEPTANCE AT BIRTH	Ps. 139:13–18
RESENTMENT	Heb. 12:15; Eph. 4:31–2; Matt. 6:14–15
SUFFERING	Rom. 5:3–5; 1 Pet. 2:18–24; Ps. 22; Lam. 3:1–33

Appendix III

EXTRACT FROM AUDREY'S DIARY
(see Chapter 16, p.209)

I found myself sharing how I felt surrounded by an invisible net that shrouded me and kept me from experiencing the Lord. There were times when a bubble of desire and eagerness to know Him would come to the surface but it evaporated quickly. I was still in my shroud of inactivity. As we prayed Rosemary encouraged me to take that image and let the Lord develop it. She asked me to see myself in the net and asked what it was like. I saw it as grey stiffened net forming a chrysalis shape. It was upright like a capsule and I was inside, able to move about but not able to break out.

Then I saw a pair of hands that had made a hole through the casing at the top; they were wanting to reach down and lift me out. But then I was aware of a dilemma because I wasn't sure that I wanted to be taken out. I felt protected even if restricted inside. If I came out I would be naked, cold and vulnerable.

Rosemary fed in these thoughts. 'Rock of Ages, cleft for me; let me hide myself in Thee; let me come to Thee for dress . . .'; and some words from Revelation to the Church at Laodicea. 'You say "I am rich, I have acquired wealth and do not need a thing": but you do not realise that you are wretched, pitiful, poor, blind and naked. I counsel you to buy from me gold refined in the fire so that you can become rich; and white clothes to wear so that you can cover your shameful nakedness . . .' Also the fact that when Adam and Eve became aware of their nakedness in the garden God gave them clothes of skin, better than their fig leaves.

Now there was a struggle going on. Did I want the Lord to lift me out or not? The struggle surprised me. I felt I ought to know what the shroud was composed of – what had caused it so that I might deal with those things, but Rosemary wisely pointed out that God was not asking me to break it up to get out but just to let Him lift me out which involved my will and my emotions. It might be that after I was free I could look at the empty shroud and see it for what it was; the cerebral part would come later.

A couple of reflections came to me. While I was in the shroud I could not see the Lord clearly – it was misty – also it muffled sound so that I could not hear Him distinctly.

But now I was beginning to see the struggle for what it was. I was afraid of failure in the future. I thought of so many things begun and not finished e.g. letters, sewing, books, collage, etc and then remembered the new beginnings with the Lord and the subsequent failure to stay close to Him. Would I not fail Him again; was it better to stay in the shroud?

I saw now that the hand was not going to reach down and take me by force however gently. It was there inviting me to climb up into it in order to be lifted out.

I yielded and the next moment I was aware of being outside the shroud, as yet naked but standing on the palm of His great hand and warmed all over by the heat of it.

'If the Son shall set you free, you shall be free indeed.'

Thank you, dear Lord.

Appendix IV

COUNSELLING IN CHURCHES

In many ways the church, with its fellowship, its love, its worship and its teaching is the ideal context for counselling. The person in need does not have to be sent outside the 'family' to which he belongs, and continuity of pastoral care after counselling can be ensured. The church leaders can be sure of the doctrinal stance of the counsellors and can easily ask about the client's progress. However there are various snags to be watched.

1) The friendliness and ease of the situation, and the fact that the counselling is probably free, may deter the client from the work and responsibility he might find it harder to evade in professional counselling.

2) In the church, counsellor and client are likely to meet in different situations and I have sometimes found real difficulty (for both of us) in the transition. On one day the counsellor and client have clear lines drawn in their relationship in the counselling room. The next day they may be co-workers in Christian service, and the level of relationship between them is quite different. The following day they might meet casually after the church service; in that setting the question, 'How are you?' expects a less detailed answer than the same question two days earlier. There is considerable potential for misunderstanding, tension and hurt unless the situation is talked over openly and the difficulties faced.

3) Confidentiality needs to be carefully guarded. Sadly, Christian circles easily become gossip shops. 'I want to ask you to pray for . . .' becomes a ready excuse to pass on a confidence. We can ask prayer for a named individual and/or an appointment at a particular time *or* for an unnamed person with a specific need.

4) Supervision may be neglected. Then 'super-spirituality' or spiritual pride may mask the counsellor's personal needs, which then obstruct the counselling. I have heard today of such a

situation where church discipline then had to be enforced; a number of church members left the church, and pain and confusion ensued.

Training

Courses can be arranged for selected church members, including leaders of house groups, either using resources already within the church or inviting other local counsellors to speak. Or church members can take part in courses elsewhere. In that case a wise church leader will check the content of the teaching to see if any counter-balance is needed. An 'apprenticeship' method of training is also useful, when an inexperienced counsellor works alongside one more experienced, learning by observation and by partnership.

Prayer ministry after services

An increasing number of churches have small teams of Christians available after services so that anyone with a need to share can go to the communion rail or to a side chapel, where he may find a friend or a total stranger. Such times are mini-counselling sessions and may incorporate all the principles of listening, teaching and praying. This can – and, I believe, usually should – include encouraging the person in need to pray for himself, not just to rely on the prayer of the 'ministers'. I was once at the communion rail after speaking at a healing service. One lady came to ask for prayer for her various physical ailments. I suggested that before I prayed for her she might pray for herself. Almost immediately she was in tears about her loneliness, which was a far deeper need than those she had originally expressed.

This prayer ministry should preferably be under the same overall leadership as all the counselling in the church, even if it is administered by a different person. Membership of such a team may be the first rung of the ladder of the counselling team in the church, with the same opportunities for training being made available. It is good if all members of the prayer ministry teams can meet regularly (perhaps monthly) for fellowship, discussion, training and prayer.

A counselling group

When a number of ordained and lay people have been selected to counsel in the church they are under the direct authority of the minister or of someone whom he has appointed for this role. As with the 'after church prayers' it is helpful for such a group to meet regularly for mutual supervision and encouragement. The group can incorporate the minister as one of its members; its meetings can have some input on a particular topic (from one of the members or from an outside professional) and an opportunity to share joys and difficulties.

The question of confidentiality is especially delicate here. It is important that no private details are divulged that will enable the client to be identified unless he has first given his permission to be discussed freely.

Everyone who is counselling should have back-up supervision and pastoral care (for the counsellor) available.

Appendix V

SOME RECOMMENDED READING

There is a wide variety of books on different aspects of Christian counselling, and I do not pretend to have read more than a fraction of them. Here is a selection of some that I have found helpful at different stages of my learning. I do not agree with everything in them; always read with a prayer that you may discern what to absorb and what to reject.

Chapters 1 and 2
Duncan Buchanan, *The Counselling of Jesus*, Hodder and Stoughton, 1985.
Myra Chave-Jones, *The Gift of Helping*, Inter-Varsity Press.
Gary Collins, *Can You Trust Counselling?*, Inter-Varsity Press, 1988.
Joyce Huggett, *Listening to Others*, Hodder and Stoughton.
Roger Hurding, *Roots and Shoots*, Hodder and Stoughton, 1986.
—, *Restoring the Image*, Paternoster Press, 1980.
John Woolmer, *Growing up to Salvation*, Triangle, 1983.

Chapters 3–6
David Augsburger, *The Freedom of Forgiveness*, Scripture Press, 1989.
Michael Green, *The Empty Cross of Jesus*, Hodder and Stoughton, 1984.
Joyce Huggett, *Conflict: Friend or Foe*, Kingsway, 1984.
Francis MacNutt, *Healing*, Hodder and Stoughton, 1989.
—, *Power to Heal*, Ave Maria Press, 1977.
Noreen Riols, *Abortion: A Woman's Birthright?*, Hodder and Stoughton, 1986.
Michael Scanlan, *Power in Penance*, Ave Maria Press, 1975.

Chapters 7–12
Rita Bennett, *Emotionally Free*, Kingsway, 1982.
James Buckingham, *Risky Living*, Kingsway, 1978.
Lawrence Crabb, *Inside Out*, Navpress, 1988.
Gruntz and Bowden, *Recovery: A Guide for Adult Children of Alcoholics*, Simon and Schuster.
Maxine Hancock and Karen Mains, *Child Sexual Abuse: a Hope for Healing*, Highland Books, 1988.
Floyd McClung, *The Father Heart of God*, Kingsway, 1985.
Leanne Payne, *The Broken Image*, Kingsway, 1988.
Mary Pytches, *Set My People Free*, Hodder and Stoughton, 1987.
—, *Yesterday's Child*, Hodder and Stoughton, 1990.
David Seamands, *Healing for Damaged Emotions*, Scripture Press, 1986.
—, *Healing of the Memories*, Scripture Press, 1986.
—, *Putting Away Childish Things*, Scripture Press, 1987.
Michael Scanlan, *Inner Healing*, Paulist Press, 1974.
Barbara Shlemon, *Healing the Hidden Self*, Ave Maria Press, 1982.
Ruth Carter Stapleton, *The Experience of Inner Healing*, Hodder & Stoughton, 1978.

Chapter 13
Lawrence Crabb, *Effective Biblical Counselling*, Marshall Pickering, 1985.
Selwyn Hughes, *The Christian Counsellor's Pocket Guide*, Kingsway, 1982.

Chapters 14–16
Rita Bennett, *How To Pray for Inner Healing*, Kingsway, 1984.
Joyce Huggett, *Listening to God*, Hodder and Stoughton, 1986.
Francis MacNutt, *The Prayer that Heals*, Ave Maria Press, 1981.
Barbara Shlemon, *Healing Prayer*, Ave Maria Press, 1976.
Charles Solomon, *The Rejection Syndrome*, Tyndale.

Chapter 17
Peter Lawrence, *The Hotline: How Can We Hear God Speak Today?*, Kingsway, 1990.
George Mallone, *Those Controversial Gifts*, Hodder & Stoughton, 1984.

Chapter 18
Michael Green, *I Believe in Satan's Downfall*, Hodder and Stoughton, 1988.
Kenneth McAll, *Healing the Family Tree*, Sheldon Press, 1986.

Other useful books
Counselling in the church
Mary Pytches, *A Healing Fellowship, Guide to Practical Counselling in the Local Church*, Hodder and Stoughton, 1988.

Depression
Myra Chave-Jones, *Coping with Depression*, Lion, 1981.
Nancy Anne Smith, *Winter Past*, Inter-Varsity Press.
John White, *The Masks of Melancholy*, Inter-Varsity Press, 1982.
Richard Winter, *The Roots of Sorrow*, Marshall Pickering.

Bereavement
Harold Bauman, *Living Through Grief*, Lion, 1989.
Robert Dykstra, *She Never Said Good-bye*, Highland Books, 1990.
Elizabeth Heike, *A Question of Grief*, Hodder and Stoughton, 1985.
Colin Murray Parkes, *Bereavement, Studies of Grief in Adult Life*, Penguin, 1986.

Suffering
Joni Eareckson, *Joni: A Biography*, Pickering and Inglis, 1980.
—, *A Step Further*, Pickering and Inglis, 1984.
Philip Yancey, *How Can I Help When Someone is Hurting?*, Lion, 1987

Singleness
Margaret Evening, *Who Walk Alone*, Hodder & Stoughton, 1980.

Marriage
Joyce Huggett, *Marriage on the Mend*, Kingsway, 1987.
Judson Swihart, *How Do You Say, I Love You?*, Kingsway.
Walter Trobisch, *I Married You*, Inter-Varsity Press, 1972.